2013

THE BEST OF
COUNTRY COOKING

Taste of Home

For other Taste of Home books and products,
visit www.ShopTasteofHome.com.

RING THE DINNER BELL FOR COUNTRY COOKING

The wholesome goodness, comforting taste and scrumptious flavor of home-style food just can't be beat. It's all right here for you inside *The Best of Country Cooking*.

This guaranteed-to-please new cookbook is packed with best-loved dishes shared by family cooks like you from coast to coast. Enjoy page after page of favorite recipes—more than 300 in all!

Savory main courses...unforgettable side dishes...heartwarming soups...golden-brown breads...standout party snacks...irresistible desserts...these satisfying specialties will have everyone running to the table. Here's more of what you'll find inside:

Contest Winners
Recipes with the blue ribbon icon (at left) are scattered throughout the book. These prized dishes won a top spot in a national *Taste of Home* recipe contest.

Fuss-Free Meals
Turn to the "Memorable Meals" chapter for the convenience of complete menus. You'll have a variety of tasty choices for breakfast, lunch and dinner.

Table for Two
When you're cooking for just a few people, you don't have to make extra food you don't want. Rely on the big "Cooking for Two" chapter for doubly delicious options that are sized right.

With all of these down-home dishes, serving up great family fare is as easy as can be. Just pick your favorite recipes, then tell everyone to "Come and get it!"

■ EDITORIAL
Editor-in-Chief **Catherine Cassidy**
Creative Director **Howard Greenberg**
Editorial Operations Director **Kerri Balliet**

Managing Editor/Print & Digital Books **Mark Hagen**
Associate Creative Director **Edwin Robles Jr.**

Editor **Michelle Rozumalski**
Art Director **Raeann Sundholm**
Layout Designer **Nancy Novak**
Editorial Production Manager **Dena Ahlers**
Copy Chief **Deb Warlaumont Mulvey**
Copy Editor **Mary C. Hanson**

Chief Food Editor **Karen Berner**
Food Editors **James Schend; Peggy Woodward, RD**
Associate Food Editor **Krista Lanphier**
Associate Editor/Food Content **Annie Rundle**
Recipe Editors **Mary King; Jenni Sharp, RD; Irene Yeh**
Content Operations Manager **Colleen King**

Test Kitchen and Food Styling Manager **Sarah Thompson**
Test Kitchen Cooks **Alicia Rooker, RD (lead); Holly Johnson; Jimmy Cababa**
Prep Cooks **Matthew Hass (lead), Nicole Spohrleder, Lauren Knoelke**
Food Stylists **Kathryn Conrad (senior), Shannon Roum, Leah Rekau**
Grocery Coordinator **Molly McCowan**

Photographers **Dan Roberts, Grace Natoli Sheldon, Jim Wieland**
Set Styling Manager **Stephanie Marchese**
Set Stylists **Melissa Haberman, Dee Dee Jacq**

■ BUSINESS
Vice President, Publisher **Jan Studin, jan_studin@rd.com**

General Manager, Taste of Home Cooking Schools **Erin Puariea**

Vice President, Brand Marketing **Jennifer Smith**
Vice President, Circulation and Continuity Marketing **Dave Fiegel**

■ READER'S DIGEST NORTH AMERICA
Vice President, Business Development **Jonathan Bigham**
President, Books and Home Entertaining **Harold Clarke**
Chief Financial Officer **Howard Halligan**
Vice President, General Manager, Reader's Digest Media **Marilynn Jacobs**
Chief Marketing Officer **Renee Jordan**
Vice President, Chief Sales Officer **Mark Josephson**
Vice President, General Manager, Milwaukee **Frank Quigley**
Vice President, Chief Content Officer **Liz Vaccariello**

■ THE READER'S DIGEST ASSOCIATION, INC.
President and Chief Executive Officer **Robert E. Guth**

© 2013 Reiman Media Group, Inc.
5400 S. 60th St., Greendale WI 53129

International Standard Book Number:
978-1-61765-224-0

International Standard Serial Number:
1097-8321

Component Number: 117000034H00

All Rights Reserved.

Taste of Home is a registered trademark of The Reader's Digest Association, Inc.

Printed In U.S.A.

1 3 5 7 9 10 8 6 4 2

PICTURED ON THE FRONT COVER Beer Macaroni & Cheese (p. 51), Connie's Tortellini Salad (p. 35), Broccoli with Orange Sauce (p. 40), Great American Brownie Pie (p. 126), Herb & Sun-Dried Tomato Muffins (p. 82).
PICTURED ON THE BACK COVER Chicken Little Sliders (p. 17), Lemon Stars (p. 103), Pickled Green Beans (p. 53).

CONTENTS

SNACKS & BEVERAGES

When the time is right for satisfying munchies and drinks, turn to the appetizing chapter here. You'll have the perfect refreshments whether you're hosting a party, watching the big game on TV or just craving a bite before dinner.

CLASSIC HUMMUS

If you have a pressure cooker, here's a great reason to pull it out! We love to pair our homemade hummus with fresh vegetables for a wholesome snack or even a light meatless meal.
—**MONICA AND DAVID EICHLER** LAWRENCE, KANSAS

PREP: 20 MIN. + SOAKING **COOK:** 25 MIN. + CHILLING
MAKES: 2½ CUPS

    1 cup dried garbanzo beans
    1 medium onion, quartered
    1 bay leaf
    4 cups water
    ¼ cup minced fresh parsley
    ¼ cup lemon juice
    ¼ cup tahini
    4 to 6 garlic cloves, minced
    1 teaspoon ground cumin
    ¾ teaspoon salt
    ⅛ teaspoon cayenne pepper
    ¼ cup olive oil
       Assorted fresh vegetables

1. Sort beans and rinse in cold water. Place beans in a large bowl; add water to cover by 2 in. Cover and let stand overnight.
2. Drain and rinse beans, discarding liquid. Transfer beans to a pressure cooker; add the onion, bay leaf and 4 cups water.
3. Close cover securely according to manufacturer's directions. Bring cooker to full pressure over high heat. Reduce heat to medium-high and cook for 12 minutes. (Pressure regulator should maintain a slow, steady rocking motion or release of steam; adjust heat if needed.)
4. Remove from the heat; allow pressure to drop on its own. Immediately cool according to manufacturer's directions until pressure is completely reduced. Drain bean mixture, reserving ½ cup cooking liquid. Discard onion and bay leaf.

5. Place the beans, parsley, lemon juice, tahini, garlic, cumin, salt and cayenne in a food processor; cover and process until smooth. While processing, gradually add oil in a steady stream. Add enough reserved cooking liquid to achieve desired consistency.
6. Cover and refrigerate for at least 1 hour. Serve with assorted fresh vegetables.

SPINACH-CORN BREAD BITES

Whether served as an appetizer or a side dish, these savory bites made in a miniature muffin pan are always popular. The recipe yields a big batch, but I never have leftovers.
—**LAURA MAHAFFEY** ANNAPOLIS, MARYLAND

PREP: 25 MIN. **BAKE:** 15 MIN./BATCH **MAKES:** 4 DOZEN

    1 package (8½ ounces) corn bread/muffin mix
    ½ cup grated Parmesan cheese
    ⅛ teaspoon garlic powder
    2 eggs
    ½ cup blue cheese salad dressing
    ¼ cup butter, melted
    1 package (10 ounces) frozen chopped spinach, thawed and
       squeezed dry
    ½ cup shredded cheddar cheese
    ½ cup finely chopped onion

1. In a large bowl, combine muffin mix, Parmesan cheese and garlic powder. In another bowl, whisk the eggs, salad dressing and butter; stir into dry ingredients just until moistened. Fold in the spinach, cheddar cheese and onion.
2. Fill greased miniature muffin cups two-thirds full. Bake at 350° for 12-14 minutes or until a toothpick inserted near the center comes out clean. Cool for 5 minutes before removing from pans to wire racks. Serve warm. Refrigerate leftovers.

PINEAPPLE SALSA

Getting bored with the same old salsa? Try a sweet and spicy twist that mixes in tangy pineapple. It's terrific not only with chips, but also as a finishing touch on top of grilled meat or fish.
—**ANGELA LONGTIN** CAVALIER, NORTH DAKOTA

PREP: 50 MIN. **PROCESS:** 15 MIN. **MAKES:** 7 PINT JARS

- 12 **medium tomatoes (about 4 pounds)**
- 2 **large red onions, chopped**
- 2 **medium green peppers, chopped**
- 2 **cans (8 ounces each) unsweetened crushed pineapple, drained**
- 1 **can (15 ounces) tomato sauce**
- 1 **can (12 ounces) tomato paste**
- 3 **cans (4 ounces each) chopped green chilies**
- 2 **cans (4 ounces each) diced jalapeno peppers, drained**
- ⅓ **cup white vinegar**
- 2 **tablespoons salt**
- 6 **garlic cloves, minced**
- 2 **teaspoons ground cumin**
- 1 **teaspoon pepper**

1. In a large saucepan, bring 8 cups water to a boil. Add the tomatoes, a few at a time; boil for 30 seconds. Drain and immediately place tomatoes in ice water. Drain and pat dry; peel and chop.

2. In a stockpot, combine the remaining ingredients. Stir in tomatoes. Bring to a boil over medium-high heat. Reduce heat; simmer, uncovered, for 15-20 minutes or to desired thickness.

3. Carefully ladle the hot mixture into hot 1-pint jars, leaving ½-in. headspace. Remove air bubbles; wipe rims and adjust lids. Process for 15 minutes in a boiling-water canner.

Editor's Note: *The processing time listed in the recipe is for altitudes of 1,000 feet or less. For altitudes up to 3,000 feet, add 5 minutes; 6,000 feet, add 10 minutes; 8,000 feet, add 15 minutes; 10,000 feet, add 20 minutes.*

FRIED CHEESE RAVIOLI

Be sure to make enough of these crispy, coated ravioli—they're bound to be a hit! The little golden-brown bundles are easy to pick up and dip in warm marinara or spaghetti sauce.
—**KATE DAMPIER** QUAIL VALLEY, CALIFORNIA

PREP: 15 MIN. **COOK:** 20 MIN. **MAKES:** ABOUT 3½ DOZEN

- 1 **package (9 ounces) refrigerated cheese ravioli**
- 2 **eggs**
- 2 **cups seasoned bread crumbs**
- ½ **cup shredded Parmesan cheese**
- 3 **teaspoons dried basil**
- ½ **cup canola oil, divided**
   Additional shredded Parmesan cheese, optional
- 1 **cup marinara sauce or meatless spaghetti sauce, warmed**

1. Cook ravioli according to package directions; drain and pat dry. In a shallow bowl, lightly beat the eggs. In another shallow bowl, combine the bread crumbs, cheese and basil. Dip ravioli in eggs, then in bread crumb mixture.

2. In a large skillet or deep-fat fryer, heat ¼ cup oil over medium heat. Fry ravioli in batches for 30-60 seconds on each side or until golden brown and crispy; drain on paper towels. Halfway through frying, replace the oil; wipe out the skillet with paper towels if necessary.

3. Sprinkle with additional cheese if desired. Serve with marinara sauce.

SWEET & SPICY JALAPENO POPPERS

There's no faster way to get a party started than with a platter of these zippy, bacon-wrapped poppers. Feel free to assemble them ahead of time and bake them just before serving.

—DAWN ONUFFER CRESTVIEW, FLORIDA

PREP/TOTAL TIME: 30 MIN.   **MAKES:** 1 DOZEN

- 6 **jalapeno peppers**
- 4 **ounces cream cheese, softened**
- 2 **tablespoons shredded cheddar cheese**
- 6 **bacon strips, halved widthwise**
- ¼ **cup packed brown sugar**
- 1 **tablespoon chili seasoning**

1. Cut jalapenos in half lengthwise and remove seeds; set aside. In a small bowl, beat cheeses until blended. Spoon into pepper halves. Wrap a half-strip of bacon around each pepper half.
2. Combine the brown sugar and chili seasoning; coat peppers with the sugar mixture. Place in a greased 15-in. x 10-in. x 1-in. baking pan.
3. Bake at 350° for 18-20 minutes or until the bacon is firm.
Editor's Note: *Wear disposable gloves when cutting hot peppers; the oils can burn skin. Avoid touching your face.*

PEPPER PREPARATION

When I need to cut a large number of jalapeno peppers, I cut off the tops of the peppers and then slice them in half the long way. To remove the seeds and membranes, I scrape them out using the small end of a melon baller. It speeds the job along.

—JULAINE SVACINA RICHLAND CENTER, WISCONSIN

SMOKY GRILLED CORN SALSA

Our backyard grill is the perfect place to cook up all of the fresh ingredients for my homemade salsa. We enjoy it with tortilla chips and as a topping for meat, poultry and fish.

—ALICIA DEWOLFE GLOUCESTER, MASSACHUSETTS

PREP/TOTAL TIME: 30 MIN.   **MAKES:** 6 CUPS

- 6 **plum tomatoes, halved**
- 4 **medium ears sweet corn, husks removed**
- 2 **medium sweet yellow peppers, halved**
- 2 **medium green peppers, halved**
- 3 **jalapeno peppers, halved and seeded**
- 1 **medium red onion, cut into ½-inch slices**
- ¼ **cup minced fresh cilantro**
- 3 **tablespoons olive oil**
- 3 **tablespoons red wine vinegar**
- 5 **garlic cloves, minced**
- 1 **teaspoon salt**
- ½ **teaspoon sugar**
- ½ **teaspoon pepper**

1. Grill the tomatoes, corn, peppers and red onion, covered, over medium heat for 10-12 minutes or until tender, turning occasionally. Allow the vegetables to cool slightly. Remove the corn from cobs; transfer to a large bowl. Chop the remaining vegetables and add to corn.
2. In a small bowl, whisk the cilantro, oil, vinegar, garlic, salt, sugar and pepper. Pour over vegetables; toss to coat. Serve warm or cold.
Editor's Note: *Wear disposable gloves when cutting hot peppers; the oils can burn skin. Avoid touching your face.*

SWEET 'N' SOUR APPETIZER MEATBALLS

A friend shared this appetizer recipe with me years ago. The tangy meatballs also make a great main dish with potatoes.

—LUCRETIA BURT TALLASSEE, ALABAMA

PREP: 30 MIN. **COOK:** 20 MIN. **MAKES:** 4 DOZEN

- 1 egg
- ½ cup quick-cooking oats
- 1 envelope onion soup mix
- 2 pounds ground beef
- 2 cans (5½ ounces each) apricot nectar
- ¾ cup packed brown sugar
- ¾ cup ketchup
- ⅓ cup cider vinegar
- 2 tablespoons prepared mustard
- 1 tablespoon prepared horseradish
  Minced fresh parsley

1. In a large bowl, combine the egg, oats and soup mix. Crumble beef over mixture and mix well. Shape into 1-in. balls.

2. Place 1 in. apart on a greased rack in a shallow baking pan. Bake at 400° for 18-20 minutes or until no longer pink. Drain on paper towels.

3. In a large skillet, combine the nectar, brown sugar, ketchup, vinegar, mustard and horseradish. Bring to a boil. Reduce heat; simmer, uncovered, for 10 minutes. Add meatballs; simmer 15 minutes longer or until heated through. Sprinkle with parsley.

HERBED GARLIC CHEESE DIP

I like to present my garden-flavored dip with a variety of bite-size vegetables. For a snack that's a little bit lighter and healthier, I use the reduced-fat version of cream cheese.

—JOSEPHINE PIRO EASTON, PENNSYLVANIA

PREP/TOTAL TIME: 30 MIN. **MAKES:** 2⅔ CUPS

- 20 garlic cloves, unpeeled
- 1⅔ cups crumbled farmer cheese (about 14 ounces)
- ¼ cup loosely packed basil leaves
- ¼ cup reduced-fat cream cheese, cubed
- ¼ cup olive oil
- 2 green onions, coarsely chopped
- 2 tablespoons packed fresh parsley leaves
- 2 tablespoons water
- 4 teaspoons minced fresh rosemary or 1 teaspoon dried rosemary, crushed
- ⅛ teaspoon cayenne pepper
  Assorted fresh vegetables

1. Place the garlic in a small saucepan and cover with water. Bring to a boil. Reduce heat; simmer for 20 minutes or until softened. Drain and rinse in cold water; peel garlic. Place in a food processor.

2. Add the farmer cheese, basil, cream cheese, oil, green onions, parsley, water, rosemary and cayenne pepper; cover and process until smooth. Transfer to a small bowl; chill until serving. Serve with vegetables.

Snacks from the Sea

Your family and friends are sure to fall hook, line and sinker for these mouthwatering appetizers. From spiced-up shrimp to creamy smoked salmon, they're the catch of the day.

SMOKED SALMON SPREAD

I often spoon this salmon spread onto endive leaves for an easy yet elegant presentation. It always goes over well at parties.
—**PATRICIA NIEH** PORTOLA VALLEY, CALIFORNIA

PREP/TOTAL TIME: 15 MIN. **MAKES:** 2 CUPS

- 12 ounces reduced-fat cream cheese, cubed
- ⅓ cup fat-free sour cream
- 4 ounces smoked salmon or lox
- 2 tablespoons capers, drained
- 3 green onions, chopped (white parts only)
- 1 tablespoon dried thyme
- 1 tablespoon lemon juice
- ¼ teaspoon hot pepper sauce
- ⅛ teaspoon pepper
- 1 tablespoon minced chives
  Assorted fresh vegetables or assorted crackers

Place the first nine ingredients in a food processor; cover and process until smooth. Chill until serving. Sprinkle with chives; serve with vegetables.

A GOOD CAPER
Capers are the immature buds from a bush native to the Middle East and Mediterranean regions that are either brined in vinegar or packed in coarse salt to preserve. They're best rinsed before using.

MEXICAN SHRIMP DIP

Our family sampled a zippy version of shrimp cocktail at a Mexican restaurant. We enjoyed it so much, I adapted the idea at home to create a dip. Now I make it at least once a month.
—**ROMONA RUTHERFORD** TAHLEQUAH, OKLAHOMA

PREP/TOTAL TIME: 15 MIN. **MAKES:** 10 SERVINGS

- 1 cup ketchup
- 1 cup salsa or picante sauce
- ¼ cup tomato juice
- 3 medium plum tomatoes, chopped
- 2 medium ripe avocados, peeled and chopped
- 1 medium red onion, finely chopped
- 1 jalapeno pepper, seeded and finely chopped
- ½ cup finely chopped green pepper
- ½ cup minced fresh cilantro
- 1 pound frozen cooked salad shrimp, thawed and well drained
  Tortilla chips

In a large bowl, combine the first nine ingredients. Spread into a 9-in. pie plate; top with shrimp. Chill until serving. Serve with tortilla chips.

Editor's Note: *Wear disposable gloves when cutting hot peppers; the oils can burn skin. Avoid touching your face.*

DEVILED CRAB

Dip your spoon into a little cup of this rich comfort food, and you might think you've gone to heaven! Generous portions of crab are blended with cream, eggs, chives, onions and more.

—**DORIS PRILLAMAN** WILMINGTON, NORTH CAROLINA

PREP: 30 MIN. **BAKE:** 20 MIN. **MAKES:** 6 SERVINGS

- ½ cup finely chopped onion
- 3 tablespoons butter
- 3 tablespoons all-purpose flour
- ½ teaspoon salt
- 1½ cups half-and-half cream
- 2 egg yolks, lightly beaten
- 3 cans (6 ounces each) crabmeat, drained, flaked and cartilage removed
- 1 tablespoon Dijon mustard
- 2 teaspoons Worcestershire sauce
- 1 teaspoon minced chives

TOPPING

- 1 cup soft bread crumbs
- 1 tablespoon butter, melted

1. In a large skillet, saute the onion in butter until tender. Stir in the flour and salt until blended. Gradually stir in the cream until smooth. Bring to a boil; cook and stir for 2 minutes or until thickened and bubbly. Remove from the heat.

2. Stir a small amount of hot mixture into egg yolks. Return all to the pan, stirring constantly. Bring to a gentle boil; cook and stir 2 minutes longer. Remove from the heat. Stir in the crab, mustard, Worcestershire sauce and chives.

3. Spoon into six greased 6-oz. ramekins or custard cups. Place on a baking sheet. Combine bread crumbs and melted butter; sprinkle over tops. Bake at 375° for 20-25 minutes or until the topping is golden brown.

BUTTERFLIED SHRIMP ROCKEFELLER

Looking for an alternative to heavy holiday fare? A platter of light, fresh shrimp bites topped with a delicious spinach mixture really stands out on an appetizer buffet. Guests can't get enough!

—**LEE BREMSON** KANSAS CITY, MISSOURI

PREP/TOTAL TIME: 30 MIN. **MAKES:** 1½ DOZEN

- 18 uncooked jumbo shrimp
- 2 shallots, finely chopped
- 1 teaspoon dried basil
- ½ teaspoon fennel seed, crushed
- ¼ teaspoon pepper
- 1 tablespoon olive oil
- 1 garlic clove, minced
- 1 package (9 ounces) fresh baby spinach, chopped
- ½ cup dry bread crumbs
- 1 tablespoon lemon juice
- 1 tablespoon grated Parmesan cheese

1. Peel and devein shrimp, leaving the tails on. Butterfly each shrimp along the outside curve; set aside.

2. In a large skillet, saute the shallots, basil, fennel seed and pepper in oil until tender. Add garlic; saute for 1 minute. Add spinach; saute 3-4 minutes longer or until wilted. Remove from the heat; stir in bread crumbs and lemon juice.

3. Arrange shrimp on a greased 15-in. x 10-in. x 1-in. baking pan. Spoon 1 tablespoon spinach mixture over each shrimp; sprinkle with Parmesan cheese. Bake at 425° for 4-6 minutes or until shrimp turn pink.

CURRIED TROPICAL NUT MIX

Here's an easy homemade gift for the Christmas season or any time at all. You'll want to make a big bowlful to serve at your next party, too. Guests can't stop munching!

—**MARY ANN DELL** PHOENIXVILLE, PENNSYLVANIA

PREP: 20 MIN. + COOLING   **MAKES:** 7½ CUPS

- 2 tablespoons curry powder
- 1 tablespoon butter
- 1 tablespoon olive oil
- 1 teaspoon ground cumin
- ½ teaspoon cayenne pepper
- 2 cups salted roasted almonds
- 2 cups salted cashew halves
- 2 cups salted peanuts
- 1 cup flaked coconut
- ½ cup dried mangoes, chopped

1. In a large microwave-safe bowl, combine the first five ingredients. Microwave, uncovered, on high for 30 seconds. Add the almonds, cashews, peanuts and coconut; toss to coat.
2. Cook, uncovered, 5-6 minutes longer or until lightly browned, stirring after each minute. Add mangoes. Spread onto waxed paper to cool. Store in an airtight container.
Editor's Note: *This recipe was tested in a 1,100-watt microwave.*

BRIE WITH ALMONDS

This almond-topped, baked round of Brie cheese looks so elegant and impressive for special occasions. No one will guess it's a snap to prepare with just a handful of ingredients.

—**MILDRED AYDT** CHANHASSEN, MINNESOTA

PREP/TOTAL TIME: 15 MIN.   **MAKES:** 6-8 SERVINGS

- 1 round Brie cheese (8 ounces)
- 2 tablespoons butter, melted
- ¼ cup sliced almonds
- 1 tablespoon brandy, optional
  Assorted crackers

1. Place Brie in an ungreased ovenproof serving dish. Combine the butter, almonds and brandy if desired; pour over Brie.
2. Bake, uncovered, at 400° for 10-12 minutes or until cheese is softened. Serve with crackers.

BACON MUSHROOM ROLL-UPS

Wrapped in toasted white bread, my creamy appetizers combine the delectable flavors of bacon and mushrooms. Just pop the little roll-ups under the broiler for a few minutes until golden brown.

—**RAYMONDE BOURGEOIS** SWASTIKA, ONTARIO

PREP: 30 MIN.   **BROIL:** 5 MIN./BATCH   **MAKES:** 20 APPETIZERS

- 8 bacon strips, chopped
- 1 medium onion, finely chopped
- 1 package (8 ounces) cream cheese, softened
- 1 can (4 ounces) mushroom stems and pieces, drained
- 20 slices sandwich bread, crusts removed
- 3 tablespoons butter, melted

1. In a small skillet, cook bacon over medium heat until crisp. Using a slotted spoon, remove to paper towels; drain, reserving 1 tablespoon drippings.
2. In the same skillet, saute the onion in drippings until tender. Transfer to a small bowl; add the cream cheese, mushrooms and bacon. Stir until blended.
3. With a rolling pin, flatten the bread slightly; spread each slice with 4½ teaspoons filling.
4. Roll up from a long side and secure with a toothpick. Place seam side down in two ungreased 15-in. x 10-in. x 1-in. baking pans; brush with butter.
5. Broil 4 in. from the heat for 3-4 minutes or until golden brown. Discard toothpicks.

CRANBERRY FIZZ

Everyone will be coming back for another glass of this wonderfully tangy punch. Be prepared to share the recipe, too!

—SUZETTE JURY KEENE, CALIFORNIA

PREP: 5 MIN. + CHILLING **MAKES:** 2 QUARTS

- 1 bottle (32 ounces) cranberry juice
- 1 cup orange juice
- 1 cup ruby red grapefruit juice
- ½ cup sugar
- 2 cups ginger ale, chilled

In a pitcher, combine the cranberry, orange and grapefruit juices and sugar. Refrigerate until chilled. Just before serving, stir in ginger ale.

JUST ENOUGH JUICE

I always keep cans of frozen orange juice concentrate in the freezer. When a recipe calls for a small amount of juice, it's simple to make if you keep in mind that the ratio to reconstitute the juice is 3 parts water to 1 part concentrate. (If a recipe calls for 1/4 cup juice, I just mix 3 tablespoons water with 1 tablespoon concentrate.) The concentrate doesn't freeze hard, so it's easy to scoop out the amount I need. Once the can is open, I store it in a resealable plastic bag.

—PEGGY S. HOT SPRINGS VILLAGE, ARKANSAS

CHICKEN NUGGETS WITH APRICOT SAUCE

Satisfying a hungry crowd is a breeze with bite-size, coated pieces of tender chicken. Pair them with a simple but sensational sauce that blends apricot preserves and mustard.

—MICHELLE KRZMARCZICK REDONDO BEACH, CALIFORNIA

PREP: 25 MIN. **BAKE:** 10 MIN. **MAKES:** 2 DOZEN (1 CUP SAUCE)

- 1 cup buttermilk, divided
- 1 pound boneless skinless chicken breasts, cut into 1-inch cubes
- ¾ cup all-purpose flour
- 1 cup crushed cornflakes
- ½ teaspoon onion powder
- ½ teaspoon garlic salt
- ¼ teaspoon salt
- ¼ teaspoon dried oregano
- ⅛ teaspoon pepper
- 2 eggs
- 1 cup apricot preserves
- 2 tablespoons prepared mustard

1. Pour ½ cup buttermilk into a large resealable plastic bag; add chicken. Seal bag and turn to coat. Place flour in another resealable plastic bag. In a third bag, combine the cornflakes, onion powder, garlic salt, salt, oregano and pepper. In a shallow bowl, whisk eggs and remaining buttermilk.

2. Drain the chicken; add to flour and shake to coat. Coat with egg mixture, then add to cornflake mixture and shake to coat. Arrange chicken in a greased 15-in. x 10-in. x 1-in. baking pan.

3. Bake at 350° for 10-15 minutes or until juices run clear. In a small bowl, combine the apricot preserves and mustard. Serve with chicken.

VEGGIE QUICHE BUNDLES

You just can't go wrong serving these crispy phyllo bundles. With a quiche-like filling, they could even be part of a brunch buffet.
—**LORRAINE CALAND** SHUNIAH, ONTARIO

PREP: 25 MIN. **BAKE:** 20 MIN. **MAKES:** 1 DOZEN

- 1 cup chopped fresh mushrooms
- ½ cup diced zucchini
- ¼ cup chopped red onion
- 1 tablespoon plus ⅓ cup butter, divided
- 1 plum tomato, seeded and diced
- 3 eggs
- ½ cup milk
- 1 tablespoon prepared pesto
- ¼ teaspoon coarsely ground pepper
- ½ cup crumbled feta cheese
- ½ cup shredded part-skim mozzarella cheese
- 12 sheets phyllo dough (14 inches x 9 inches)

1. In a small skillet, saute the mushrooms, zucchini and red onion in 1 tablespoon butter until the mushrooms are tender; stir in the tomato. In a small bowl, whisk the eggs, milk, pesto and pepper. In another bowl, combine the feta and mozzarella cheeses.

2. Melt the remaining butter. Place one sheet of phyllo dough on a work surface; brush with melted butter. Repeat with three more sheets of phyllo, brushing each layer. Cut phyllo in half widthwise, then cut in half lengthwise. (Keep remaining phyllo covered with plastic wrap and a damp towel to prevent it from drying out.)

3. Repeat with remaining phyllo and butter. Carefully place each stack in a greased muffin cup. Fill each with 4 teaspoons vegetable mixture, 1 tablespoon cheese mixture and 4 teaspoons egg mixture. Pinch the corners of the phyllo together and twist to seal.

4. Bake at 325° for 20-25 minutes or until golden brown. Serve warm. Refrigerate leftovers.

ALMOND "FETA" WITH HERB OIL

Looking for something a bit different? Blanched almonds give my herb-flavored appetizer a rich texture. Unbaked, it's smooth and spreadable, while baking makes it crumbly like feta.
—MARY RAYMOND CHESTERFIELD, MISSOURI

PREP: 25 MIN. + SOAKING **BAKE:** 35 MIN. + CHILLING
MAKES: 1½ CUPS

- 1 cup blanched almonds
- ½ cup water
- ¼ cup lemon juice
- 5 tablespoons olive oil, divided
- 1 garlic clove
- 1¼ teaspoons salt
- 1½ teaspoons minced fresh thyme or ½ teaspoon dried thyme
- ½ teaspoon minced fresh rosemary or ⅛ teaspoon dried rosemary, crushed
  Assorted crackers

1. Rinse almonds in cold water. Place in a large bowl; add water to cover by 3 in. Cover and let stand overnight.
2. Drain and rinse the almonds, discarding liquid. Transfer to a food processor. Add ½ cup water, lemon juice, 3 tablespoons oil, garlic and salt; cover and process for 5-6 minutes or until pureed.
3. Line a large strainer with four layers of cheesecloth and place over a large bowl. Pour almond mixture into prepared strainer; bring up the corners of cloth and tie with string to form a bag. Refrigerate overnight.
4. Squeeze out any liquid; remove the cheesecloth and discard the liquid from bowl. Transfer ball to a parchment paper-lined baking sheet; flatten slightly into a 6-in. circle.
5. Bake at 200° for 35-40 minutes or until firm. Cool. Refrigerate until chilled.
6. In a small skillet, heat the thyme, rosemary and remaining oil over medium heat for 2 minutes. Cool to room temperature. Drizzle over almond mixture. Serve with crackers.

RASPBERRY CHIPOTLE DIP

It's almost hard to believe that such a delicious, crowd-pleasing dip comes from only three basic ingredients. Just add a basket of your favorite crackers, and you'll have the hit of the party!
—PAT STEVENS GRANBURY, TEXAS

PREP/TOTAL TIME: 5 MIN. **MAKES:** 3 CUPS

- 3 cartons (8 ounces each) whipped cream cheese
- 1 cup raspberry chipotle salsa
- ½ cup pecan halves, toasted
  Assorted crackers

Spread cream cheese onto a small serving platter. Top with salsa and pecans. Refrigerate until serving. Serve with crackers.
Editor's Note: *This recipe was tested with Mrs. Renfro's raspberry chipotle salsa.*

SANGRIA WINE

Wonderful anytime, this icy drink goes over especially well on hot summer days. Lemon and lime slices give each glass extra flair.
—COLLEEN STURMA MILWAUKEE, WISCONSIN

PREP/TOTAL TIME: 10 MIN. **MAKES:** 10 SERVINGS

- 1 bottle (750 milliliters) dry red wine
- 1 cup lemon-flavored rum
- 2 cans (12 ounces each) lemon-lime soda, chilled
- 2 medium lemons, sliced
- 2 medium limes, sliced
  Ice cubes

In a pitcher, combine the wine, rum and soda; add lemon and lime slices. Serve over ice.

CRANBERRY GLOGG

A cold winter's day is the perfect time to cozy up with a hot beverage, and this is a family favorite. We love the tangy cranberry juice spiced with cinnamon, cardamom and cloves.

—**JUNE LINDQUIST** HAMMOND, WISCONSIN

PREP/TOTAL TIME: 30 MIN. **MAKES:** 7 SERVINGS

- 4 cups cranberry juice
- 2 cups ruby port wine or grape juice
- 1 cup golden raisins
- ¼ cup sugar
- 2 cinnamon sticks (3 inches)
- 4 cardamom pods, crushed
- 6 whole cloves
  Additional cinnamon sticks, optional

1. In a large saucepan, combine the cranberry juice, wine, raisins and sugar. Place the cinnamon, cardamom and cloves on a double thickness of cheesecloth; bring up corners of cloth and tie with string to form a bag. Add to the pan.
2. Bring just to a simmer (do not boil). Reduce heat; simmer gently, uncovered, for 15 minutes or until flavors are blended. Discard spice bag. Serve warm in mugs with additional cinnamon if desired.

APRICOT BRIE

Want an appetizer that looks elegant but is easy to make? Simply dress up a round of Brie cheese. It's wonderful topped with an apricot sauce and served with sliced French bread.

— **ALICEGOGGIN@MSN.COM**

PREP/TOTAL TIME: 20 MIN. **MAKES:** 8 SERVINGS

- ½ cup apricot preserves
- 1 tablespoon grated orange peel
- 1 tablespoon lemon juice
- 1 tablespoon orange juice

- ⅛ teaspoon ground cinnamon
- 1 round (8 ounces) Brie cheese
  Sliced French bread

In a small microwave-safe bowl, combine the first five ingredients. Cook, uncovered, on high for 1 minute or until heated through. Pour into a shallow 3-cup microwave-safe serving dish. Place cheese on preserve mixture. Cook 1 to 1½ minutes longer or until cheese is softened. Serve with bread.
Editor's Note: *This recipe was tested in a 1,100-watt microwave.*

PARMESAN PRETZEL RODS

These cheesy, zesty snacks are irresistible. The coated pretzels get a kick from garlic powder, cayenne pepper and oregano.

—**CINDY WINTER-HARLEY** CARY, NORTH CAROLINA

PREP: 10 MIN. **BAKE:** 20 MIN. + COOLING
MAKES: ABOUT 2½ DOZEN

- 1 cup grated Parmesan cheese
- 1 teaspoon garlic powder
- 1 teaspoon dried oregano
- ½ teaspoon cayenne pepper
- 6 tablespoons butter, cubed
- ¼ cup olive oil
- 1 package (12 ounces) pretzel rods

1. In a small bowl, combine the cheese, garlic powder, oregano and cayenne; set aside. In a small saucepan, heat butter and oil until butter is melted. Coat two-thirds of each pretzel rod with butter mixture, then roll in cheese mixture. Reheat butter mixture if needed.
2. Place in an ungreased 15-in. x 10-in. x 1-in. baking pan. Bake at 275° for 20-25 minutes or until golden brown, turning once. Cool. Store in an airtight container.

CHICKEN LITTLE SLIDERS

A fruity homemade salsa and flavored mayonnaise really brighten up my little chicken sandwiches. They're great when you need to tide over a hungry crowd before mealtime.

—**LAURA MCALLISTER** MORGANTON, NORTH CAROLINA

PREP: 30 MIN. **GRILL:** 10 MIN. **MAKES:** 1½ DOZEN

SALSA
- 3 plum tomatoes, seeded and chopped
- ¼ cup minced fresh basil or 1 tablespoon dried basil
- ¼ cup canned crushed pineapple
- ¼ cup chopped red onion
- 1 jalapeno pepper, seeded and finely chopped
- 2 tablespoons lemon juice
- 1 teaspoon grated lemon peel
- ⅛ teaspoon salt
- ⅛ teaspoon pepper

MAYO
- ⅓ cup reduced-fat mayonnaise
- 2 tablespoons chopped roasted sweet red pepper
- ½ teaspoon grated lemon peel
- Dash salt

BURGERS
- 1 egg, beaten
- ½ cup finely chopped roasted sweet red peppers
- 2 tablespoons plus 2 teaspoons fat-free milk
- 1½ teaspoons Dijon mustard
- 1⅓ cups soft bread crumbs
- ¾ teaspoon salt
- ¼ teaspoon pepper
- 1½ pounds ground chicken

SERVING
- ½ cup crumbled feta cheese
- 18 heat-and-serve rolls, split
- 18 small lettuce leaves

1. In two small bowls, combine the salsa and mayo ingredients; chill until serving.

2. In a large bowl, combine the egg, peppers, milk, mustard, bread crumbs, salt and pepper. Crumble chicken over mixture and mix well. Shape into 18 patties.

3. If grilling the burgers, coat grill rack with cooking spray before starting the grill. Grill burgers, covered, over medium heat or broil 4 in. from the heat for 3-4 minutes on each side or until a thermometer reads 165° and juices run clear.

4. Stir the feta cheese into the prepared salsa. Spread the rolls with the prepared mayo; top each with a lettuce leaf, burger and 2 tablespoons salsa mixture.

Editor's Note: *Wear disposable gloves when cutting hot peppers; the oils can burn skin. Avoid touching your face.*

MANGO MELBA SHAKES

When we go camping, we treat drop-in visitors to these refreshing shakes. There's no yummier way to cool off in our Florida heat!

—**JOHN SLIVON** MILTON, FLORIDA

PREP/TOTAL TIME: 5 MIN. **MAKES:** 3 SERVINGS

- ¼ cup 2% milk
- 1½ cups vanilla ice cream
- 1 cup frozen unsweetened sliced peaches
- ½ cup chopped peeled mango
- ½ cup fresh raspberries

In a blender, combine all ingredients; cover and process for 30 seconds or until smooth. Pour into chilled glasses; serve immediately.

POPCORN DELIGHT

Whenever I take this sweet popcorn mix to a get-together, I bring copies of the recipe because people always ask for it. They quickly realize that once you start munching, it's hard to stop!
—CHERYL BULL BLUE GRASS, IOWA

PREP: 15 MIN. + CHILLING **MAKES:** ABOUT 6 QUARTS

- 14 **cups popped popcorn**
- 2 **cups salted peanuts**
- 2 **cups crisp rice cereal**
- 2 **cups miniature marshmallows**
- 1 **pound white candy coating, coarsely chopped**
- 3 **tablespoons creamy peanut butter**

1. In a large bowl, combine the popcorn, peanuts, cereal and miniature marshmallows. In a microwave, melt candy coating and peanut butter; stir until smooth. Pour over the popcorn mixture; toss to coat.

2. Spread onto waxed paper-lined baking sheets; refrigerate for 15 minutes or until set. Break into pieces. Store in an airtight container in the refrigerator.

ENLIGHTENED SPICY AVOCADO DIP

My avocado dip features hints of citrus and spice. Its lively green color suits the Christmas season perfectly.
—JESSIE GREARSON-SAPAT FALMOUTH, MAINE

PREP/TOTAL TIME: 15 MIN. **MAKES:** 1½ CUPS

- 2 **medium ripe avocados, peeled and pitted**
- ¼ **cup fresh cilantro leaves**
- ¼ **cup reduced-fat sour cream**

- ¼ **cup lime juice**
- 2 **tablespoons olive oil**
- 1 **garlic clove, minced**
- ¼ **to ½ teaspoon prepared wasabi**
  Assorted fresh vegetables

Place the first seven ingredients in a food processor; cover and process until smooth. Chill until serving. Serve with vegetables.

ALMOND-BACON CHEESE CROSTINI

Try these baked bites when you want an alternative to the usual toasted tomato appetizer. For a unique presentation, slice the baguette at an angle instead of making a straight cut.
—LEONDRE HERMANN STUART, FLORIDA

PREP: 30 MIN. **BAKE:** 15 MIN. **MAKES:** 3 DOZEN

- 1 **French bread baguette (1 pound), cut into 36 slices**
- 2 **cups (8 ounces) shredded Monterey Jack cheese**
- ⅔ **cup mayonnaise**
- ½ **cup sliced almonds, toasted**
- 6 **bacon strips, cooked and crumbled**
- 1 **green onion, chopped**
  Dash salt
  Additional toasted almonds, optional

1. Place bread slices on an ungreased baking sheet. Bake at 400° for 8-9 minutes or until lightly browned.

2. Meanwhile, in a large bowl, combine the cheese, mayonnaise, almonds, bacon, onion and salt. Spread over bread. Bake for 7-8 minutes or until cheese is melted. Sprinkle with additional almonds if desired. Serve warm.

CHICKEN SALAD IN BASKETS

Every time I prepare these cute little bread baskets filled with a refreshing chicken salad, they're a big hit. My husband frequently asks me to fix them for meetings and parties.
—**GWENDOLYN FAE TRAPP** STRONGSVILLE, OHIO

PREP: 15 MIN. **BAKE:** 15 MIN. + CHILLING **MAKES:** 20 APPETIZERS

- 1 **cup diced cooked chicken**
- 3 **bacon strips, cooked and crumbled**
- ⅓ **cup chopped mushrooms**
- 2 **tablespoons chopped pecans**
- 2 **tablespoons diced peeled apple**
- ¼ **cup mayonnaise**
- ⅛ **teaspoon salt**
  Dash pepper
- 20 **slices bread**
- 6 **tablespoons butter, melted**
- 2 **tablespoons minced fresh parsley**

1. In a small bowl, combine the first five ingredients. Combine the mayonnaise, salt and pepper; add to chicken mixture and stir to coat. Cover and refrigerate until serving.
2. Cut each slice of bread with a 3-in. round cookie cutter; brush both sides with butter. Press into ungreased mini muffin cups. Bake at 350° for 11-13 minutes or until golden brown and crisp.

3. Cool for 3 minutes before removing from pans to wire racks to cool completely. Spoon 1 tablespoonful chicken salad into each bread basket. Cover and refrigerate for up to 2 hours. Just before serving, sprinkle with parsley.

CHOCOLATE CHAI FRAPPES

Blend chocolate milk with fresh-brewed chai tea, and what do you get? A glass of pure comfort! You won't want to buy a frappe at a coffee shop when you can easily create your own at home.
—**HEIDI BLANKEN** SEDRO-WOOLLEY, WASHINGTON

PREP/TOTAL TIME: 20 MIN. **MAKES:** 4 SERVINGS

- 4 **individual chai tea bags**
- ½ **cup boiling water**
- 2 **cups 2% chocolate milk**
- ½ **cup ice cubes**
- 4 **dashes ground cinnamon**
- 4 **dashes ground nutmeg**

1. Place tea bags in a small bowl; add boiling water. Let stand for 15 minutes or until lukewarm.
2. Discard tea bags. Pour tea into a blender; add the milk and ice. Cover and process for 30 seconds or until slushy. Pour into chilled glasses. Sprinkle with dashes of cinnamon and nutmeg; serve immediately.

SOUPS, SALADS & SANDWICHES

A hearty bowl of chili... fresh-tasting potluck salad...burger with the works...the sensational recipes in this chapter are true standouts. Serve them as part of a larger feast or all by themselves. Either way, you can't go wrong!

CAJUN CHICKEN & RICE SOUP

My family loves to see a big pot of spicy chicken soup simmering on the stove. I serve generous bowlfuls with warm corn bread.
—**LISA HAMMOND** HIGGINSVILLE, MISSOURI

PREP: 20 MIN. **COOK:** 2 HOURS **MAKES:** 8 SERVINGS (3 QUARTS)

- 1 **stewing chicken (about 6 pounds)**
- 2 **bay leaves**
- 1 **teaspoon salt**
- 1 **teaspoon poultry seasoning**
- 1 **teaspoon pepper**
- 1 **medium onion, chopped**
- 2 **celery ribs, chopped**
- 1 **tablespoon butter**
- 12 **garlic cloves, minced**
- 1 **can (10 ounces) diced tomatoes and green chilies, drained**
- ¾ **cup orange juice**
- 2 **tablespoons minced fresh cilantro**
- 2 **teaspoons Cajun seasoning**
- 1 **teaspoon dried oregano**
- ½ **teaspoon dried thyme**
- ½ **teaspoon ground cumin**
- ½ **teaspoon paprika**
- 2 **cups cooked rice**
- 1 **can (15 ounces) pinto beans, rinsed and drained**

1. Place the chicken in a large stockpot; cover with water. Add the bay leaves, salt, poultry seasoning and pepper. Bring to a boil. Reduce heat; cover and simmer for 1½ hours or until the chicken is tender.

2. Remove the chicken from the broth; set aside to cool. Strain the broth, discarding the seasonings. Set aside 6 cups broth for the soup; save remaining broth for another use. Skim fat from soup broth. When cool enough to handle, remove chicken from bones; discard bones. Shred and set aside 3 cups chicken (save remaining chicken for another use).

3. In a large stockpot, saute the onion and celery in butter until onion is crisp-tender. Add garlic; cook 1 minute longer. Stir in tomatoes, orange juice, cilantro, seasonings and reserved broth. Bring to a boil. Reduce heat; cover and simmer for 15 minutes or until vegetables are tender. Stir in the rice, beans and reserved chicken; heat through.

HAM 'N' SWISS ENVELOPES

These clever envelopes will make your guests eager to look inside! The hot pockets shaped with refrigerated crescent roll dough are stuffed with a delicious ham-and-Swiss filling.
—**TAMMY BURGESS** LOVELAND, OHIO

PREP/TOTAL TIME: 30 MIN. **MAKES:** 4 SERVINGS

- ¾ **cup diced fully cooked ham**
- 4 **teaspoons finely chopped onion**
- 1 **teaspoon canola oil**
- ¾ **cup shredded Swiss cheese**
- 1 **package (3 ounces) cream cheese, cubed**
- 2 **tubes (8 ounces each) refrigerated crescent rolls**

1. In a large skillet, saute the ham and onion in oil until onion is tender. Add the cheeses; cook for 3-4 minutes or until melted. Remove from the heat; set aside.

2. Unroll crescent dough and separate into four rectangles; seal perforations. Place 2 tablespoons of ham mixture in the center of each rectangle. Starting with a short side, fold a third of the dough over filling. On the other short side, bring both corners together in the center to form a point. Fold over to resemble an envelope. Pinch seams to seal.

3. Place on an ungreased baking sheet. Bake at 400° for 10-12 minutes or until golden brown.

ITALIAN GRILLED CHEESE SANDWICHES

I created an Italian-style grilled cheese recipe for the students in the foods and nutrition class I teach. The kids told me that they like it so much, they prepare it at home for their families.

—BETH HIOTT YORK, SOUTH CAROLINA

PREP/TOTAL TIME: 25 MIN. **MAKES:** 4 SERVINGS

- 8 slices Italian bread
- 4 tablespoons prepared pesto
- 4 slices provolone cheese
- 4 slices part-skim mozzarella cheese
- 5 teaspoons olive oil
  Marinara sauce warmed, optional

1. Spread four bread slices with pesto. Layer with cheeses; top with remaining bread. Spread outsides of sandwiches with oil.
2. In a large skillet over medium heat, toast the sandwiches for 3-4 minutes on each side or until cheese is melted. Serve with marinara if desired.

CURRIED OLIVE EGG SALAD

Want to give your humble egg salad sandwich a boost? Simply mix in some olives, curry powder and celery seed.

—ANITA DOYLE DODGEVILLE, WISCONSIN

PREP/TOTAL TIME: 15 MIN. **MAKES:** 4 SERVINGS

- 6 hard-cooked eggs, chopped
- ½ cup reduced-fat mayonnaise
- ⅓ cup chopped sweet onion
- ¼ cup chopped pimiento-stuffed olives
- ½ teaspoon celery seed
- ½ teaspoon curry powder
- ¼ teaspoon sugar
- ¼ teaspoon pepper
- ⅛ teaspoon salt

- 8 pita pocket halves
- 8 lettuce leaves

In a large bowl, combine the first nine ingredients. Line pita halves with lettuce; fill each with ¼ cup egg salad.

TEX-MEX CHILI

Years ago, I dreamed up this beefy, zesty Southwestern chili. It's still the go-to favorite in our family cookbook.

—MARTHA HOOK TYLER, TEXAS

PREP: 20 MIN. **COOK:** 4 HOURS **MAKES:** 9 SERVINGS

- 1½ pounds ground beef
- 1 medium onion, chopped
- 5 garlic cloves, minced
- 1 can (14½ ounces) diced tomatoes, undrained
- 1 cup water
- 1 cup V8 juice
- ¼ cup brewed coffee
- 2 envelopes chili seasoning
- 1 can (16 ounces) refried beans
- 1 can (15 ounces) Ranch Style beans (pinto beans in seasoned tomato sauce)
- 2 tablespoons ground cumin
- 2 tablespoons chili powder
- ¼ teaspoon lemon juice

1. In a large skillet, cook the beef and onion over medium heat until the meat is no longer pink. Add the garlic; cook 1 minute longer. Drain. Stir in the tomatoes, water, V8 juice, coffee and chili seasoning.
2. Transfer to a 4-qt. slow cooker. Stir in remaining ingredients. Cover and cook on low for 4-5 hours to allow flavors to blend.

RIVEL SOUP

For years, I'd been trying to figure out how my grandmother made her rivel soup. I was fascinated to discover that the recipe wasn't just something she came up with to feed her family. It's a treasured home-style soup, and many people have their own special version.
—**KATHY KEGLEY** RURAL RETREAT, VIRGINIA

PREP/TOTAL TIME: 10 MIN. **MAKES:** 6 SERVINGS

- 1 cup all-purpose flour
- ½ teaspoon salt
- 1 egg
- 4 cups 2% milk
  Minced fresh parsley and coarsely ground pepper

1. In a small bowl, combine flour and salt. Cut in egg with a fork until crumbly.
2. In a large saucepan, heat the milk over medium heat until bubbles form around the sides of the pan. Gradually add flour mixture; bring to a gentle boil, stirring constantly. Cook and stir for 1-2 minutes or until rivels are cooked through. Sprinkle servings with parsley and pepper.

RUNDOWN ON RIVEL

German in origin, rivel soup is made extensively in areas with Pennsylvania Dutch, Mennonite and Amish communities. Rivel means "lump," referring to the crumbly little egg dumplings. The soup is sometimes referred to by different names, such as dough-ball soup and farmer's rice.

JALAPENO POPPER MEGA BURGERS

If you like a little spice in your food, these big burgers stuffed with cheese and jalapenos are the ones for you. Just be sure to have plenty of frosty drinks on hand to serve with them!
—**KRIS SWIHART** PERRYSBURG, OHIO

PREP: 25 MIN. **GRILL:** 15 MIN. **MAKES:** 4 SERVINGS

- 1 medium ripe avocado, peeled and cubed
- 1 medium tomato, finely chopped
- 1 small onion, finely chopped
- 1 can (4 ounces) diced jalapeno peppers, drained, divided
- 1 tablespoon lime juice
- 1 garlic clove, minced
- 2 pounds ground beef
- 4 ounces reduced-fat cream cheese
- 1 cup (4 ounces) shredded Monterey Jack cheese
- 1 tablespoon steak seasoning
- 4 kaiser rolls, split
- 4 Bibb lettuce leaves

1. In a small bowl, combine the avocado, tomato, onion, ¼ cup jalapenos, lime juice and garlic; set aside.
2. Shape beef into eight patties. In another bowl, combine the cheeses and remaining jalapenos. Spoon onto the center of four patties. Top with remaining patties and press edges firmly to seal; sprinkle burgers with steak seasoning.
3. Grill burgers, covered, over medium heat for 6-7 minutes on each side or until a thermometer reads 160°. Serve on rolls with lettuce leaves and avocado mixture.

Editor's Note: *This recipe was tested with McCormick's Montreal Steak Seasoning. Look for it in the spice aisle.*

SPICY COWBOY CHILI

When making my chili, I always add the step of toasting the ancho and chipotle peppers. It releases their earthy flavors.

— **RACHEL SPRINKEL** HILO, HAWAII

PREP: 45 MIN. **COOK:** 7 HOURS
MAKES: 14 SERVINGS (3½ QUARTS)

- 1 **whole garlic bulb**
- 2 **to 3 tablespoons olive oil, divided**
- 2 **dried ancho chilies**
- 2 **dried chipotle chilies**
- 1 **bottle (12 ounces) dark beer**
- 3 **pounds beef stew meat, cut into ¾-inch pieces**
- 2 **large onions, chopped**
- 3 **cans (16 ounces each) kidney beans, rinsed and drained**
- 3 **cans (14½ ounces each) diced tomatoes, undrained**
- 2 **cans (8 ounces each) tomato sauce**
- 2 **tablespoons Worcestershire sauce**
- 1 **tablespoon chili powder**
- 1 **teaspoon pepper**
- ½ **teaspoon salt**
  Shredded cheddar cheese, optional

1. Remove the papery outer skin from the garlic bulb, but do not peel or separate the cloves. Cut off the top of the garlic bulb, exposing the individual cloves. Brush cut cloves with 1 teaspoon oil. Wrap in foil. Bake at 425° for 30-35 minutes or until cloves are soft. Unwrap and cool slightly. Squeeze garlic from the skins; mash with a fork.

2. Meanwhile, in a large dry skillet over medium-high heat, toast chilies on both sides until puffy, about 3-6 minutes. (Do not blacken.) Cool. Remove the stems and seeds; coarsely chop chilies. Place in a small bowl; cover with beer. Let stand to soften, about 30 minutes.

3. In the same skillet, heat 1 tablespoon oil over medium-high heat. Brown the beef in batches, adding additional oil if needed; transfer to a 6-qt. slow cooker. In the skillet, heat 2 teaspoons oil over medium heat. Add the onions; cook and stir until tender. Add to the beef.

4. Stir in the remaining ingredients, mashed garlic and dried chilies mixture. Cover and cook on low for 7-9 hours or until the meat is tender. If desired, serve with cheese.

Editor's Note: *One-half teaspoon ground chipotle pepper may be substituted for the dried chipotle chilies; add ground chipotle with mashed garlic and beer mixture to slow cooker.*

ANDOUILLE-SHRIMP CREAM SOUP

This zippy, creamy soup is a variation on a southern Louisiana corn stew. The boldness of the andouille sausage blends beautifully with the shrimp, vegetables and subtle spices.
—**JUDY ARMSTRONG** PRAIRIEVILLE, LOUISIANA

PREP: 20 MIN. **COOK:** 30 MIN. **MAKES:** 7 SERVINGS

- ½ **pound fully cooked andouille sausage links, thinly sliced**
- 1 **medium onion, chopped**
- 2 **celery ribs, thinly sliced**
- 1 **medium sweet red pepper, chopped**
- 1 **medium green pepper, chopped**
- 1 **jalapeno pepper, seeded and chopped**
- ¼ **cup butter, cubed**
- 3 **garlic cloves, minced**
- 2 **cups fresh or frozen corn, thawed**
- 4 **plum tomatoes, chopped**
- 1 **cup vegetable broth**
- 2 **tablespoons minced fresh thyme or 2 teaspoons dried thyme**
- 1 **teaspoon chili powder**
- ½ **teaspoon salt**
- ½ **teaspoon pepper**
- ¼ to ½ **teaspoon cayenne pepper**
- 1 **pound uncooked medium shrimp, peeled and deveined**
- 1 **cup heavy whipping cream**

1. In a large skillet, saute the first six ingredients in butter until the vegetables are tender. Add the garlic; cook 1 minute longer. Add the corn, tomatoes, vegetable broth, thyme, chili powder, salt, pepper and cayenne. Bring to a boil. Reduce heat; simmer, uncovered, for 10 minutes.

2. Stir in the shrimp and cream. Bring to a gentle boil. Simmer, uncovered, for 8-10 minutes or until shrimp turn pink.

Editor's Note: *Wear disposable gloves when cutting hot peppers; the oils can burn skin. Avoid touching your face.*

CORN AND SPINACH SALAD

As a child, I liked the combination of fresh spinach, crunchy nuts, cheese and red onions in a salad. When I was older, I visited different restaurants to see how chefs prepared similar dishes. Here's my own version with a homemade dressing.
—**ROBIN HAAS** CRANSTON, RHODE ISLAND

PREP/TOTAL TIME: 30 MIN.
MAKES: 8 SERVINGS (½ CUP DRESSING)

- ½ **cup chopped walnuts**
- 1 **tablespoon sugar**
- 1½ **teaspoons cider vinegar**
- 1 **package (6 ounces) fresh baby spinach**
- 1 **medium sweet red pepper, diced**
- 1 **medium red onion, diced**
- 1 **cup fresh or frozen corn, thawed**
- 1 **cup crumbled goat cheese**
- ¼ **cup dried cranberries**

DRESSING
- 3 **tablespoons cider vinegar**
- 2 **tablespoons orange marmalade**
- 2 **tablespoons mayonnaise**
- ½ **teaspoon salt**
- ½ **teaspoon pepper**
- ¼ **teaspoon Worcestershire sauce**

1. In a small heavy skillet, cook the walnuts over medium heat until toasted, about 3 minutes. Sprinkle with sugar and vinegar. Cook and stir for 2-4 minutes or until sugar is melted. Spread on foil to cool.

2. In a large bowl, combine the spinach, red pepper, onion, corn, cheese and cranberries; sprinkle with walnuts. In a small bowl, whisk the dressing ingredients. Serve with salad.

TURKEY BURGERS WITH BLUEBERRY BBQ SAUCE

I created these change-of-pace cheeseburgers to take advantage of the nutrition benefits—and refreshing flavor—of blueberries. The fruity barbecue sauce really complements the turkey patties.

—LORI MERRICK DANVERS, ILLINOIS

PREP/TOTAL TIME: 30 MIN. **MAKES:** 4 SERVINGS

- ¼ cup chopped onion
- 1 garlic clove, minced
- 1 teaspoon olive oil
- 2 cups fresh or frozen blueberries, thawed
- 2 tablespoons brown sugar
- 1 chipotle pepper in adobo sauce, chopped
- 2 tablespoons red wine vinegar
- 1 tablespoon Dijon mustard
- 1 tablespoon Worcestershire sauce

BURGERS
- 1 pound lean ground turkey
- ½ teaspoon salt
- ½ teaspoon pepper
- 1 cup sliced fresh mushrooms
- 4 slices reduced-fat provolone cheese
- 4 whole wheat hamburger buns, split
- ½ cup fresh baby spinach

1. In a large skillet, cook onion and garlic in oil over medium heat until tender. Stir in the blueberries, brown sugar, pepper, vinegar, mustard and Worcestershire sauce. Cook and stir until thickened, about 10 minutes. Cool slightly. Transfer to a food processor; cover and process until smooth.

2. Shape the turkey into four patties; sprinkle with salt and pepper. Place mushrooms on a double thickness of heavy-duty foil (about 12 in. square). Fold the foil around mushrooms and seal tightly.

3. Grill burgers and mushroom packet, covered, over medium heat for 5-7 minutes on each side or until a thermometer inserted into the burgers reads 165° and juices run clear. Top burgers with cheese; cover and grill 1-2 minutes longer or until cheese is melted.

4. Place the buns, cut side down, on grill for 1-2 minutes or until toasted. Serve burgers on buns with mushrooms, spinach and blueberry sauce.

Editor's Note: *Wear disposable gloves when cutting hot peppers; the oils can burn skin. Avoid touching your face.*

LAYERED BROCCOLI SALAD

My veggie salad is one of our mealtime staples. The colorful layers look festive, and the crisp broccoli, sunflower seeds and crumbled bacon contrast nicely with the chewy dried cranberries.

—DARLENE BRENDEN SALEM, OREGON

PREP/TOTAL TIME: 20 MIN. **MAKES:** 8 SERVINGS

- 6 cups chopped fresh broccoli florets
- 1 small red onion, thinly sliced
- ⅔ cup dried cranberries
- ½ cup plain yogurt
- 2 tablespoons mayonnaise
- 2 tablespoons honey
- 2 tablespoons cider vinegar
- 1½ cups (6 ounces) shredded cheddar cheese
- ¼ cup sunflower kernels
- 2 bacon strips, cooked and crumbled

In a large glass bowl, layer the broccoli, onion and cranberries. Combine the yogurt, mayonnaise, honey and vinegar; drizzle over salad. Sprinkle with cheese, sunflower kernels and bacon.

MANGO CHICKEN WRAPS

When I want to make sandwiches for my family, I frequently turn to these deliciously different wraps. The spiced-up chicken strips taste amazing with the tangy mango sauce.
—**JAN WARREN-RUCKER** CLEMMONS, NORTH CAROLINA

PREP: 30 MIN. **COOK:** 10 MIN. **MAKES:** 5 SERVINGS

- 1½ cups chopped peeled mangoes
- ¼ cup chopped red onion
- 1 jalapeno pepper, seeded and chopped
- 2 tablespoons lime juice
- 1 teaspoon honey
- ¼ cup fresh cilantro leaves
- 2 packages (6 ounces each) ready-to-use grilled chicken breast strips
- 1½ teaspoons ground cumin
- ¾ teaspoon garlic powder
- ¾ teaspoon chili powder
- ⅛ teaspoon cayenne pepper
  Dash dried oregano
- 4 teaspoons olive oil
- 5 whole wheat tortillas (8 inches)
- ¾ cup shredded Monterey Jack cheese
- 1 small sweet red pepper, julienned
- ¾ cup chopped tomatoes
- 1 cup torn leaf lettuce

1. In a food processor, combine the mangoes, onion, jalapeno, lime juice and honey. Cover and process until pureed. Stir in the cilantro; set aside.

2. In a large skillet, saute the chicken, cumin, garlic powder, chili powder, cayenne pepper and oregano in oil until heated through. Spread the mango sauce over the tortillas. Layer with the chicken, Monterey Jack cheese, red pepper, tomatoes and lettuce; roll up.

Editor's Note: *Wear disposable gloves when cutting hot peppers; the oils can burn skin. Avoid touching your face.*

PEARL PASTA SALAD

I sampled a pearl pasta dish at a Sacramento hotel and just loved it. Here's my version. It's great to take on camping trips or picnics.
—**RACHAEL ZAVALA** PLEASANT HILL, CALIFORNIA

PREP/TOTAL TIME: 25 MIN. **MAKES:** 15 SERVINGS

- 2 cups uncooked acini di pepe pasta
- 3 cups frozen corn
- 1 jar (14 ounces) oil-packed sun-dried tomatoes, drained and chopped
- 1 jar (6 ounces) prepared pesto
- ½ cup grated Parmesan cheese
- ¼ cup olive oil
- ⅛ teaspoon salt
- ⅛ teaspoon pepper

1. In a large saucepan, cook the pasta according to the package directions, adding the corn during the last 2 minutes. Drain and rinse in cold water.

2. In a large bowl, combine tomatoes, pesto, Parmesan cheese, oil, salt and pepper. Add pasta and corn; toss to coat. Refrigerate until serving.

MOJITO PULLED PORK

Citrus juices give this slow-cooked pulled pork the flair of popular mojito drinks. Serve the flavorful, fork-tender meat on a bun, in a tortilla or even spooned over cooked rice.

—MINDY OSWALT WINNETKA, CALIFORNIA

PREP: 20 MIN. **COOK:** 7 HOURS **MAKES:** 16 SERVINGS

- 1 boneless pork shoulder roast (4 to 5 pounds)
- 2 teaspoons salt
- 2 teaspoons dried oregano
- 2 teaspoons each ground cumin, paprika and pepper
- 1 bunch fresh cilantro, divided
- 2 medium onions, halved and sliced
- ¼ cup canned chopped green chilies
- 4 garlic cloves, minced
- 2 cans (14½ ounces each) reduced-sodium chicken broth
- ⅔ cup orange juice
- ½ cup lime juice
- 16 sandwich buns, split
   Barbecue sauce

1. Cut roast in half. Combine the salt, oregano, cumin, paprika and pepper; rub over pork. Place in a 4- or 5-qt. slow cooker.
2. Mince cilantro to measure ¼ cup; set aside. Trim remaining cilantro, discarding stems. Add the whole cilantro leaves, onions, chilies and garlic to the slow cooker. Combine the broth, orange juice and lime juice; pour over roast. Cover and cook on low for 7-9 hours or until meat is tender.
3. Remove roast; cool slightly. Skim fat from cooking juices; set aside 3 cups juices. Discard remaining juices. Shred pork with two forks and return to slow cooker. Stir in minced cilantro and reserved cooking juices; heat through. Spoon ½ cup meat onto each bun. Serve with barbecue sauce.

SIMPLY ELEGANT TOMATO SOUP

If the only tomato soup you've eaten came from a can, you're going to be blown away when you try a bowl of this simple homemade blend. It's velvety, creamy and so good!

—HEIDI BLANKEN SEDRO-WOOLLEY, WASHINGTON

PREP: 25 MIN. **COOK:** 20 MIN. **MAKES:** 4 SERVINGS

- 4 pounds tomatoes (about 10 medium)
- 1 tablespoon butter
- 3 tablespoons minced chives, divided
- 1 teaspoon salt
- ½ teaspoon pepper
- 2 cups half-and-half cream

1. In a large saucepan, bring 8 cups water to a boil. Using a slotted spoon, place tomatoes, one at a time, in boiling water for 30-60 seconds. Remove each tomato and immediately plunge in ice water. Peel and quarter tomatoes; remove seeds.
2. In another large saucepan, melt the butter. Add the tomatoes, 2 tablespoons chives, salt and pepper. Bring to a boil. Reduce the heat; simmer, uncovered, for 6-7 minutes or until tender, stirring occasionally. Remove from the heat. Cool slightly.
3. In a blender, process the soup until blended. Return to the pan. Stir in the half-and-half cream; heat through. Sprinkle each serving with remaining chives.

Pass the Potato Salad!

For backyard barbecues, church picnics and other get-togethers, a big bowl of potato salad is guaranteed to please. So dig into a heaping helping of the spud selections here.

SMOKY SPANISH POTATO SALAD

I originally created this dish for red potatoes, but I discovered that fingerlings and Yukon Golds work well, too. With artichoke hearts and smoked Spanish paprika, it's sure to liven up any menu.
—**HELEN CONWELL** PORTLAND, OREGON

PREP: 1 HOUR + COOLING **MAKES:** 8 SERVINGS

> 1¾ pounds red potatoes (about 7 medium)
> 2 tablespoons olive oil
> 1 teaspoon smoked Spanish paprika
> ½ teaspoon salt
> 1 jar (6 ounces) marinated quartered artichoke hearts
> 1 cup (8 ounces) sour cream
> ¼ cup mayonnaise
> 1 celery rib, thinly sliced
> 2 tablespoons capers, drained
> 2 green onions, sliced
> 3 tablespoons minced fresh basil

1. Scrub the potatoes; cut into 1-in. pieces. Place in a large bowl; drizzle with oil and sprinkle with smoked Spanish paprika and salt. Toss to coat. Transfer to a greased 15-in. x 10-in. x 1-in. baking pan. Bake at 425° for 35-40 minutes or until tender, stirring occasionally. Cool.

2. Drain the artichokes, reserving 2 tablespoons marinade; place artichokes and potatoes in a large bowl. In another bowl, combine sour cream, mayonnaise, celery, capers, green onions, basil and reserved marinade. Pour over potato mixture and toss to coat. Chill until serving.

CREAMY GERMAN POTATO SALAD

My mother's recipe has been a salad staple in our family for years. The whipping cream gives it a wonderful richness.
—**TRACY ZETTELMEIER** MUKWONAGO, WISCONSIN

PREP/TOTAL TIME: 30 MIN. **MAKES:** 13 SERVINGS (¾ CUP EACH)

> 4½ pounds red potatoes (about 18 medium)
> ½ pound bacon strips, diced
> 1 medium onion, chopped
> 4 teaspoons all-purpose flour
> ¾ cup sugar
> ¾ cup cider vinegar
> 1 cup heavy whipping cream

1. Cut potatoes into ½-in. cubes; place in a stock pot and cover with water. Bring to a boil. Reduce heat; cover and simmer for 10-12 minutes or until tender.

2. In a Dutch oven, cook bacon over medium heat until crisp. Using a slotted spoon, remove to paper towels; drain, reserving 5 tablespoons drippings. Set bacon aside.

3. In the same pan, saute onion in drippings until tender. Stir in flour until blended. Gradually stir in sugar and vinegar. Bring to a boil; cook and stir for 2 minutes until thickened.

4. Remove from the heat; gradually whisk in cream. Set aside. Drain potatoes. Transfer to a large bowl; add the reserved onion mixture and bacon. Stir gently to coat. Serve warm.

ROASTED SWEET AND GOLD POTATO SALAD

To make this medley extra colorful and festive, I mix in Mexicorn and black beans. Tossed with a zesty dressing, it's the best!

—JEANNE TRUDELL DEL NORTE, COLORADO

PREP: 1½ HOURS **MAKES:** 16 SERVINGS (¾ CUP EACH)

- 2½ pounds Yukon Gold potatoes (about 8 medium)
- 1½ pounds sweet potatoes (about 2 large)
- 2 tablespoons olive oil
- 1 tablespoon ground cumin
- 2 teaspoons chili powder
- 2 teaspoons garlic powder
- 4 thick-sliced bacon strips, chopped
- 4 green onions, sliced
- 1 medium sweet red pepper, finely chopped
- ½ cup minced fresh cilantro
- 2 hard-cooked eggs, chopped
- ¾ cup mayonnaise
- 1 tablespoon chopped chipotle pepper in adobo sauce
- 2 teaspoons sugar
- 1 large ripe avocado, peeled and finely chopped
- 2 tablespoons lime juice

1. Peel and cut the potatoes and sweet potatoes into ¾-in. cubes. Place in a large bowl; drizzle with oil and sprinkle with seasonings. Toss to coat. Transfer to two greased 15-in. x 10-in. x 1-in. baking pans. Bake at 450° for 45-55 minutes or until tender, stirring occasionally. Cool slightly.

2. In a small skillet, cook bacon over medium heat until crisp. Remove to paper towels with a slotted spoon; drain.

3. In a large bowl, combine the potatoes, bacon, onions, red pepper, cilantro and eggs. Combine the mayonnaise, chipotle and sugar; pour over potato mixture and toss to coat. In a small bowl, toss avocado with lime juice; gently stir into salad. Serve warm or cold.

CHIPOTLE PEPPER POTATO SALAD

The next time you're planning to serve potato salad, think outside the picnic basket and head south of the border with this crunchy, munchy and flavorful variation. It gets a tongue-tingling kick from chipotle peppers in adobo sauce and cumin.

—JENNIFER WALKER DENVER, COLORADO

PREP: 40 MIN. + CHILLING **MAKES:** 8 SERVINGS

- 2 pounds red potatoes, peeled and cut into 1-inch cubes
- 1 cup chopped red onion
- 2 green onions, sliced
- ½ cup fresh or frozen corn, thawed
- ½ cup chopped sweet yellow pepper
- ½ cup chopped sweet red pepper
- 2 hard-cooked eggs, chopped
- ¼ cup minced fresh cilantro
- 1 cup mayonnaise
- ¼ cup lime juice
- 4 chipotle peppers in adobo sauce, finely chopped, plus 2 teaspoons adobo sauce
- 2 garlic cloves, minced
- 2 teaspoons grated lime peel
- 1 teaspoon ground cumin
- ½ teaspoon salt
- ½ teaspoon pepper

1. Place potatoes in a large saucepan; cover with water. Bring to a boil. Reduce heat; cover and cook for 10-15 minutes or until tender. Drain and cool to room temperature.

2. In a large bowl, lightly mash 1½ cups potatoes. Add onions, corn, sweet peppers, eggs, cilantro and remaining potatoes.

3. In a small bowl, combine the mayonnaise, lime juice, chipotle peppers and adobo sauce, garlic, lime peel, cumin, salt and pepper. Pour over potato mixture and toss to coat. Refrigerate for 1 hour or until chilled.

CRAN-RASPBERRY GELATIN SALAD

Just like Mom's, this pretty gelatin mold has refreshing berry flavor without being too tart. It's perfect for Thanksgiving dinner.

—**ROSEMARY BURCH** PHOENIX, ARIZONA

PREP: 15 MIN. + CHILLING **MAKES:** 10 SERVINGS

- 2 **packages (3 ounces each) raspberry gelatin**
- 1 **cup boiling water**
- 1 **can (14 ounces) whole-berry cranberry sauce**
- 1 **can (8 ounces) crushed pineapple, undrained**
- 1 **cup orange juice**

1. In a large bowl, dissolve gelatin in boiling water. Stir in the cranberry sauce, pineapple and orange juice. Pour into a 6-cup ring mold coated with cooking spray.
2. Cover and refrigerate for 4 hours or until set. Unmold onto a serving platter.

SUNFLOWER NOODLE COLESLAW

Dressed up with sunflower oil and kernels, my slaw is a mainstay at family get-togethers. Using a convenient packaged mix and basic pantry items, I can whip up a big batch in 15 minutes.

—**EILEEN HERMAN** BRINSMADE, NORTH DAKOTA

PREP/TOTAL TIME: 15 MIN. **MAKES:** 10 SERVINGS

- 1 **package (3 ounces) chicken ramen noodles**
- 1 **package (14 ounces) coleslaw mix**
- ½ **cup unsalted sunflower kernels**
- ¼ **cup chopped green pepper**
- ⅓ **cup sunflower oil**
- ¼ **cup white vinegar**
- 3 **tablespoons sugar**
- 1 **tablespoon poppy seeds**
- ¾ **teaspoon pepper**

1. Break noodles into small pieces. In a large bowl, combine the noodles, coleslaw mix, sunflower kernels and green pepper.
2. In a small bowl, whisk oil, vinegar, sugar, poppy seeds, pepper and contents of seasoning packet. Pour over the salad and toss to coat. Chill until serving.

CREAM OF CRAB SOUP

A friend of mine brought her creamy crab soup to a potluck. After just one delectable spoonful, I had to have the recipe!

—**MARILYN SHAW** MIDDLETOWN, DELAWARE

PREP: 20 MIN. **COOK:** 20 MIN.
MAKES: 14 SERVINGS (3½ QUARTS)

- 1 **large onion, finely chopped**
- 1 **medium green pepper, finely chopped**
- 2 **tablespoons butter**
- 2 **garlic cloves, minced**
- 3 **pints half-and-half cream**
- 2 **cups frozen shredded hash brown potatoes, thawed**
- 1 **can (10¾ ounces) condensed cream of mushroom soup, undiluted**
- 1 **can (10¾ ounces) condensed cream of asparagus soup, undiluted**
- 2 **cans (6 ounces each) lump crabmeat, drained**
- 1 **package (8 ounces) imitation crabmeat, chopped**
- 1½ **cups frozen corn, thawed**
- 1 **tablespoon dried parsley flakes**
- 1½ **teaspoons dill weed**
- 1½ **teaspoons seafood seasoning**
- 1 **teaspoon pepper**

In a Dutch oven, saute onion and green pepper in butter until tender. Add garlic; saute 1 minute longer. Stir in the remaining ingredients. Cook and stir over medium-low heat until heated through (do not boil).

ITALIAN-STYLE ONION SOUP

On a chilly winter's day, warm everyone from head to toe with a steaming pot of this well-seasoned soup. Each bowl boasts a slice of cheesy, tomato-topped toast as the crowning touch.

—**DEBBIE MILLER** OLDSMAR, FLORIDA

PREP: 20 MIN. **COOK:** 45 MIN. **MAKES:** 5 SERVINGS

- 2 tablespoons butter
- 1 tablespoon olive oil
- 6 medium sweet onions, thinly sliced (about 6 cups)
- ½ teaspoon minced fresh rosemary
- ¼ teaspoon salt, divided
- ¼ teaspoon pepper, divided
- 6 cups beef broth
- ½ cup white wine or additional beef broth
- 1 tablespoon balsamic vinegar
- 1 cup grape tomatoes, quartered
- ½ cup fresh basil leaves, thinly sliced
- ¼ cup grated Parmesan cheese
- ½ teaspoon garlic powder
- 5 slices day-old French bread (1½ inches thick), toasted
- 5 slices part-skim mozzarella cheese

1. In a Dutch oven over medium heat, melt butter with the oil. Add the onions, rosemary, ⅛ teaspoon salt and ⅛ teaspoon pepper. Cook for 30 minutes or until lightly browned, stirring occasionally. Add the broth, wine and vinegar; heat through.

2. Meanwhile, in a small bowl, combine the tomatoes, basil, Parmesan cheese, garlic powder and remaining salt and pepper. Spoon tomato mixture over bread slices; top with mozzarella. Place on a baking sheet.

3. Broil 3-4 in. from the heat for 2-3 minutes or until the cheese is melted. Ladle the soup into bowls; top with the toast. Serve immediately.

ORZO VEGETABLE SALAD

Heading to a cookout and need something to share? Combine tiny orzo pasta and fresh vegetables with a homemade lemon dressing, and you'll have a crowd-pleasing summer dish.

—**TERRI CRANDALL** GARDNERVILLE, NEVADA

PREP/TOTAL TIME: 30 MIN. **MAKES:** 6 SERVINGS

- ½ cup uncooked orzo pasta
- 3 plum tomatoes, chopped
- 1 cup marinated quartered artichoke hearts, chopped
- 1 cup coarsely chopped fresh spinach
- 2 green onions, chopped
- ½ cup crumbled feta cheese
- 1 tablespoon capers, drained

DRESSING

- ⅓ cup olive oil
- 4 teaspoons lemon juice
- 1 tablespoon minced fresh tarragon or 1 teaspoon dried tarragon
- 2 teaspoons grated lemon peel
- 2 teaspoons rice vinegar
- ½ teaspoon salt
- ¼ teaspoon pepper

1. Cook the orzo pasta according to the package directions.

2. Meanwhile, in a large bowl, combine tomatoes, artichokes, spinach, onions, cheese and capers. In a small bowl, whisk the dressing ingredients.

3. Drain the orzo and rinse in cold water. Add to the vegetable mixture. Pour the dressing over the salad; toss to coat. Chill salad until serving.

GOLDEN GOUDA MUSHROOM SOUP

Here's a fantastic first course for guests—or a heartwarming meal any time with fresh-baked rolls. The rich, cheesy and creamy soup looks extra-special garnished with chives and paprika.
—**CHARLOTTE ROGERS** VIRGINIA BEACH, VIRGINIA

PREP/TOTAL TIME: 30 MIN. **MAKES:** 6 SERVINGS

- ½ cup butter, cubed
- ½ cup all-purpose flour
- ½ teaspoon pepper
- ½ teaspoon ground allspice
- 1 carton (32 ounces) chicken broth
- ½ cup sherry or additional chicken broth
- ½ cup heavy whipping cream
- ½ pound sliced fresh mushrooms
- 4 garlic cloves, minced
- 2 cups (8 ounces) shredded smoked Gouda cheese
  Chives and smoked paprika

1. In a large saucepan, melt butter. Stir in the flour, pepper and allspice until smooth; gradually add the broth, sherry and cream. Bring to a boil. Add mushrooms and garlic. Reduce heat; cover and simmer for 5-6 minutes or until mushrooms are tender.
2. Add cheese; cook and stir until melted. Garnish servings with chives and paprika.

SMOKED SALMON BAGEL SANDWICHES

When I tried a memorable pesto salmon in Hawaii, I was inspired to experiment and came up with my own sandwiches. Pack them for lunch or serve them at your next brunch buffet.
—**SHERRYL VERA** HURLBURT FIELD, FLORIDA

PREP/TOTAL TIME: 10 MIN. **MAKES:** 2 SERVINGS

- 2 tablespoons prepared pesto
- 2 whole wheat bagels, split and toasted
- ⅛ teaspoon coarsely ground pepper
- 4 to 5 ounces smoked salmon or lox

- 2 slices tomato
- 2 Bibb or Boston lettuce leaves

Spread pesto over bagel bottoms; sprinkle with pepper. Layer with salmon, tomato and lettuce leaves. Replace tops.

BBQ BEEF SANDWICHES

After years of searching, I discovered a slow cooker recipe for shredded barbecue beef that my friends and relatives really love. It's easy to freeze, too—assuming there's any left over!
—**REBECCA ROHLAND** MEDFORD, WISCONSIN

PREP: 15 MIN. **COOK:** 8 HOURS **MAKES:** 14 SERVINGS

- 2 cups ketchup
- 1 medium onion, chopped
- ¼ cup cider vinegar
- ¼ cup molasses
- 2 tablespoons Worcestershire sauce
- 2 garlic cloves, minced
- ½ teaspoon salt
- ½ teaspoon ground mustard
- ½ teaspoon pepper
- ¼ teaspoon garlic powder
- ¼ teaspoon crushed red pepper flakes
- 1 boneless beef chuck roast (3 pounds)
- 14 sesame seed hamburger buns, split

1. In a large bowl, combine the first 11 ingredients. Cut roast in half; place in a 5-qt. slow cooker. Pour ketchup mixture over roast. Cover; cook on low for 8-10 hours or until meat is tender.
2. Remove the meat and shred with two forks. Skim the fat from the cooking juices. Return meat to slow cooker; heat through. Using a slotted spoon, serve beef on buns.

CHILLED CORN AND SHRIMP SOUP

Hot days call for cool foods, like this chilled seafood favorite. It's so pretty and unique, your guests are sure to remember it.
—**MARY MARLOWE LEVERETTE** COLUMBIA, SOUTH CAROLINA

PREP: 30 MIN. + CHILLING **MAKES:** 4 SERVINGS

- ½ cup chopped sweet onion
- 3 tablespoons olive oil
- 1½ pounds uncooked small shrimp, peeled and deveined
- 2 garlic cloves, minced
- 1 teaspoon curry powder
- 2 cups buttermilk
- 1 package (16 ounces) frozen shoepeg corn, thawed, divided
- 1 cup (8 ounces) reduced-fat sour cream
- 1 teaspoon hot pepper sauce
- 1 teaspoon salt
- ½ teaspoon coarsely ground pepper
- 2 tablespoons minced chives

1. In a large skillet, saute the onion in oil until tender. Add the shrimp, garlic and curry; saute 4-6 minutes longer or until the shrimp turn pink. Remove from the heat and set aside.
2. In a blender, combine buttermilk, 2 cups corn, sour cream, pepper sauce, salt and pepper. Cover and process until smooth; transfer to a large bowl. Add the remaining corn and shrimp mixture. Cover soup and refrigerate for at least 3 hours. Garnish each serving with chives.

ORANGE-POPPY SEED COLESLAW

This crisp, crunchy coleslaw features a refreshing orange dressing. We like it best with a main course of pot roast.
—**NANCY LATULIPPE** SIMCOE, ONTARIO

PREP/TOTAL TIME: 15 MIN. **MAKES:** 6 SERVINGS

- 3 cups finely shredded red cabbage
- 1 celery rib, thinly sliced
- 1 medium orange, peeled, sectioned and cut into bite-size pieces
- 4 green onions, chopped
- 3 tablespoons orange juice
- 1 tablespoon olive oil
- 1 tablespoon honey
- 2 teaspoons poppy seeds
- 1 teaspoon Dijon mustard
- ¼ teaspoon salt
- ¼ teaspoon pepper

In a large bowl, combine the cabbage, celery, orange and onions. In a small bowl, whisk the remaining ingredients. Pour over the coleslaw and toss to coat. Refrigerate until serving.

CONNIE'S TORTELLINI SALAD

My salad is nice for lazy weekends, when family members can just grab some whenever they're hungry. The tortellini makes it filling.
— **CONNIE EATON** PITTSBURGH, PENNSYLVANIA

PREP/TOTAL TIME: 30 MIN. **MAKES:** 16 SERVINGS (¾ CUP EACH)

- 1 package (13 ounces) dried cheese tortellini
- 1 medium zucchini, halved and sliced
- 1 cup Italian salad dressing
- 1 pint grape tomatoes
- 1 can (14 ounces) water-packed artichoke hearts, rinsed, drained and quartered
- 1 jar (11.1 ounces) pitted Greek olives, drained
- 1 carton (8 ounces) miniature fresh mozzarella cheese balls, drained

In a large saucepan, cook the tortellini according to the package directions. Drain; transfer to a large bowl. Immediately add the zucchini and salad dressing; toss to coat. Stir in the remaining ingredients. Serve warm or refrigerate and serve cold.

COLORFUL BEAN SALAD

My husband loves all varieties of beans, and I experimented with many different salad combinations before hitting on the right one. Corn and other veggies add to the color and texture.

—**DALE BENOIT** MONSON, MASSACHUSETTS

PREP: 30 MIN. + CHILLING **MAKES:** 13 SERVINGS (¾ CUP EACH)

- 2 cups fresh or frozen corn, thawed
- 1 can (16 ounces) kidney beans, rinsed and drained
- 1 can (16 ounces) red beans, rinsed and drained
- 1 can (15½ ounces) white kidney or cannellini beans, rinsed and drained
- 1 can (15¼ ounces) lima beans, rinsed and drained
- 1 can (15 ounces) black beans, rinsed and drained
- 1 can (2¼ ounces) sliced ripe olives, drained
- 1 large green pepper, chopped
- 1 small onion, chopped
- ½ cup chili sauce
- ¼ cup olive oil
- ¼ cup red wine vinegar
- 2 garlic cloves, minced
- 2 teaspoons dried oregano
- ½ teaspoon pepper

1. In a large bowl, combine the first nine ingredients. In a small bowl, whisk the chili sauce, oil, red wine vinegar, garlic, oregano and pepper. Pour over bean mixture; toss to coat.

2. Refrigerate salad for at least 1 hour before serving.

GOLDEN SUMMER PEACH GAZPACHO

Because peaches and tomatoes are in season together, I thought of pairing them in a cool, refreshing gazpacho for summer. Leftovers keep well in the refrigerator—if you have any.

—**JULIE HESSION** LAS VEGAS, NEVADA

PREP: 20 MIN. + CHILLING **MAKES:** 8 SERVINGS

- 3 cups sliced peeled fresh or frozen peaches, thawed
- 3 medium yellow tomatoes, chopped
- 1 medium sweet yellow pepper, chopped
- 1 medium cucumber, peeled and chopped
- ½ cup chopped sweet onion
- 1 garlic clove, minced
- ⅓ cup lime juice
- 2 tablespoons rice vinegar
- 1 tablespoon marinade for chicken
- 1 teaspoon salt
- ¼ teaspoon hot pepper sauce
- 1 to 3 teaspoons sugar, optional
  Thin cucumber slices

1. Place the first six ingredients in a food processor; cover and process until blended. Add the lime juice, vinegar, marinade for chicken, salt and pepper sauce; cover and process until smooth. Stir in sugar if desired.

2. Cover and refrigerate for at least 4 hours. Garnish servings with cucumber.

Editor's Note: *This recipe was tested with Lea & Perrins Marinade for Chicken.*

ZESTY ITALIAN SOUP

While I was visiting my sister-in-law, we had a terrific Italian soup at a local restaurant. We decided to try duplicating it at home and came up with this version. Feel free to vary the seasonings and types of canned tomatoes you use to suit your family's tastes.

—MYRNA SIPPEL THOMPSON, ILLINOIS

PREP: 15 MIN. **COOK:** 7 HOURS
MAKES: 10 SERVINGS (3½ QUARTS)

1 **pound bulk Italian sausage**
3 **cans (14½ ounces each) reduced-sodium chicken broth**
1 **can (15 ounces) black beans, rinsed and drained**
1 **can (15 ounces) pinto beans, rinsed and drained**
1 **can (14½ ounces) diced tomatoes and green chilies, undrained**
1 **can (14½ ounces) Italian diced tomatoes**
1 **large carrot, chopped**
1 **jalapeno pepper, seeded and chopped**
1½ **teaspoons Italian seasoning**
1 **teaspoon dried minced garlic**
1½ **cups cooked elbow macaroni**

1. In a large skillet, cook the sausage over medium heat until no longer pink; drain.

2. Transfer to a 5-qt. slow cooker. Stir in chicken broth, beans, tomatoes, carrot, jalapeno, Italian seasoning and garlic.

3. Cover and cook on low for 7-8 hours or until heated through. Just before serving, stir in macaroni.

Editor's Note: *Wear disposable gloves when cutting hot peppers; the oils can burn skin. Avoid touching your face.*

PASTA POINTER

If added to a slow cooker when dry, pasta tends to become very sticky. When preparing Zesty Italian Soup (above left) or similar slow cooker recipes that call for pasta, it's better to cook the pasta according to the package directions and stir it into the slow cooker just before serving.

SIDE DISHES & CONDIMENTS

As good as a main course may be, a meal just isn't complete without equally tasty accompaniments. Rely on this chapter to round out any menu, from a fast family dinner on a busy weeknight to a special holiday feast.

SPICY SWEET POTATO FRIES

You'll want to pile these sweet-and-spicy favorites high on each plate. Served with a creamy mayonnaise dip that gets a kick from cayenne pepper, these fries create cravings for more.
—**MARY JONES** WILLIAMSTOWN, WEST VIRGINIA

PREP: 25 MIN. **BAKE:** 30 MIN. **MAKES:** 5 SERVINGS

- 1 teaspoon coriander seeds
- ½ teaspoon fennel seed
- ½ teaspoon dried oregano
- ½ teaspoon crushed red pepper flakes
- ½ teaspoon salt
- 2 pounds sweet potatoes (about 4 medium), peeled and cut into wedges
- 2 tablespoons canola oil

SPICY MAYONNAISE DIP

- 1¼ cups mayonnaise
- 2 tablespoons lime juice
- 2 tablespoons minced fresh cilantro
- 2 garlic cloves, minced
- 1 teaspoon ground mustard
- ¼ teaspoon cayenne pepper
- ⅛ teaspoon salt

1. In a spice grinder or with a mortar and pestle, combine the coriander, fennel, oregano and red pepper flakes; grind until the mixture becomes a fine powder. Stir in salt.

2. In a large bowl, combine the potatoes, oil and ground spices; toss to coat. Transfer to a greased 15-in. x 10-in. x 1-in. baking pan.

3. Bake, uncovered, at 400° for 30-35 minutes or until crisp and golden brown, turning occasionally. Meanwhile, in a small bowl, combine the dip ingredients; chill until serving. Serve with fries.

BROCCOLI WITH ORANGE SAUCE

Broccoli doesn't have to be boring! Drape crisp-tender spears with a refreshing citrus yogurt sauce for a change-of-pace treat.
—**DORIS HEATH** FRANKLIN, NORTH CAROLINA

PREP/TOTAL TIME: 20 MIN. **MAKES:** 8 SERVINGS

- 3 pounds fresh broccoli, cut into spears
- 4½ teaspoons butter
- 4½ teaspoons all-purpose flour
- ⅓ cup orange juice
- ½ teaspoon grated orange peel
- ⅓ cup mandarin oranges, drained
- ¼ teaspoon dried tarragon
- ⅓ cup plain yogurt

1. Place broccoli in a large saucepan; add 1 in. of water. Bring to a boil. Reduce heat; cover and cook for 5-8 minutes or until crisp-tender.

2. Meanwhile, in a small saucepan, melt the butter. Whisk in the flour until smooth. Gradually stir in orange juice. Add the orange peel, mandarin oranges and tarragon. Bring to a boil; cook and stir for 2 minutes or until thickened. Remove from the heat; stir in yogurt. Drain broccoli; serve with sauce.

LEMON FRESH

Don't like the smell of broccoli, cauliflower or cabbage as it cooks? To reduce the odor, simply add a slice of lemon to the water.
—**ELIZABETH E.** BELLEVILLE, ONTARIO

INTERNATIONAL POTATO CAKE

When I need a side for a lunch or dinner party, I rely on my potato cake. I've also made it with lamb and ham in place of the salami.
—**JUDY BATSON** TAMPA, FLORIDA

PREP: 40 MIN. **BAKE:** 35 MIN. + STANDING **MAKES:** 12 SERVINGS

- ¼ cup seasoned bread crumbs
- 3 pounds potatoes (about 9 medium), peeled and cut into wedges
- ½ cup heavy whipping cream
- ¼ cup butter, cubed
- 3 eggs, beaten
- 1 teaspoon Greek seasoning
- ¼ teaspoon garlic salt
- ¼ teaspoon lemon-pepper seasoning
- ¼ pound thinly sliced fontina cheese
- ¼ pound thinly sliced hard salami, coarsely chopped

TOPPING
- ⅓ cup grated Parmesan cheese
- 1 tablespoon seasoned bread crumbs
- 1 tablespoon butter, melted

1. Sprinkle the bread crumbs onto the bottom of a greased 9-in. springform pan; set aside.

2. Place the potatoes in a large saucepan and cover with water. Bring to a boil. Reduce heat; cover and simmer for 15-20 minutes or until tender. Drain; transfer to a large bowl. Mash potatoes with cream, butter, eggs, and seasonings.

3. Spoon half of potatoes into prepared pan. Layer with cheese and salami; top with remaining potatoes. Combine the topping ingredients; spoon over potatoes.

4. Cover and bake at 350° for 30 minutes. Uncover; bake 5-10 minutes longer or until the topping is golden brown and a thermometer reads 160°. Cool on a wire rack for 10 minutes. Carefully run a knife around edge of pan to loosen; remove sides of pan. Serve warm.

GARLIC-ROASTED BRUSSELS SPROUTS WITH MUSTARD SAUCE

Don't be afraid to bring out the Brussels sprouts! Mellowed by roasting and jazzed up with a tangy Dijon mustard sauce, these will please even people who normally don't care for vegetables. Plus, the recipe comes together in just 20 minutes.
—**BECKY WALCH** ORLAND, CALIFORNIA

PREP/TOTAL TIME: 20 MIN. **MAKES:** 6 SERVINGS

- 1½ pounds fresh Brussels sprouts, halved
- 2 tablespoons olive oil
- 3 garlic cloves, minced
- ½ cup heavy whipping cream
- 3 tablespoons Dijon mustard
- ⅛ teaspoon white pepper
  Dash salt

1. Place Brussels sprouts in an ungreased 15-in. x 10-in. x 1-in. baking pan. Combine the oil and garlic; drizzle over sprouts and toss to coat.

2. Bake, uncovered, at 450° for 10-15 minutes or until tender, stirring occasionally.

3. Meanwhile, in a small saucepan, combine the heavy whipping cream, mustard, white pepper and salt. Bring to a gentle boil; cook for 1-2 minutes or until slightly thickened. Spoon over the Brussels sprouts.

TEXAS GARLIC MASHED POTATOES

These creamy mashed potatoes get a burst of flavor from garlic and caramelized onions. They're great with just about any meal.

—**RICHARD MARKLE** MIDLOTHIAN, TEXAS

PREP: 30 MIN. **BAKE:** 30 MIN. **MAKES:** 6 SERVINGS

- 1 whole garlic bulb
- 1 teaspoon plus 1 tablespoon olive oil, divided
- 1 medium white onion, chopped
- 4 medium potatoes, peeled and quartered
- ¼ cup butter, softened
- ¼ cup sour cream
- ¼ cup grated Parmesan cheese
- ¼ cup 2% milk
- ½ teaspoon salt
- ¼ teaspoon pepper

1. Remove the papery outer skin from the garlic (do not peel or separate cloves). Cut top off of garlic bulb. Brush with 1 teaspoon oil. Wrap bulb in heavy-duty foil. Bake at 425° for 30-35 minutes or until softened.

2. Meanwhile, in a large skillet over low heat, cook the onion in remaining oil for 15-20 minutes or until golden brown, stirring occasionally. Transfer to a food processor. Cover and process until blended; set aside.

3. Place the potatoes in a large saucepan and cover with water. Bring to a boil. Reduce heat; cover and cook for 15-20 minutes or until tender. Drain. Place potatoes in a large bowl. Squeeze softened garlic into bowl; add the butter, sour cream, cheese, milk, salt, pepper and onion. Beat until mashed.

SQUASH DRESSING

My husband's cousin gave me her wonderful dressing recipe. She always prepared it for her mother at Thanksgiving.

—**ANNA MAYER** FORT BRANCH, INDIANA

PREP: 30 MIN. + COOLING **BAKE:** 40 MIN. **MAKES:** 8 SERVINGS

- 1 package (8½ ounces) corn bread/muffin mix
- ½ cup water
- 4 cups chopped yellow summer squash
- ½ cup butter
- ½ cup each chopped onion, celery and green pepper
- 1 can (10¾ ounces) condensed cream of chicken soup, undiluted
- 1 cup milk
- 1 teaspoon salt
- ½ teaspoon pepper

1. Prepare corn bread according to package directions. Cool and crumble into a large bowl; set aside.

2. In a large saucepan, bring ½ cup of water to a boil. Add the squash; cook, covered, for 3-5 minutes or until crisp-tender. Drain. Meanwhile, in a large skillet, melt the butter. Add onion, celery and green pepper; saute until tender.

3. Add the vegetable mixture and squash to the corn bread. In a small bowl, combine the soup, milk, salt and pepper; add to corn bread and stir until blended. Transfer to a greased 11-in. x 7-in. baking dish.

4. Bake, uncovered, at 350° for 40-45 minutes or until golden brown.

JALAPENO-PEAR CHUTNEY

With hot peppers, pears, tomatoes, onions and more, this versatile chutney is a tongue-tingling treat. Serve it alongside your favorite meat entree...as a sandwich spread...over cream cheese for an appetizer...or even with chips as a salsa-style dip.

—DEB THOMSON GRAND ISLAND, NEBRASKA

PREP: 45 MIN. + SIMMERING **PROCESS:** 10 MIN.
MAKES: 5 HALF-PINTS

- 2 **pounds pears, peeled and chopped**
- 2 **pounds tomatoes, peeled, seeded and chopped**
- 2 **cups chopped onions**
- 1 **cup finely chopped seeded jalapeno peppers**
- 1 **cup cider vinegar**
- 1 **cup packed brown sugar**
- 4 **teaspoons minced fresh gingerroot**
- 1 **to 2 teaspoons crushed red pepper flakes**
- 1 **teaspoon ground mustard**

1. In a Dutch oven, combine all ingredients. Bring to a boil. Reduce heat; simmer, uncovered, for 45-60 minutes or until thickened, stirring occasionally.

2. Carefully ladle hot mixture into hot half-pint jars, leaving ½-in. headspace. Remove air bubbles; wipe rims and adjust lids. Process for 10 minutes in a boiling-water canner.

Editor's Note: *Wear disposable gloves when cutting hot peppers; the oils can burn skin. Avoid touching your face.*

ROASTED VEGETABLES WITH GREMOLATA

Traditional gremolata, an herb condiment, is made with parsley, lemon peel and garlic. Here, walnuts and Parmesan cheese add richness and crunch that enhance the potatoes and parsnips.

—FRAN FEHLING STATEN ISLAND, NEW YORK

PREP: 20 MIN. **BAKE:** 45 MIN. **MAKES:** 9 SERVINGS

- 3 **pounds sweet potatoes (about 4 large), peeled and cut into 1-inch cubes**
- 1 **pound parsnips, peeled and cut into 1-inch lengths**
- 6 **shallots, quartered**
- 5 **tablespoons olive oil, divided**
- 1 **teaspoon salt**
- ½ **teaspoon pepper**
- 1 **tablespoon lemon juice**

GREMOLATA
- ¾ **cup chopped walnuts, toasted**
- ⅓ **cup grated Parmesan cheese**
- 3 **tablespoons minced fresh parsley**
- 1 **tablespoon grated lemon peel**
- 1 **tablespoon lemon juice**
- 1 **tablespoon olive oil**
- 1 **garlic clove, minced**
- ¼ **teaspoon ground nutmeg**

1. Place the potatoes, parsnips and shallots in a greased shallow roasting pan. Drizzle with 4 tablespoons oil; sprinkle with salt and pepper. Bake at 425° for 45-50 minutes or until tender, stirring occasionally. Drizzle with lemon juice and remaining oil.

2. For gremolata, place walnuts in a food processor; cover and process until coarsely ground. Transfer to a small bowl; stir in the cheese, parsley, lemon peel and juice, oil, garlic and nutmeg. Sprinkle over vegetables. Serve warm.

GOURMET POTATOES AU GRATIN

Here's a different take on a classic potato dish. Bursting with the goodness of sun-dried tomatoes, it's special enough for guests.

—**KATHERINE BARRETT** BELLEVUE, WASHINGTON

PREP: 55 MIN. **BAKE:** 70 MIN. **MAKES:** 12 SERVINGS (⅔ CUP EACH)

- ½ cup sun-dried tomatoes (not packed in oil), chopped
- 1 cup boiling water
- 1 large onion, sliced
- 3 tablespoons butter
- 1 tablespoon minced fresh oregano
- ½ teaspoon salt
- ¼ teaspoon pepper
- ¼ cup all-purpose flour
- 2¼ cups fat-free milk
- 1 cup grated Parmesan cheese
- 3 pounds potatoes (about 9 medium), peeled and thinly sliced

1. Place tomatoes in a small bowl. Cover with boiling water; let stand for 5 minutes. Drain and set aside.

2. In a large skillet over medium heat, cook onion in butter until tender. Add the oregano, salt, pepper and reserved tomatoes; cook 2 minutes longer. Sprinkle with flour; stir until blended. Gradually add milk. Bring to a boil; cook and stir for 2 minutes or until thickened. Remove from the heat; stir in cheese.

3. Place potatoes in a greased 13-in. x 9-in. baking dish; top with sauce. Cover and bake at 350° for 1 hour. Uncover; bake 10-15 minutes longer or until potatoes are tender.

MOCHA CASHEW BUTTER

Blended with coffee, semisweet chocolate and cashews, this easy spread is a yummy alternative to the usual peanut butter. Whip up a jar for yourself and a few more for gifts.

—**MARY HOUCHIN** LEBANON, ILLINOIS

PREP/TOTAL TIME: 25 MIN. **MAKES:** 2¼ CUPS

- 3 cups salted cashews
- ½ cup butter, softened, divided
- ½ cup semisweet chocolate chips
- 2 teaspoons instant coffee granules
- 2 teaspoons water
    Additional salted cashews, optional

1. Place the cashews in a food processor. Cover and process until finely ground. Add half of the butter; process until smooth. Transfer to a small bowl.

2. In a small saucepan, combine the chocolate chips, instant coffee granules, water and remaining butter. Cook and stir over low heat until smooth.

3. Stir into the cashew mixture. Top with additional cashews if desired. Store in the refrigerator.

CHUCK WAGON BEANS

I was inspired by the cooks of the Old Western cattle ranges to create my sweet and smoky beans. The addition of sliced kielbasa or Polish sausage makes them extra hearty.

—**NANCY MOORE** BUCKLIN, KANSAS

PREP: 15 MIN. **COOK:** 8 HOURS
MAKES: 24 SERVINGS (⅔ CUP EACH)

- 2 cans (28 ounces each) baked beans
- 3 cans (16 ounces each) kidney beans, rinsed and drained
- 2 cans (15 ounces each) pinto beans, rinsed and drained
- 1 pound smoked kielbasa or Polish sausage, sliced
- 1 jar (12 ounces) pickled jalapeno slices, drained
- 1 medium onion, chopped
- 1 cup barbecue sauce
- ½ cup spicy brown mustard
- ¼ cup steak seasoning

In a greased 6-qt. slow cooker, combine all ingredients. Cover and cook on low for 8-10 hours or until heated through.

Editor's Note: *This recipe was tested with McCormick's Montreal Steak Seasoning. Look for it in the spice aisle.*

CARROT FRITTERS

Crispy and mild-flavored, this unusual but fun finger food always gets snatched up in a flash. Leftovers reheat well, so if I have any, I save them for a quick snack the next day.

—SUSAN WITT FAIRBURY, NEBRASKA

PREP/TOTAL TIME: 30 MIN. **MAKES:** 20 FRITTERS

- 1 cup all-purpose flour
- 1 teaspoon salt
- 1 teaspoon baking powder
- 2 eggs
- ½ cup milk
- 1 teaspoon canola oil
- 3 cups shredded carrots
  Oil for deep-fat frying

1. In a large bowl, combine the flour, salt and baking powder. Combine the eggs, milk and oil; add to dry ingredients just until moistened. Fold in carrots.
2. In an electric skillet, heat ¼ in. of oil to 375°. Drop the batter by 2 tablespoonfuls into the hot oil; press lightly to flatten. Fry until golden brown, about 1-2 minutes on each side. Drain on paper towels.

DEEP-FRIED DO'S

To keep fried foods warm until the entire recipe is cooked, drain the fried foods on paper towel, then place them on an ovenproof platter. Cover them loosely with foil and place them in a 200° oven.

YELLOW SUMMER SQUASH RELISH

Every year, I look forward to the growing season and the arrival of fresh-picked yellow summer squash, onions and green peppers for my relish. It really jazzes up plain hot dogs.

—RUTH HAWKINS JACKSON, MISSISSIPPI

PREP: 1 HOUR + MARINATING **PROCESS:** 15 MIN.
MAKES: 6 PINTS

- 10 cups shredded yellow summer squash (about 4 pounds)
- 2 large onions, chopped
- 1 large green pepper, chopped
- 6 tablespoons canning salt
- 4 cups sugar
- 3 cups cider vinegar
- 1 tablespoon each celery seed, ground mustard and ground turmeric
- ½ teaspoon ground nutmeg
- ½ teaspoon pepper

1. In a large container, combine the squash, onions, green pepper and salt. Cover and refrigerate overnight. Drain; rinse and drain again.
2. In a Dutch oven, combine the sugar, vinegar and seasonings; bring to a boil. Add squash mixture; return to a boil. Reduce heat; simmer for 15 minutes. Remove from the heat.
3. Carefully ladle the hot mixture into six hot pint jars, leaving ½-in. headspace. Remove air bubbles; wipe rims and adjust lids. Process for 15 minutes in a boiling-water canner. Refrigerate the remaining relish for up to 1 week.
Editor's Note: *The processing time listed in the recipe is for altitudes of 1,000 feet or less. For altitudes up to 3,000 feet, add 5 minutes; 6,000 feet, add 10 minutes; 8,000 feet, add 15 minutes; 10,000 feet, add 20 minutes.*

Pick of the Corn Crop

From golden farm fields to your family's table, a harvest of corn brings fresh-picked goodness to any meal. Try the creative recipes here, and you'll reap earfuls of raves!

ASIN CORN SUCCOTASH

Because I'm not a fan of lima beans, I prepare my succotash with edamame (green soybeans) instead. You won't want to skip the homemade, Asian-inspired vinaigrette.

—DIERDRE CALLAWAY PARKVILLE, MISSOURI

PREP/TOTAL TIME: 25 MIN. **MAKES:** 3 SERVINGS

- 1 cup frozen shelled edamame
- 2 cups fresh corn
- ¼ cup chopped red onion
- ¼ cup chopped sweet red pepper

VINAIGRETTE
- ¼ cup rice vinegar
- ¼ cup olive oil
- 1 tablespoon sugar
- ½ teaspoon sesame oil
- ¼ teaspoon reduced-sodium soy sauce
- ⅛ teaspoon salt
- ⅛ teaspoon pepper
    Dash hot pepper sauce

1. Place edamame in a saucepan and cover with 3 cups water. Bring to a boil. Cover and cook for 4-5 minutes or until tender, adding the corn during the last 2 minutes of cooking. Drain and rinse under cold water. Transfer to a large bowl; add the onion and pepper.

2. In a small bowl, combine the vinaigrette ingredients. Pour over corn mixture and toss to coat. Chill until serving.

CRANBERRY CORN BREAD CASSEROLE

What could be better on a chilly fall day than the combination of a sweet, warm bread and a creamy casserole? This dish starts with a mix and comes together quickly. Just bake, scoop and eat!

—VALERY ANDERSON STERLING HEIGHTS, MICHIGAN

PREP: 15 MIN. **BAKE:** 20 MIN. **MAKES:** 9 SERVINGS

- ½ cup dried cranberries
- ½ cup boiling water
- 1 package (8½ ounces) corn bread/muffin mix
- 1 teaspoon onion powder
- ¼ teaspoon rubbed sage
- 1 egg
- 1 can (14¾ ounces) cream-style corn
- 2 tablespoons butter, melted
- ¼ cup chopped pecans
- ½ teaspoon grated orange peel

1. Place cranberries in a small bowl; cover with boiling water. Let stand for 5 minutes; drain and set aside.

2. In a small bowl, combine the muffin mix, onion powder and sage. In another bowl, whisk the egg, corn and butter; stir into dry ingredients just until moistened. Fold in the pecans, orange peel and cranberries.

3. Transfer to a greased 8-in. square baking dish. Bake, uncovered, at 400° for 20-25 minutes or until set.

SHOEPEG CORN SUPREME

I dress up canned corn with vegetables, sour cream, celery soup and sharp cheddar. With a yummy cracker coating on top, this is comfort food no one will be able to resist!

—**LINDA ROBERSON** COLLIERVILLE, TENNESSEE

PREP: 10 MIN. **BAKE:** 25 MIN. **MAKES:** 8 SERVINGS

- 1 small green pepper, chopped
- 1 small onion, chopped
- 1 celery rib, chopped
- 2 tablespoons olive oil
- 3 cans (7 ounces each) white or shoepeg corn, drained
- 1 can (10¾ ounces) condensed cream of celery soup, undiluted
- 1 cup (8 ounces) sour cream
- ½ cup shredded sharp cheddar cheese
- ¼ teaspoon pepper
- 1½ cups crushed butter-flavored crackers
- 3 tablespoons butter, melted

1. In a large skillet, saute the green pepper, onion and celery in oil until tender. Remove from the heat; stir in the corn, soup, sour cream, cheese and pepper. Transfer to a greased 11-in. x 7-in. baking dish.

2. Combine cracker crumbs and butter; sprinkle over the top. Bake, uncovered, at 350° for 25-30 minutes or until bubbly.

SHOEPEG FOR SURE

The term "shoepeg corn" dates back to before the United States Civil War. The corn was named for its peg-like shape. Shoepeg corn has smaller kernels and is sweeter than yellow corn.

 ## FIESTA GRILLED CORN

We love Mexican flavors and corn on the cob, so I came up with a recipe that celebrates both. For an Italian variation, use Parmesan cheese and butter blended with oregano and basil.

—**MACKENZIE SEVERSON** GERMANTOWN, MARYLAND

PREP: 25 MIN. + SOAKING **GRILL:** 25 MIN. **MAKES:** 6 SERVINGS

- ½ cup butter, softened
- ¼ cup minced fresh cilantro
- 2 teaspoons grated lime peel
- ½ teaspoon garlic powder
- 6 large ears sweet corn in husks
- ½ cup mayonnaise
- 1 tablespoon chili powder
- ½ teaspoon paprika
- ½ cup queso fresco or fresh goat cheese, crumbled

1. In a small bowl, combine the butter, cilantro, lime peel and garlic powder. Shape into a log; wrap in plastic wrap. Refrigerate for 30 minutes or until firm.

2. Carefully peel back corn husks to within 1 in. of bottoms; remove silk. Place in a Dutch oven; cover with cold water. Soak for 20 minutes; drain. In a small bowl, combine the mayonnaise, chili powder and paprika. Spread over corn. Rewrap corn in husks and secure with kitchen string.

3. Grill corn, covered, over medium heat for 25-30 minutes or until tender, turning often. Serve with butter slices and sprinkle with cheese.

POTATO BACON CASSEROLE

 The combination of bacon and potatoes is hard to beat. I pair them in an easy casserole that goes with most main courses.
—JOANNE PANZETTA BUSHNELL, FLORIDA

PREP: 20 MIN. **BAKE:** 35 MIN. **MAKES:** 8 SERVINGS

4 cups frozen shredded hash brown potatoes, thawed
½ cup finely chopped onion
8 bacon strips, cooked and crumbled
1 cup (4 ounces) shredded cheddar cheese
1 egg
1 can (12 ounces) evaporated milk
½ teaspoon seasoned salt

1. In a greased 8-in. square baking dish, layer half of the shredded hash brown potatoes, onion, bacon and cheddar cheese. Repeat the layers.
2. In a small bowl, whisk the egg, milk and seasoned salt; pour over the potato mixture. Cover and bake at 350° for 30 minutes. Uncover; bake 5-10 minutes longer or until a knife inserted near the center comes out clean.

JALAPENO BREAD & BUTTER PICKLES

Even those who normally don't care for spicy-hot food will want to dip into these zippy bread and butter pickles. They're great!
—KAREN OWEN RISING SUN, INDIANA

PREP: 45 MIN. + STANDING **PROCESS:** 15 MIN. **MAKES:** 7 PINTS

4 pounds cucumbers, sliced
5 small onions, sliced
4 jalapeno peppers, sliced and seeded
½ cup canning salt
5 cups sugar
4 cups white vinegar
2 tablespoons mustard seed
2 teaspoons celery seed
1½ teaspoons ground turmeric
½ teaspoon ground cloves

1. In a large container, combine cucumbers, onions, jalapeno peppers and salt. Cover with crushed ice and mix well. Let stand for 3 hours. Drain; rinse and drain again.
2. In a Dutch oven, combine the sugar, vinegar and seasonings; bring to a boil. Add cucumber mixture; return to a boil. Remove from the heat.
3. Carefully ladle hot mixture into hot pint jars, leaving ½-in. headspace. Remove air bubbles; wipe rims and adjust lids. Process for 15 minutes in a boiling-water canner.
Editor's Notes: *When cutting hot peppers, disposable gloves are recommended. Avoid touching your face. The processing time listed in this recipe is for altitudes of 1,000 feet or less. For altitudes up to 3,000 feet, add 5 minutes; 6,000 feet, add 10 minutes; 8,000 feet, add 15 minutes; 10,000 feet, add 20 minutes.*

GINGERED ORANGE CARROTS

Want a side dish for poultry, pork or beef? Try carrots and onions flavored with ginger, orange juice and red currant jelly. Every time I serve these to guests, they ask for the recipe.
—LAURIE HICKS TROY, MONTANA

PREP/TOTAL TIME: 25 MIN. **MAKES:** 6 SERVINGS

8 medium carrots, cut into ¼-inch slices
2 medium onions, halved and thinly sliced
¼ teaspoon ground ginger
2 tablespoons butter
¼ cup orange juice
¼ cup red currant jelly
¼ teaspoon salt
1 tablespoon minced fresh parsley

1. In a large skillet, saute carrots, onions and ginger in butter for 8-10 minutes or until crisp-tender.
2. Add the orange juice, currant jelly and salt. Cook and stir for 2-3 minutes or until sauce is slightly thickened. Sprinkle with parsley. Serve with a slotted spoon.

SUMMER RISOTTO

My mother always liked to make a hearty risotto to use up her late-summer garden vegetables. I sometimes toss in sauteed mushrooms and serve it as an entree with a salad and bread.
—**SHIRLEY HODGE** BANGOR, PENNSYLVANIA

PREP: 25 MIN. **COOK:** 30 MIN. **MAKES:** 12 SERVINGS

- 5½ to 6 cups reduced-sodium chicken broth
- 1 small onion, finely chopped
- 2 tablespoons olive oil
- 1 tablespoon butter
- 2 cups uncooked arborio rice
- 3 large tomatoes, chopped
- 2 cups fresh or frozen corn, thawed
- ½ cup crumbled feta cheese
- 2 tablespoons minced fresh thyme or 2 teaspoons dried thyme
- 2 tablespoons minced fresh rosemary or 2 teaspoons dried rosemary, crushed
- 2 tablespoons minced fresh basil or 2 teaspoons dried basil
- ¼ teaspoon salt
- ¼ teaspoon pepper
  Shredded Parmesan cheese

1. In a large saucepan, heat broth and keep warm. In a large skillet, saute onion in oil and butter until tender. Add rice; cook and stir for 2-3 minutes or until lightly browned. Stir in 1 cup warm broth. Cook and stir until all of the liquid is absorbed.

2. Add remaining broth, ½ cup at a time, stirring constantly. Allow the liquid to be absorbed between additions. Cook until risotto is creamy and rice is almost tender (total cooking time will be about 20 minutes).

3. Add the tomatoes, corn, feta cheese, herbs, salt and pepper; heat through. Sprinkle with the Parmesan cheese. Serve immediately.

BOSTON BAKED BEANS

Simmered in molasses, sugar and spices, these slow-cooked beans are guaranteed crowd-pleasers and the perfect contribution to potluck get-togethers. With a sauce that's this sweet, dark and rich, you won't want to miss a single spoonful!
—**DARLENE DUNCAN** LANGHORNE, PENNSYLVANIA

PREP: 20 MIN. + SOAKING **COOK:** 10 HOURS
MAKES: 10 SERVINGS

- 1 pound dried navy beans
- 6 cups water, divided
- ¼ pound diced salt pork or 6 bacon strips, cooked and crumbled
- 1 large onion, chopped
- ½ cup packed brown sugar
- ½ cup molasses
- ¼ cup sugar
- 1 teaspoon ground mustard
- 1 teaspoon salt
- ½ teaspoon ground cloves
- ½ teaspoon pepper

1. Sort beans and rinse in cold water. Place beans in a 3- or 4-qt. slow cooker; add 4 cups water. Cover and let stand overnight.

2. Drain and rinse beans, discarding the liquid. Return beans to slow cooker; add salt pork.

3. In a small bowl, combine the onion, brown sugar, molasses, sugar, mustard, salt, cloves, pepper and remaining water. Pour mixture over beans; stir to combine.

4. Cover and cook on low for 10-12 hours or until the beans are tender.

DURANGO POTATO CASSEROLE

Like things spicy? It's easy to turn up the heat on this loaded potato casserole by adding more chili powder or jalapenos.
—**PATRICIA HARMON** BADEN, PENNSYLVANIA

PREP: 35 MIN. **BAKE:** 25 MIN. **MAKES:** 12 SERVINGS (⅔ CUP EACH)

- 2½ pounds potatoes (about 8 medium), peeled and cut into 1-inch cubes
- 8 thick-sliced bacon strips
- 1 can (14½ ounces) diced tomatoes and green chilies, drained
- 3 cups (12 ounces) shredded Mexican cheese blend
- 4 green onions, chopped
- ⅓ cup chopped green pepper
- ⅓ cup chopped sweet red pepper
- 1½ cups reduced-fat mayonnaise
- 2 tablespoons lime juice
- 1 teaspoon seasoned salt
- ¼ teaspoon pepper
- 1½ teaspoons chili powder
- 2 tablespoons minced fresh cilantro

1. Place the potatoes in a large saucepan and cover with water. Bring to a boil. Reduce heat; cover and simmer for 10-15 minutes or until tender.

2. In a large skillet, cook bacon over medium heat until partially cooked but not crisp. Remove to paper towels to drain; set aside.

3. Drain potatoes and transfer to a large bowl; add the tomatoes, cheese, onions and peppers.

4. In a small bowl, whisk the mayonnaise, lime juice, seasoned salt and pepper; add to potatoes and gently stir to coat. Transfer to a greased 13-in. x 9-in. baking dish. Coarsely chop bacon; sprinkle over the top. Sprinkle casserole with chili powder.

5. Bake, uncovered, at 350° for 25-30 minutes or until heated through. Sprinkle with the cilantro. Let stand for 5 minutes before serving.

THREE-FRUIT MARMALADE

I make all my own jams, but my marmalade is a favorite. It blends the warm flavors of peaches and pears with citrus.
—**LORRAINE WRIGHT** GRAND FORKS, BRITISH COLUMBIA

PREP: 30 MIN. **PROCESS:** 5 MIN. **MAKES:** 4 PINTS

- 1 medium orange
- 2 cups chopped peeled fresh peaches
- 2 cups chopped peeled fresh pears
- 1 package (1¾ ounces) powdered fruit pectin
- 5 cups sugar

1. Finely grate peel from the orange; peel and section the fruit. Place peel and sections in a Dutch oven. Add peaches and pears. Stir in pectin. Bring to a boil over high heat, stirring constantly. Stir in sugar; bring to a full rolling boil. Boil for 1 minute, stirring constantly. Remove from the heat; skim off foam.

2. Ladle the hot mixture into hot sterilized pint jars, leaving ¼-in. headspace. Remove air bubbles; wipe rims and adjust lids. Process for 5 minutes in a boiling-water canner.

Editor's Note: *The processing time listed in the recipe is for altitudes of 1,000 feet or less. Add 1 minute to the processing time for each 1,000 feet of additional altitude.*

ROASTED FALL VEGETABLES

I love serving a bowl of these tender roasted vegetables as part of a warm-you-up dinner on a chilly autumn night. The cayenne pepper lends some zip without being overpowering.

—JULI MEYERS HINESVILLE, GEORGIA

PREP: 30 MIN. **BAKE:** 40 MIN. **MAKES:** 14 SERVINGS

- 1 large acorn squash, peeled and cut into 1½-inch cubes
- 1 large rutabaga, peeled and cut into 1-inch cubes
- 1 medium pie pumpkin or butternut squash, peeled and cut into 1-inch cubes
- 3 large carrots, peeled and cut into 1½-inch pieces
- 1 medium parsnip, peeled and cut into 1-inch cubes
- ¼ cup grated Parmesan cheese
- ¼ cup canola oil
- 3 tablespoons minced fresh parsley
- 2 tablespoons paprika
- 2 teaspoons salt
- 1 teaspoon garlic powder
- ½ teaspoon cayenne pepper

1. In a large bowl, combine the first five ingredients. In a small bowl, combine the remaining ingredients. Pour over vegetables; toss to coat.

2. Transfer to two greased 15-in. x 10-in. x 1-in. baking pans. Bake, uncovered, at 425° for 40-50 minutes or until tender, stirring occasionally.

BEER MACARONI & CHEESE

At our big family meals, we enjoy mac and cheese jazzed up with bacon, garlic and a hint of beer. It's terrific!

— LAUREN PETERSEN EVERETT, WASHINGTON

PREP: 20 MIN. **BAKE:** 15 MIN. **MAKES:** 12 SERVINGS

- 1 package (16 ounces) elbow macaroni
- ¼ cup butter
- 2 garlic cloves, minced
- ¼ cup all-purpose flour
- 1 tablespoon ground mustard
- 1 teaspoon salt
- ¾ teaspoon pepper
- 2½ cups 2% milk
- ¾ cup amber beer
- ¼ cup heavy whipping cream
- 3 cups (12 ounces) shredded cheddar cheese, divided
- 2 cups (8 ounces) shredded fontina cheese
- 2 tablespoons grated Parmesan cheese, divided
- 2 tablespoons minced chives
- 5 bacon strips, cooked and crumbled

1. Cook macaroni according to package directions for al dente.

2. Meanwhile, in a Dutch oven, heat butter over medium-high heat. Add the garlic; cook and stir for 1 minute. Stir in the flour, mustard, salt and pepper until smooth; gradually whisk in the milk, beer and cream. Bring to a boil; cook and stir for 2 minutes or until thickened.

3. Reduce heat. Stir in 2 cups cheddar cheese, fontina cheese and 1 tablespoon Parmesan cheese until melted. Add chives.

4. Drain the macaroni; stir into the sauce. Transfer to a greased 3-qt. baking dish. Sprinkle with the remaining cheddar and Parmesan cheeses.

5. Bake, uncovered, at 400° for 15-20 minutes or until golden brown and heated through. Top with crumbled bacon. Let stand for 5 minutes before serving.

POLENTA FRIES WITH BLUE CHEESE DIP

These change-of-pace fries made with polenta bake up crispy and golden in the oven. Tangy blue cheese dip is the perfect accent.
—**REBEKAH BEYER** SABETHA, KANSAS

PREP: 35 MIN. + CHILLING **COOK:** 10 MIN./BATCH
MAKES: 15 SERVINGS (1¾ CUPS DIP)

- 7 cups 2% milk
- 2 cups water
- 2 tablespoons butter
- ¾ teaspoon salt
- ½ teaspoon pepper
- 2¼ cups yellow cornmeal
- 1 cup (4 ounces) shredded smoked Gouda cheese
- 2 tablespoons minced fresh basil or 2 teaspoons dried basil
- 2 tablespoons minced fresh thyme or 2 teaspoons dried thyme
- 1 cup mayonnaise
- ½ cup crumbled blue cheese
- 2 ounces cream cheese, softened
- 1 cup all-purpose flour
- 1 cup canola oil

1. In a Dutch oven, bring the milk, water, butter, salt and pepper to a boil. Reduce the heat to a gentle boil; slowly whisk in the cornmeal. Cook and stir with a wooden spoon for 15-20 minutes or until the polenta is thickened and pulls away cleanly from the sides of the pan.
2. Stir in Gouda cheese, basil and thyme. Spread into a greased 15-in. x 10-in. x 1-in. baking pan. Refrigerate for 1 hour.
3. Meanwhile, in a small bowl, combine the mayonnaise, blue cheese and cream cheese; chill until serving.
4. Cut the polenta into 3¼-in. x ½-in. strips. Place the flour in a shallow bowl. Dip polenta in flour; shake off excess.
5. In a large skillet, cook the polenta in oil in batches for 3-4 minutes on each side or until golden brown. Serve with dip.

CREAMED KOHLRABI

I'm a big fan of kohlrabi. My creamed version might look like potato salad, but it's actually kohlrabi cubes covered in a white, velvety sauce and accented with minced chives.
—**LORRAINE FOSS** PUYALLUP, WASHINGTON

PREP/TOTAL TIME: 30 MIN. **MAKES:** 6 SERVINGS

- 4 cups cubed peeled kohlrabies (about 6 medium)
- 2 tablespoons butter
- 2 tablespoons all-purpose flour
- 2 cups whole milk
- ½ teaspoon salt
- ¼ teaspoon pepper
  Dash paprika
- 1 egg yolk, lightly beaten
  Minced chives and additional paprika

1. Place kohlrabies in a large saucepan; add 1 in. of water. Bring to a boil. Reduce heat; cover and simmer for 6-8 minutes or until crisp-tender.
2. Meanwhile, in a small saucepan, melt butter. Stir in flour until smooth; gradually add milk. Bring to a boil. Stir in the salt, pepper and paprika. Gradually stir a small amount of hot mixture into egg yolk; return all to the pan, stirring constantly. Bring to a gentle boil; cook and stir for 2 minutes.
3. Drain kohlrabies and place in a serving bowl; add sauce and stir to coat. Sprinkle with chives and additional paprika.

PICKLED GREEN BEANS

With this handy recipe, I preserve the fresh-picked green beans from my garden for months to come—if they last that long, that is! I crank up the heat a bit with cayenne pepper.

—**MARISA MCCLELLAN** PHILADELPHIA, PENNSYLVANIA

PREP: 20 MIN. **PROCESS:** 10 MIN. **MAKES:** 4 PINTS

1¾ pounds fresh green beans, trimmed
1 teaspoon cayenne pepper
4 garlic cloves, peeled
4 teaspoons dill seed or 4 fresh dill heads
2½ cups water
2½ cups white vinegar
¼ cup canning salt

1. Pack beans into four hot 1-pint jars to within ½ in. of the top. Add the cayenne, garlic and dill seed to jars.
2. In a large saucepan, bring the water, vinegar and salt to a boil.
3. Carefully ladle the hot mixture over the beans, leaving ½-in. headspace. Remove the air bubbles; wipe the rims and adjust the lids. Process for 10 minutes in a boiling-water canner.
Editor's Note: *The processing time listed in the recipe is for altitudes of 1,000 feet or less. For altitudes up to 3,000 feet, add 5 minutes; 6,000 feet, add 10 minutes; 8,000 feet, add 15 minutes; 10,000 feet, add 20 minutes.*

TRIMMING GREEN BEANS

To trim fresh green beans quickly, line up the ends of the beans; then, using a chef's knife, slice several at a time. Or, use a kitchen shears.

TWICE-BAKED MASHED POTATOES

Dressing up an all-time-favorite comfort food is a snap with sour cream, onion, cheddar cheese and crumbled bacon. It's also easy to double the ingredients and make a larger amount for a crowd.
—**ANNA MAYER** FORT BRANCH, INDIANA

PREP: 30 MIN. **BAKE:** 30 MIN. **MAKES:** 6 SERVINGS

2½ pounds medium potatoes, peeled
1 cup (8 ounces) sour cream
¼ cup milk
2 tablespoons butter, melted
1½ cups (6 ounces) shredded cheddar cheese, divided
½ cup chopped onion
5 bacon strips, cooked and crumbled
½ teaspoon salt
⅛ teaspoon pepper

1. Place the potatoes in a large saucepan and cover with water. Bring to a boil. Reduce heat; cover and cook for 15-20 minutes or until tender. Drain.
2. In a large bowl, mash the potatoes. Add the sour cream, milk, butter and 1 cup cheddar cheese. Stir in the onion, bacon, salt and pepper. Spoon into a greased 2-qt. baking dish. Sprinkle with remaining cheese.
3. Bake, uncovered, at 350° for 30-35 minutes or until heated through.

BLUEBERRY JAM

Summer just doesn't feel complete to me without at least one trip to the berry patch and a batch of homemade blueberry jam. Enjoy this on fresh-baked scones, toast or biscuits.
—**MARISA MCCLELLAN** PHILADELPHIA, PENNSYLVANIA

PREP: 35 MIN. **PROCESS:** 10 MIN./BATCH **MAKES:** 9 HALF-PINTS

- 8 cups fresh blueberries
- 6 cups sugar
- 3 tablespoons lemon juice
- 2 teaspoons ground cinnamon
- 2 teaspoons grated lemon peel
- ½ teaspoon ground nutmeg
- 2 pouches (3 ounces each) liquid fruit pectin

1. Place the blueberries in a food processor; cover and process until blended. Transfer to a stockpot. Stir in the sugar, lemon juice, cinnamon, lemon peel and nutmeg. Bring to a full rolling boil over high heat, stirring constantly. Stir in the pectin. Boil for 1 minute, stirring constantly.

2. Remove from the heat; skim off foam. Ladle hot mixture into hot sterilized half-pint jars, leaving ¼-in. headspace. Remove air bubbles; wipe rims and adjust lids. Process for 10 minutes in a boiling-water canner.

Editor's Note: *The processing time listed in the recipe is for altitudes of 1,000 feet or less. Add 1 minute to the processing time for each 1,000 feet of additional altitude.*

 ## RUSSIAN POTATOES

Popular at potlucks, these creamy mashed potatoes topped with sour cream always disappear from the pan in no time flat. I like to serve them with a main course of beef roast or prime rib.
—**JUDY WILSON** SUN CITY WEST, ARIZONA

PREP: 1¼ HOURS **BAKE:** 30 MIN. **MAKES:** 12 SERVINGS

- 6 cups chopped sweet onions
- ¼ cup olive oil
- ⅓ cup plus ½ cup butter, cubed, divided
- 1 tablespoon sugar
- 4 pounds potatoes, peeled and cubed
- 4 cans (14½ ounces each) chicken broth or 8 cups water plus 8 teaspoons chicken bouillon granules
- 3 cups sour cream, divided
- 1 cup heavy whipping cream
- 4 eggs, beaten
- 1 teaspoon dill weed

1. In a large skillet, saute onions in oil and ⅓ cup butter until softened. Stir in the sugar. Reduce heat to medium-low; cook, stirring occasionally, for 40 minutes or until deep golden brown.

2. Meanwhile, place potatoes in a large saucepan and cover with chicken broth. Bring to a boil. Reduce heat; cover and cook for 15-20 minutes or until tender. Drain potatoes; transfer to a large bowl. Add 1 cup sour cream, the whipping cream, eggs, dill and remaining butter. Beat until mashed.

3. Spread half of potatoes into a greased 13-in. x 9-in. baking dish; layer with onions and remaining potatoes. Gently spread remaining sour cream over the top. Bake, uncovered, at 350° for 30-35 minutes or until a thermometer reads 160°.

seasoning, rosemary, salt, pepper and mushroom mixture to the sausage. Whisk egg and broth; pour over bread mixture and toss to coat. Transfer to a greased 13-in. x 9-in. baking dish (the dish will be full).

3. Bake, uncovered, at 350° for 30-35 minutes until top is lightly browned and a thermometer reads at least 160°.

MAPLE & BACON GLAZED BRUSSELS SPROUTS

Even children will happily gobble up these glazed Brussels sprouts. The maple syrup and smoky bacon complement the vegetables perfectly and make them taste like a treat.
—**JAN VALDEZ** CHICAGO, ILLINOIS

PREP: 15 MIN. **COOK:** 20 MIN. **MAKES:** 4 SERVINGS

- 5 bacon strips, chopped
- 1 pound fresh Brussels sprouts, trimmed
- 3 tablespoons butter
- ½ cup chicken broth
- ¼ cup chopped pecans
- ¼ cup maple syrup
- ¼ teaspoon salt
- ¼ teaspoon pepper

1. In a small skillet, cook bacon over medium heat until crisp. Remove to paper towels with a slotted spoon; drain.

2. Meanwhile, cut an "X" in the core of each Brussels sprout. In a large skillet, saute Brussels sprouts in butter for 4-5 minutes or until lightly browned.

3. Stir in the broth, pecans, maple syrup, salt and pepper. Bring to a boil. Reduce heat; cover and simmer for 5 minutes. Uncover; cook and stir 8-10 minutes longer or until Brussels sprouts are tender. Sprinkle with bacon.

SAUSAGE SOURDOUGH STUFFING

Sourdough's tangy chewiness gives my hearty sausage stuffing a pleasant texture, while mushrooms and cranberries lend an earthy sweetness. Try it for a holiday dinner or other special occasion.
—**JENNIFER BRAZELL** LEWISTON, IDAHO

PREP: 30 MIN. **BAKE:** 30 MIN.
MAKES: 18 SERVINGS (¾ CUP EACH)

- 1 pound bulk pork sausage
- 1 pound sliced baby portobello mushrooms
- 1 large sweet onion, chopped
- 2 celery ribs, chopped
- 2 tablespoons canola oil
- 3 garlic cloves, minced
- 1 loaf (1 pound) day-old sourdough bread, cubed
- 2 jars (7½ ounces each) marinated quartered artichoke hearts, drained and chopped
- 1 cup grated Parmesan cheese
- ½ cup dried cranberries
- 1½ teaspoons poultry seasoning
- 1 teaspoon dried rosemary, crushed
- ½ teaspoon salt
- ½ teaspoon pepper
- 1 egg
- 1½ cups reduced-sodium chicken broth

1. In a Dutch oven, cook the sausage over medium heat until no longer pink; drain. Transfer to a large bowl. In the same pan, saute the mushrooms, onion and celery in oil until tender. Add garlic; cook 1 minute longer.

2. Add the bread, artichokes, cheese, dried cranberries, poultry

MAIN DISHES

Thanks to these savory main courses, finding just the right entree for your menu is as easy as can be. Choose from a mouthwatering array of beef, chicken, turkey, pork, fish, seafood and meatless options—this chapter has them all!

ALL-DAY RED BEANS & RICE

My family loves New Orleans-style food, so I make my red beans and rice often. As a busy working woman, I appreciate the fact that I can get it started before I leave in the morning.
—**CELINDA DAHLGREN** NAPA, CALIFORNIA

PREP: 20 MIN. + SOAKING **COOK:** 8½ HOURS **MAKES:** 6 SERVINGS

- 1 cup dried red beans
- 7 cups water, divided
- 2 smoked ham hocks
- 1 medium onion, chopped
- 1½ teaspoons minced garlic
- 1 teaspoon ground cumin
- 1 medium tomato, chopped
- 1 medium green pepper, chopped
- 1 teaspoon salt
- 4 cups hot cooked rice

1. Sort beans and rinse in cold water. Place beans in a 3-qt. slow cooker. Add 4 cups water; cover and let stand overnight.
2. Drain and rinse the beans, discarding liquid. Return beans to the slow cooker; add the ham hocks, onion, garlic, cumin and remaining water. Cover and cook on low for 8-10 hours or until beans are tender.
3. Remove the ham hocks; cool slightly. Remove the meat from the bones. Finely chop meat and return to slow cooker; discard bones. Stir in the tomato, pepper and salt; cover and cook on high for 30 minutes or until pepper is tender. Serve with rice.
Stovetop All-Day Red Beans & Rice: *Prepare beans as directed using a Dutch oven. Add the ham hocks, onion, garlic, cumin and*

remaining water. Bring to a boil. Reduce heat; cover and simmer for 1 hour. Prepare ham as directed. Stir in the tomato, pepper and salt. Bring to a boil. Reduce heat; cover and simmer for 45 minutes. Uncover and simmer 10-15 minutes longer or until beans reach desired consistency.

COLA BARBECUE RIBS

Enjoy the smoky goodness of a summer barbecue all year long by preparing these moist and tender spareribs in your slow cooker. The cola-spiked sauce is a hit with everyone.
—**KAREN SHUCK** EDGAR, NEBRASKA

PREP: 10 MIN. **COOK:** 9 HOURS **MAKES:** 4 SERVINGS

- ¼ cup packed brown sugar
- 2 garlic cloves, minced
- 1 teaspoon salt
- ½ teaspoon pepper
- 3 tablespoons Liquid Smoke, optional
- 4 pounds pork spareribs, cut into serving-size pieces
- 1 medium onion, sliced
- ½ cup cola
- 1½ cups barbecue sauce

1. In a small bowl, combine the brown sugar, garlic, salt, pepper and Liquid Smoke if desired; rub over ribs.
2. Layer the ribs and onion in a greased 5- or 6-qt. slow cooker; pour cola over ribs. Cover and cook on low for 8-10 hours or until ribs are tender. Drain liquid. Pour barbecue sauce over ribs and cook 1 hour longer.

TERIYAKI STEAK

My brother-in-law, Stanley, gave me his special recipe for flank steak over 30 years ago. He was an officer in the Army, and fellow officers considered his teriyaki-flavored entree a treat.

—**DAN MAYER** OLNEY, ILLINOIS

PREP: 20 MIN. + MARINATING **COOK:** 15 MIN. **MAKES:** 6 SERVINGS

- 1   beef flank steak (1½ to 2 pounds)
- ½   cup plus ⅓ cup reduced-sodium soy sauce, divided
- ¼   cup balsamic vinegar
- ¼   cup honey
- 1   teaspoon ground ginger
- 2   garlic cloves, minced
- 2   tablespoons butter, divided
- 3   eggs, beaten
- 2   cups cold cooked rice
- 1   package (9 ounces) frozen peas and pearl onions

1. Place the steak in a large resealable plastic bag. In a small bowl, whisk ½ cup soy sauce, balsamic vinegar, honey, ginger and garlic. Pour half of the marinade over the steak. Seal the bag and turn to coat; refrigerate overnight. Cover and refrigerate the remaining marinade.

2. Drain and discard the marinade. Grill steak, covered, over medium heat or broil 3-4 in. from the heat for 7-9 minutes on each side or until meat reaches desired doneness (for medium-rare, a thermometer should read 145°; medium, 160°; well-done, 170°). Let stand for 10 minutes before slicing.

3. Meanwhile, transfer reserved marinade to a small saucepan. Bring to a boil; cook until liquid is reduced by half. Set aside.

4. In a large skillet, heat 1 tablespoon butter over medium-high heat. Pour eggs into skillet. As eggs set, lift edges, letting uncooked portion flow underneath. When eggs are completely cooked, remove to plate. Chop eggs into small pieces; set aside.

5. In the same skillet, stir-fry rice in the remaining butter over medium-high heat. Stir in the peas, onions and remaining soy sauce. Add the eggs; cook and stir until heated through. Thinly slice the steak across the grain; serve over rice. Drizzle with the sauce mixture.

GARDEN CHEDDAR FRITTATA

This meatless dish is wonderful not only for breakfast, but also for dinner. I've replaced the cheddar with goat cheese and had equally good results. Feel free to substitute other vegetables as well.

—**EVA AMUSO** CHESHIRE, MASSACHUSETTS

PREP: 30 MIN. **BAKE:** 15 MIN. **MAKES:** 6 SERVINGS

- 2   small potatoes, peeled and cut into ½-inch cubes
- 8   eggs, lightly beaten
- 2   tablespoons water
- ¼   teaspoon salt
- ⅛   teaspoon garlic powder
- ⅛   teaspoon chili powder
- ⅛   teaspoon pepper
- 1   small zucchini, chopped
- ¼   cup chopped onion
- 1   tablespoon butter
- 1   tablespoon olive oil
- 2   plum tomatoes, thinly sliced
- 1   cup (4 ounces) shredded sharp cheddar cheese
     Minced chives and additional shredded cheddar cheese

1. Place potatoes in small saucepan and cover with water. Bring to a boil. Reduce heat; cover and simmer for 5 minutes. Drain. In a large bowl, whisk the eggs, water, salt, garlic powder, chili powder and pepper; set aside.

2. In a 10-in. ovenproof skillet, saute the zucchini, onion and potatoes in the butter and oil until tender. Reduce heat. Pour 1½ cups egg mixture into skillet. Arrange half of the tomatoes over top; sprinkle with ½ cup cheese. Top with remaining egg mixture, tomatoes and cheese.

3. Bake, uncovered, at 425° for 14-18 minutes or until eggs are completely set. Let stand for 5 minutes. Sprinkle with chives and additional cheddar cheese. Cut into wedges.

TWO-CHEESE SPAGHETTI BAKE

My kids and grandkids love this pasta casserole loaded with ground beef and two kinds of cheese. I prepare it at least once a month.
—**JANET KNORR** GOLDEN, ILLINOIS

PREP: 30 MIN. **BAKE:** 25 MIN. **MAKES:** 6 SERVINGS

- 6 ounces uncooked spaghetti, broken into thirds
- 1 pound ground beef
- ¼ cup chopped onion
- 1 jar (14 ounces) spaghetti sauce
- 2 tablespoons butter
- 4 teaspoons all-purpose flour
- ¼ teaspoon salt
- ¾ cup evaporated milk
- ⅓ cup water
- 4 ounces process cheese (Velveeta), cubed, divided
- 2 tablespoons grated Parmesan cheese

1. Cook spaghetti according to package directions. Meanwhile, in a large skillet, cook beef and onion over medium heat until meat is no longer pink; drain. Add spaghetti sauce; bring to a boil. Reduce heat; simmer, uncovered, for 10 minutes. Drain spaghetti; stir into beef mixture. Set aside.

2. In a small saucepan, melt butter. Stir in flour and salt; gradually stir in milk and water. Bring to a boil; cook and stir until thickened and bubbly. Add ½ cup process cheese and Parmesan cheese; stir until melted.

3. Spread half of the spaghetti mixture into a greased 11-in. x 7-in. baking dish. Cover with cheese sauce; top with remaining spaghetti mixture and process cheese.

4. Bake, uncovered, at 350° for 25-30 minutes or until heated through.

SLOW-COOKED THAI PEANUT CHICKEN

In the mood for Thai? Skip the trip to an Asian restaurant and whip up an exotic chicken specialty in your own kitchen.
—**BLAIR LONERGAN** ROCHELLE, VIRGINIA

PREP: 25 MIN. **COOK:** 4 HOURS **MAKES:** 8 SERVINGS

- 1 cup all-purpose flour
- 8 boneless skinless chicken thighs (about 2 pounds)
- ¾ cup creamy peanut butter
- ½ cup orange juice
- ¼ cup orange marmalade
- 2 tablespoons sesame oil
- 2 tablespoons soy sauce
- 2 tablespoons teriyaki sauce
- 2 tablespoons hoisin sauce
- 1 can (13.66 ounces) light coconut milk
- 1 cup uncooked basmati rice
- ¾ cup water
- ½ cup chopped salted peanuts

1. Place the flour in a large resealable plastic bag. Add chicken, a few pieces at a time, and shake to coat. Transfer to a greased 4- or 5-qt. slow cooker.

2. In a small bowl, combine peanut butter, orange juice, orange marmalade, oil, soy sauce, teriyaki sauce, hoisin sauce and ¾ cup coconut milk; pour over chicken. Cover and cook on low for 4-5 hours or until chicken is tender.

3. In a small saucepan, bring the rice, water and remaining coconut milk to a boil. Reduce heat; cover and simmer for 15-20 minutes or until the rice is tender. Fluff with a fork. Serve with chicken and sauce; sprinkle with peanuts.

TILAPIA WITH CITRUS SAUCE

Here's a great way to enhance the mild, delicate flavor of tilapia fillets. The zesty sauce features fruit juices, garlic and onion.
—**FRANCIS GARLAND** ANNISTON, ALABAMA

PREP/TOTAL TIME: 30 MIN. **MAKES:** 4 SERVINGS

- ½ cup 2% milk
- ½ cup all-purpose flour
- ½ teaspoon salt
- ½ teaspoon pepper
- 4 tilapia fillets (4 ounces each)
  Olive oil-flavored cooking spray
- 3 garlic cloves, minced
- 1 tablespoon butter
- 2 teaspoons olive oil
- ½ small lemon, sliced
- ½ medium lime, sliced
- ½ small navel orange, sliced
- 3 tablespoons lemon juice
- 3 tablespoons lime juice
- 2 tablespoons orange juice
- 2 green onions, finely chopped

1. Place the milk in a shallow bowl. In another shallow bowl, combine the flour, salt and pepper. Dip fish in milk, then coat with flour mixture.

2. Spray fillets with cooking spray. In a large nonstick skillet coated with cooking spray, cook fish over medium-high heat for 3-4 minutes on each side or until fish flakes easily with a fork. Remove and keep warm.

3. In the same pan, saute garlic in butter and oil for 1 minute. Add the lemon, lime and orange slices, juices and onions; cook 1 minute longer. Serve with fish.

SAUSAGE MUSHROOM PIE

A convenient ready-to-bake pie shell speeds up the preparation of this delicious, hearty brunch dish. After cooking the sausage and onion, I combine the filling ingredients and spoon into the pastry. All that's left to do is bake and sprinkle on some cheddar.
—**VALERIE PUTSEY** WINAMAC, INDIANA

PREP: 20 MIN. **BAKE:** 40 MIN. **MAKES:** 6-8 SERVINGS

- 1 pound bulk pork sausage
- ¼ cup chopped onion
- 2 packages (10 ounces each) frozen chopped spinach, thawed and squeezed dry
- 2 cans (8 ounces each) mushroom stems and pieces, drained
- 2 eggs, lightly beaten
- 3 cups (12 ounces) shredded part-skim mozzarella cheese
- 1 unbaked deep-dish pastry shell (9 inches)
- 1 cup (4 ounces) shredded cheddar cheese

1. In a large skillet, cook the sausage and onion over medium heat until the meat is no longer pink; drain. Stir in spinach and mushrooms. Combine the eggs and mozzarella cheese; fold into sausage mixture. Spoon into pastry shell.

2. Cover and bake at 400° for 30 minutes. Uncover; sprinkle with cheddar cheese. Bake 10-15 minutes longer or until a knife inserted near the center comes out clean.

TURKEY ENCHILADAS VERDES

Planning a Mexican fiesta night? If you have leftover turkey in the fridge, look here! The authentic-tasting enchiladas in spicy green sauce are sure to please your whole family.
—**KARYN "KIKI" POWER** ARLINGTON, TEXAS

PREP: 45 MIN. **BAKE:** 30 MIN. **MAKES:** 16 SERVINGS

    32 corn tortillas (6 inches)
    ⅓ cup plus 1 tablespoon canola oil, divided
    1 medium onion, chopped
    3 cups cubed cooked turkey
    1 can (14½ ounces) Mexican diced tomatoes, undrained
    1 tablespoon chopped pickled jalapeno slices
    1 envelope taco seasoning
    1 teaspoon ground cumin
    ½ teaspoon dried oregano
    ½ teaspoon dried basil
    3 cans (10 ounces each) green enchilada sauce
    1 can (10¾ ounces) condensed cream of chicken soup, undiluted
    3 cups (12 ounces) shredded Monterey Jack cheese
       Sour cream and additional pickled jalapeno slices, optional

1. In a large skillet, fry tortillas in batches, using ⅓ cup oil, for 5 seconds on each side or until golden. Drain on paper towels.
2. In the same skillet, saute onion in remaining oil until tender. Stir in the turkey, tomatoes, jalapenos, taco seasoning, cumin, oregano and basil; heat through.
3. Combine enchilada sauce and soup. Spread ½ cup mixture into each of two 13-in. x 9-in. baking dishes. Place 2 tablespoons turkey mixture down the center of each tortilla; top with 1 tablespoon cheese. Roll up and place seam side down in prepared dishes. Pour remaining sauce over the top.
4. Cover and bake at 350° for 25-30 minutes or until heated through. Uncover; sprinkle with the remaining cheese. Bake 5 minutes longer or until cheese is melted. Garnish with sour cream and additional jalapenos if desired.

SPINACH LASAGNA ROLL-UPS

With five kinds of cheese—ricotta, mozzarella, Parmesan, Gruyere and cream cheese—these meatless roll-ups are a wonderfully rich indulgence. Serve them with fresh-baked breadsticks and a tossed green salad, and you'll have an Italian feast to remember!
—**MARY JANE JONES** WILLIAMSTOWN, WEST VIRGINIA

PREP: 35 MIN. **BAKE:** 30 MIN. + STANDING **MAKES:** 10 SERVINGS

    10 uncooked lasagna noodles
    1 package (8 ounces) cream cheese, softened
    2 packages (10 ounces each) frozen chopped spinach, thawed and squeezed dry
    1 carton (15 ounces) ricotta cheese
    2 cups (8 ounces) shredded part-skim mozzarella cheese
    1 cup grated Parmesan cheese
    1½ teaspoons Italian seasoning
    ¼ teaspoon salt
SAUCE
    3 tablespoons butter
    4 tablespoons all-purpose flour
    ½ teaspoon pepper
    ¼ teaspoon salt
    2 cups chicken broth
    1 cup heavy whipping cream
TOPPING
    ½ cup shredded Gruyere cheese
    ½ cup grated Parmesan cheese

1. Cook the lasagna noodles according to package directions; drain. In a large bowl, beat the cream cheese until smooth. Stir in the spinach, ricotta, mozzarella, Parmesan, Italian seasoning and salt. Spread ½ cup cheese mixture over each lasagna noodle; carefully roll up.
2. For the sauce, in a large saucepan, melt butter over medium heat. Whisk in the flour, pepper and salt until smooth. Gradually whisk in the chicken broth. Bring to a boil; cook and stir for 2 minutes or until thickened. Remove from the heat; stir in the heavy whipping cream.
3. Pour 1 cup sauce into a greased 13-in. x 9-in. baking dish. Cut the lasagna roll-ups in half widthwise; place cut side down in dish. Top with the remaining sauce; sprinkle with Gruyere and Parmesan.
4. Cover and bake at 350° for 20-25 minutes. Uncover; bake 10 minutes longer or until bubbly. Let stand for 15 minutes before serving.

USING YOUR NOODLE

Whenever I've cooked more lasagna noodles than needed, I cut the leftovers into ¼-inch or ½-inch strips. Then I put them in a heavy-duty resealable plastic bag and store them in the freezer. The trimmed-down noodles freeze well and make quick, hearty additions to soups and stews.
—**EMMA M.** AMSTERDAM, NEW YORK

SLOW-COOKED MOROCCAN CHICKEN

Here's a great way to change up everyday chicken. Plenty of herbs, spices and dried fruit give it an exotic twist.
—**KATHY MORGAN** RIDGEFIELD, WASHINGTON

PREP: 20 MIN. **COOK:** 6 HOURS **MAKES:** 4 SERVINGS

- 4 medium carrots, sliced
- 2 large onions, halved and sliced
- 1 broiler/fryer chicken (3 to 4 pounds), cut up, skin removed
- ½ teaspoon salt
- ½ cup chopped dried apricots
- ½ cup raisins
- 2 tablespoons all-purpose flour
- 1 can (14½ ounces) reduced-sodium chicken broth
- ¼ cup tomato paste
- 2 tablespoons lemon juice
- 2 garlic cloves, minced
- 1½ teaspoons ground ginger
- 1½ teaspoons ground cumin
- 1 teaspoon ground cinnamon
- ¾ teaspoon pepper
   Hot cooked couscous

1. Place the carrots and onions in a greased 5-qt. slow cooker. Sprinkle chicken with salt; add to slow cooker. Top with apricots and raisins. In a small bowl, combine the flour and broth until smooth; whisk in the tomato paste, lemon juice, garlic, ginger, cumin, cinnamon and pepper. Pour over chicken.

2. Cover and cook on low for 6 to 7 hours or until chicken is tender. Serve with couscous.

PORK ROAST WITH PEACH SAUCE

My husband loves this savory, saucy pork that combines the kick of chili sauce with the sweetness of peaches. It's always a popular choice, especially when it's cold here in the Northwoods.
—**JANICE CHRISTOFFERSON** EAGLE RIVER, WISCONSIN

PREP: 20 MIN. **COOK:** 6 HOURS
MAKES: 8 SERVINGS (2½ CUPS SAUCE)

- 1 boneless pork loin roast (3 to 4 pounds)
- 2 teaspoons canola oil
- ¼ teaspoon onion salt
- ¼ teaspoon pepper
- 1 can (15¼ ounces) sliced peaches
- ½ cup chili sauce
- ⅓ cup packed brown sugar
- 3 tablespoons cider vinegar
- 1 teaspoon pumpkin pie spice
- 2 tablespoons cornstarch
- 2 tablespoons cold water

1. Cut roast in half. In a large skillet, brown pork in oil on all sides. Transfer to a 4- or 5-qt. slow cooker. Sprinkle with onion salt and pepper.

2. Drain peaches, reserving juice in a small bowl; stir the chili sauce, brown sugar, vinegar and pie spice into the juice. Spoon peaches over roast; top with juice mixture. Cover and cook on low for 6-8 hours or until meat is tender.

3. Remove meat and peaches to a serving platter; keep warm. Skim the fat from cooking juices; transfer to a small saucepan. Bring liquid to a boil. Combine the cornstarch and water until smooth; gradually stir into pan. Bring to a boil; cook and stir for 2 minutes or until thickened. Serve with pork and peaches.

What do you get when you stuff delicious seafood, poultry and veggies with equally delicious fillings? Twice-as-nice recipes you and your family will find doubly delightful!

INTERNATIONAL STUFFED ZUCCHINI

Tender zucchini boats create fun holders for a mix of ground beef and cheese. It's a quick, easy and wholesome dinner.

—TRACEY ROSATO MARKHAM, ONTARIO

PREP: 20 MIN. **BAKE:** 20 MIN. **MAKES:** 4 SERVINGS

- 2 **large zucchini**
- 1 **pound ground beef**
- 1 **garlic clove, minced**
- 1 **cup (4 ounces) shredded Havarti cheese with jalapeno or Havarti cheese**
- ¾ **cup crumbled feta cheese, divided**
- 2 **tablespoons minced fresh basil or oregano**
- ¼ **teaspoon salt**
- ⅛ **teaspoon pepper**

1. Cut each zucchini in half lengthwise; cut a thin slice from the bottoms so they sit flat. Scoop out pulp, leaving ¼-in. shells. Place zucchini shells in an ungreased 8-in. square microwave-safe dish. Cover and microwave on high for 3 minutes or until crisp-tender; drain and set aside.

2. In a large skillet over medium heat, cook beef and garlic until meat is no longer pink; drain. Stir in the Havarti cheese, ½ cup feta cheese, basil, salt and pepper.

3. Place zucchini in an ungreased 15-in. x 10-in. x 1-in. baking pan; fill with meat mixture. Bake at 400° for 15 minutes. Top with remaining feta; bake 5 minutes longer or until zucchini is tender and cheese is melted.

Editor's Note: *This recipe was tested in a 1,100-watt microwave.*

CRAB & SHRIMP STUFFED SOLE

The most casual cookout will seem elegant when it includes this delicate fish combined with seafood stuffing and a lemony sauce. Complete the meal with a green salad and warm baguette.

—BRYN NAMAVARI CHICAGO, ILLINOIS

PREP: 25 MIN. **GRILL:** 15 MIN. **MAKES:** 4 SERVINGS

- 1 **can (6 ounces) crabmeat, drained, flaked and cartilage removed**
- ½ **cup chopped cooked peeled shrimp**
- ¼ **cup soft bread crumbs**
- ¼ **cup butter, melted, divided**
- 2 **tablespoons whipped cream cheese**
- 2 **teaspoons minced chives**
- 1 **garlic clove, minced**
- 1 **teaspoon grated lemon peel**
- 1 **teaspoon minced fresh parsley**
- 4 **sole fillets (6 ounces each)**
- 1½ **cups cherry tomatoes**
- 2 **tablespoons dry white wine or chicken broth**
- 2 **tablespoons lemon juice**
- ½ **teaspoon salt**
- ½ **teaspoon pepper**

1. In a small bowl, combine the crab, shrimp, bread crumbs, 2 tablespoons butter, cream cheese, chives, garlic, lemon peel and parsley. Spoon about ¼ cup stuffing onto each fillet; roll up and secure with toothpicks.

2. Place each fillet on a double thickness of heavy-duty foil (about 18 in. x 12 in.). Combine the tomatoes, wine, lemon juice, salt, pepper and remaining butter; spoon over fillets. Fold foil around fish and seal tightly.

3. Grill, covered, over medium heat for 12-15 minutes or until the fish flakes easily with a fork. Open the foil carefully to allow steam to escape.

SPINACH-STUFFED CHICKEN BREASTS

Here's a company-worthy dish that comes together surprisingly quickly. I frequently double the recipe, then freeze the leftovers in individual-size portions. They're great for busy weekdays when I'm working late and don't have time to cook.
—**SANDY FRIEDE** NEWBURYPORT, MASSACHUSETTS

PREP: 30 MIN. **BAKE:** 40 MIN. **MAKES:** 6 SERVINGS

- ¼ cup chopped onion
- 4½ teaspoons plus ¼ cup butter, divided
- 1 garlic clove, minced
- 1 package (10 ounces) frozen chopped spinach, thawed and squeezed dry
- 6 ounces cream cheese, cubed
- ¼ cup seasoned bread crumbs
- 6 boneless skinless chicken breast halves (6 ounces each)
- ½ teaspoon salt
- ½ teaspoon pepper
- ¼ cup honey
- 2 tablespoons stone-ground mustard
- 1 tablespoon lemon juice

1. In a large skillet, saute onion in 4½ teaspoons butter until tender. Add garlic; saute 1 minute longer. Add spinach and cream cheese; cook and stir over low heat until blended. Remove from the heat; stir in bread crumbs.

2. Flatten chicken to ¼-in. thickness; sprinkle both sides with salt and pepper. Place about ¼ cup spinach mixture down the center of each chicken breast half. Fold chicken over filling and secure with toothpicks.

3. Place seam side down in a greased 11-in. x 7-in. baking dish. Melt remaining butter; stir in the honey, mustard and lemon juice. Pour over chicken.

4. Bake, uncovered, at 350° for 40-50 minutes or until the meat is no longer pink, basting every 15 minutes with the pan juices. Discard toothpicks.

■ FESTIVE STUFFED CORNISH GAME HENS

These plump, golden-brown birds are so beautiful and impressive on a holiday table. Moistened by juicy orange sections, the crusty ciabatta bread makes a wonderful stuffing.
—**LISA SPEER** PALM BEACH, FLORIDA

PREP: 30 MIN. **BAKE:** 1 HOUR + STANDING **MAKES:** 4 SERVINGS

- ½ cup chopped sweet onion
- ¼ cup chopped celery
- 2 tablespoons butter
- 3 tablespoons olive oil, divided
- 1 garlic clove, minced
- ¾ teaspoon salt, divided
- ¾ teaspoon pepper, divided
- 2 cups cubed ciabatta bread
- 3 medium navel oranges, peeled and sectioned
- ½ cup dried cranberries
- ½ cup chopped pecans, toasted
- 1 teaspoon grated orange peel
- 4 Cornish game hens (20 to 24 ounces each)
- ½ cup orange juice

1. In a large skillet, saute the onion and celery in butter and 1 tablespoon oil until tender. Add the garlic, ¼ teaspoon salt and ¼ teaspoon pepper; cook 1 minute longer.

2. In a large bowl, combine bread, oranges, cranberries, pecans and orange peel. Add onion mixture; toss to coat.

3. Loosely stuff the hens with stuffing. Tuck wings under hens; tie drumsticks together. Rub with remaining oil; sprinkle with remaining salt and pepper. Place breast side up on a rack in a shallow roasting pan.

4. Bake, uncovered, at 350° for 1 to 1½ hours or until a thermometer reads 180° for the hens and 165° for the stuffing, basting occasionally with the orange juice. Cover loosely with foil if hens brown too quickly. Cover and let stand for 10 minutes before serving.

BBQ BRISKET FLATBREAD PIZZAS

Preparing this beef brisket pizza takes a little bit of time, but you'll be glad you did. Each smoky, rich, juicy bite is amazing!
—**AARON REYNOLDS** FOX RIVER GROVE, ILLINOIS

PREP: 3 HOURS + MARINATING **GRILL:** 20 MIN.
MAKES: 2 FLATBREAD PIZZAS (6 SLICES EACH)

- 2 cups barbecue sauce, divided
- ½ cup cider vinegar
- ½ cup chopped green onions, divided
- ½ cup minced fresh cilantro, divided
- 2 pounds fresh beef brisket
- 1 teaspoon salt
- 1 teaspoon pepper
- 1 large red onion, cut into thick slices
- 1 teaspoon olive oil
- 2 cups (8 ounces) shredded smoked Gouda cheese

DOUGH
- 2¾ to 3¼ cups all-purpose flour
- 1 tablespoon sugar
- 3 teaspoons salt
- 1 package (¼ ounce) quick-rise yeast
- 1¼ cups warm water (120° to 130°)
- 2 tablespoons olive oil

1. In a large resealable plastic bag, combine 1 cup barbecue sauce, vinegar, ¼ cup green onions and ¼ cup cilantro. Sprinkle brisket with salt and pepper; add to the bag. Seal bag and turn to coat. Refrigerate for 8 hours or overnight.

2. Drain and discard marinade. Prepare grill for indirect heat, using a drip pan. Place the brisket over pan; grill, covered, over indirect low heat for 1 hour. Add 10 briquettes to coals. Cover and grill about 1¼ hours longer or until the meat is fork-tender, adding more briquettes if needed. When cool enough to handle, shred meat with two forks; set aside.

3. Meanwhile, in a large bowl, combine 2¾ cups flour, sugar, salt and yeast. Add water and oil; beat just until smooth. Stir in enough remaining flour to form a soft dough (dough will be sticky).

4. Turn onto a floured surface; knead until smooth and elastic, about 6-8 minutes. Place in a greased bowl, turning once to grease the top. Cover and let rise in a warm place until doubled, about 1 hour. Punch dough down; divide into two portions. Roll each into a 15-in. circle.

5. Grill each circle, covered, over medium heat for 1-2 minutes on one side or until lightly browned. Set aside. Brush onion with oil; grill for 4-5 minutes or until tender, turning once. Remove from the heat; chop and set aside.

6. Spread the grilled side of each crust with remaining barbecue sauce. Top with shredded brisket, onion, cheese and remaining green onions and cilantro.

7. Place a pizza on grill; cover and cook over indirect medium heat for 8-10 minutes or until crust is lightly browned and cheese is melted. Rotate pizza halfway through cooking to ensure an evenly browned crust. Repeat with remaining pizza.

DUTCH BABY TROPICALE

Want something different for breakfast? Simple but impressive, a Dutch baby is a cross between a pancake, soufflé and omelet. The eggy batter puffs up to a beautiful golden brown.
—**CINDY RAPPUHN** STARTUP, WASHINGTON

PREP: 15 MIN. **BAKE:** 20 MIN. **MAKES:** 8 SERVINGS

- 5 eggs
- 1 cup 2% milk
- 1 cup all-purpose flour
- ⅓ cup butter, cubed

FILLING
- 3 tablespoons butter
- 2 large bananas, sliced
- 1 medium papaya, peeled and sliced
  Lime wedges, optional

1. In a blender, combine the eggs, milk and flour; cover and process just until smooth. Place cubed butter in an ungreased 13-in. x 9-in. baking dish. Place in a 425° oven for 5 minutes or until melted.

2. Pour batter into hot dish. Bake, uncovered, for 20 minutes or until puffy and golden brown.

3. Meanwhile, for the filling, melt butter in a large skillet. Add the bananas and papaya. Cook over medium heat until tender, stirring frequently. Spoon into Dutch baby. Serve immediately with lime wedges.

PAPAYA POINTERS

Select papayas that have a golden-yellow skin. To prepare a papaya for cooking, wash it and slice it lengthwise in half. Scoop out the seeds (which are edible but are generally discarded). Then peel the papaya and slice or cube it as needed for the recipe.

PUMPKIN PANCAKES WITH APPLE CIDER COMPOTE

For an extra-special treat on autumn or winter mornings, try these spiced-up pumpkin pancakes. The accompanying compote made with apple pie filling is the crowning touch.

—MARGE MITCHELL PORTLAND, OREGON

PREP: 25 MIN. **COOK:** 10 MIN./BATCH
MAKES: 14 PANCAKES (5 CUPS COMPOTE)

- 1 **cup sugar**
- 2 **tablespoons cornstarch**
- ½ **teaspoon ground cinnamon**
- 2 **cups apple cider or juice**
- 2 **tablespoons orange juice**
- 1 **can (21 ounces) apple pie filling**
- 2 **tablespoons butter**

PANCAKES
- 1 **cup old-fashioned oats**
- 1¼ **cups all-purpose flour**
- 2 **tablespoons brown sugar**
- 2 **teaspoons baking powder**
- 1 **teaspoon pumpkin pie spice**
- 1 **teaspoon ground cinnamon**
- ¼ **teaspoon salt**
- 1 **egg**
- 1½ **cups milk**
- 1 **cup canned pumpkin**
- 3 **tablespoons maple syrup**
- 2 **tablespoons canola oil**
- 1 **cup chopped pecans, toasted, divided**

1. In a large saucepan, combine the sugar, cornstarch and cinnamon. Stir in apple cider and orange juice until smooth. Bring to a boil; cook and stir for 2 minutes or until thickened. Stir in apple pie filling and butter. Remove from the heat; set aside and keep warm.

2. For pancakes, place the oats in a food processor; cover and process until ground. Transfer to a large bowl; add the flour, brown sugar, baking powder, pie spice, cinnamon and salt. In another bowl, whisk the egg, milk, pumpkin, syrup and oil. Stir into dry ingredients just until moistened; fold in ½ cup pecans.

3. Pour the batter by ¼ cupfuls onto a hot griddle; flatten with the back of a spoon. Turn when the undersides are browned; cook until the second sides are golden brown. Serve with apple cider compote and remaining pecans. Store leftover compote in the refrigerator.

Editor's Note: *Leftover compote may be served with hot cereal or vanilla ice cream. It's also a tasty condiment for pork chops.*

ROBUST ITALIAN SAUSAGE & PASTA

With my sausage and pasta entree, I can sit back and let the slow cooker do most of the work. The noodles aren't cooked separately, so there's one less pot to wash after supper.

—LADONNA REED PONCA CITY, OKLAHOMA

PREP: 15 MIN. **COOK:** 6½ HOURS **MAKES:** 4 SERVINGS

- 4 **Italian sausage links (4 ounces each), halved**
- 1 **jar (25.6 ounces) Italian sausage spaghetti sauce**
- 1 **can (10 ounces) diced tomatoes and green chilies, undrained**
- 1 **large green pepper, julienned**
- 1 **medium onion, diced**
- 2 **garlic cloves, minced**
- 1 **teaspoon Italian seasoning**
- 2 **cups uncooked spiral pasta**

1. In a large nonstick skillet, brown sausage links. Transfer to a 3-qt. slow cooker. Add the spaghetti sauce, tomatoes, green pepper, onion, garlic and Italian seasoning.

2. Cover and cook on low for 6 hours. Stir in pasta. Cover and cook on high for 30-40 minutes or until pasta is tender.

CANADIAN BACON ONION QUICHE

For more than 20 years, we sold our homegrown specialty onions at the local farmers market. I handed out copies of this favorite quiche recipe to all of our customers.

—**JANICE REDFORD** CAMBRIDGE, WISCONSIN

PREP: 30 MIN. **BAKE:** 40 MIN. **MAKES:** 6-8 SERVINGS

- 1 **cup all-purpose flour**
- ¾ **teaspoon salt, divided**
- ½ **cup plus 3 tablespoons cold butter, divided**
- ½ **cup 4% small-curd cottage cheese**
- 3 **large sweet onions, sliced (about 6 cups)**
- 4 **ounces Canadian bacon, diced**
- ¼ **teaspoon pepper**
- 3 **eggs, lightly beaten**
- 1 **cup (4 ounces) shredded cheddar cheese**

1. In a small bowl, combine flour and ¼ teaspoon salt; cut in ½ cup butter until crumbly. Gradually add the cottage cheese, tossing with a fork until dough forms a ball.

2. Roll out pastry to fit a 9-in. pie plate. Transfer pastry to pie plate. Trim pastry to ½ in. beyond edge of plate; flute edges.

3. In large skillet, saute onions in remaining butter until golden brown. Stir in the Canadian bacon, pepper and remaining salt. Remove from the heat; add eggs and cheddar cheese. Pour into pastry shell.

4. Bake at 350° for 40-45 minutes or until a knife inserted near the center comes out clean.

GARLIC POT ROAST

My family absolutely loves garlic—the more, the better! Ever since I came up with this zippy pot roast, they've been requesting it for Sunday dinner. The veggies make it a complete meal.

—**RHONDA HAMPTON** COOKEVILLE, TENNESSEE

PREP: 20 MIN. **BAKE:** 2½ HOURS **MAKES:** 8 SERVINGS

- 1 **boneless beef chuck roast (3 pounds)**
- 4 **garlic cloves, peeled and halved**
- 3 **teaspoons garlic powder**
- 3 **teaspoons Italian salad dressing mix**
- ½ **teaspoon pepper**
- 1 **tablespoon canola oil**
- 3 **cups water**
- 1 **envelope onion soup mix**
- 1 **teaspoon reduced-sodium beef bouillon granules**
- 5 **medium potatoes, peeled and quartered**
- 1 **pound fresh baby carrots**
- 1 **large onion, cut into 1-inch pieces**

1. Using the point of a sharp knife, make eight slits in the roast. Insert garlic into slits. Combine the garlic powder, salad dressing mix and pepper; rub over roast. In a Dutch oven, brown roast in oil on all sides; drain.

2. Combine the water, onion soup mix and bouillon; pour over roast. Cover and bake at 325° for 1½ hours.

3. Add the potatoes, carrots and onion. Cover and bake 1 hour longer or until the meat and vegetables are tender. Thicken pan juices if desired.

ITALIAN BAKED CHICKEN

Here's a winning main dish for just about any occasion. Serve the saucy entree with a green salad and bread for an Italian feast.
—**MARCELLO BASCO** DEERFIELD BEACH, FLORIDA

PREP: 25 MIN. **BAKE:** 35 MIN. **MAKES:** 4 SERVINGS

- ½ cup all-purpose flour
- ½ teaspoon salt
- ⅛ teaspoon pepper
- 4 boneless skinless chicken breast halves (6 ounces each)
- 3 tablespoons olive oil, divided
- 5 garlic cloves, minced
- 1 teaspoon dried oregano
- 1 teaspoon dried basil
- 2 cups chicken broth
- 1 cup tomato puree
- 4 slices mozzarella cheese
- 4 tomato slices
- 4 teaspoons grated Parmesan cheese
  Hot cooked angel hair pasta
  Minced fresh parsley

1. In a large resealable plastic bag, combine the flour, salt and pepper; add chicken, one piece at a time, and shake to coat. In a large skillet over medium heat, brown chicken in 2 tablespoons oil on each side. Transfer to a greased 11-in. x 7-in. baking dish.
2. In the same skillet, saute the garlic, oregano and basil in the remaining oil for 1 minute. Add the chicken broth and tomato puree. Bring to a boil. Remove from the heat; pour over the chicken. Cover and bake at 400° for 25-30 minutes or until a thermometer reads 170°.
3. Remove chicken and set aside. Pour sauce into a small bowl and keep warm. Return chicken to the pan; top each with a cheese and tomato slice. Sprinkle with Parmesan cheese.
4. Bake, uncovered, for 6-8 minutes or until cheese is melted. Arrange pasta on a large serving platter; top with chicken. Pour sauce over chicken and sprinkle with parsley.

AT-ATTENTION GRILLED CHICKEN

I've been fixing this for years and have yet to taste a better grilled chicken. The cooking technique makes it so juicy and tender, you won't want to prepare a whole chicken any other way.
—**SHIRLEY HODGE** BANGOR, PENNSYLVANIA

PREP: 15 MIN. + MARINATING **GRILL:** 1¼ HOURS + STANDING
MAKES: 6 SERVINGS

- 3 tablespoons minced fresh thyme or 1 tablespoon dried thyme
- 1 tablespoon grated lemon peel
- 1 tablespoon ground cumin
- 1 teaspoon salt
- 1 teaspoon ground allspice
- 1 teaspoon chili powder
- 1 teaspoon pepper
- ½ teaspoon ground nutmeg
- 1 broiler/fryer chicken (3 to 4 pounds)
- 1 tablespoon olive oil
- 1 can (12 ounces) beer or nonalcoholic beer

1. Combine the first eight ingredients. Gently loosen skin from chicken breasts; rub olive oil and 2 tablespoons spice mixture under the skin. Rub remaining spice mixture over skin. Place chicken in a large resealable plastic bag; seal bag. Refrigerate for at least 1 hour or overnight.
2. Prepare grill for indirect heat, using a drip pan. Pour out a third of the beer. Carefully poke additional holes in the top of can with a can opener. Holding the chicken with legs pointed down, lower chicken over the can so it fills the body cavity.
3. Place the chicken over drip pan; grill, covered, over indirect medium heat for 1¼ to 1½ hours or until a thermometer reads 180°. Remove the chicken from grill; cover and let stand for 10 minutes. Remove chicken from can.

CRAB QUICHE WITH HOLLANDAISE

While on a motorcycle road trip with my husband, we stopped at a diner that served an amazing crab quiche. It was so good, I tried to duplicate it at home. Our family loved the results!

—**AMY KNIGHT** LAKE LINDEN, MICHIGAN

PREP: 25 MIN. **BAKE:** 35 MIN. **MAKES:** 6 SERVINGS (⅔ CUP SAUCE)

    Pastry for single-crust pie (9 inches)
1 can (6 ounces) crabmeat, drained, flaked and cartilage removed
1 cup (4 ounces) shredded cheddar-Monterey Jack cheese
¾ cup frozen asparagus stir-fry vegetable blend, thawed
¼ cup finely chopped onion
3 eggs
1 cup evaporated milk
½ teaspoon salt
¼ teaspoon pepper
¼ teaspoon seafood seasoning
⅛ teaspoon hot pepper sauce

SAUCE
3 egg yolks
1 tablespoon water
1 tablespoon lemon juice
½ cup butter, melted
    Dash pepper

1. Roll out pastry to fit a 9-in. pie plate. Transfer pastry to pie plate. Trim pastry to ½ in. beyond the edge of plate; flute edges. Line unpricked pastry with a double thickness of heavy-duty foil. Bake at 450° for 8 minutes. Remove the foil; bake 5 minutes longer. Place on a wire rack.

2. In a small bowl, combine the crab, cheese, vegetable blend and onion; transfer to the crust. In another bowl, whisk the eggs, milk, salt, pepper, seafood seasoning and pepper sauce. Pour over crab mixture.

3. Bake at 375° for 35-40 minutes or until a knife inserted near the center comes out clean. Cover edges with foil during the last 15 minutes to prevent overbrowning if necessary. Let stand for 5 minutes before cutting.

4. In a double boiler or metal bowl over simmering water, constantly whisk the egg yolks, water and lemon juice until the mixture reaches 160° or is thick enough to coat the back of a metal spoon. Reduce heat to low. Slowly drizzle in warm melted butter, whisking constantly. Whisk in pepper. Serve immediately with quiche.

SMOKY SAUSAGE & APPLE PIZZA

I top this homemade pie with savory chicken sausage, chopped apple, veggies and cheddar cheese. It's a great way to enjoy pizza without sabotaging a healthy eating plan.

—**LINDSAY WILLIAMS** HASTINGS, MINNESOTA

PREP: 40 MIN. + STANDING **BAKE:** 15 MIN. **MAKES:** 4 SERVINGS

½ cup all-purpose flour
½ to ¾ cup whole wheat flour
1 teaspoon quick-rise yeast
½ teaspoon salt
    Dash sugar
½ cup warm water (120° to 130°)
4½ teaspoons olive oil
1 tablespoon honey

TOPPINGS
1 small onion, chopped
3 teaspoons cider vinegar, divided
2 teaspoons maple syrup, divided
    Dash salt
    Dash cayenne pepper
2 teaspoons olive oil
1½ teaspoons chopped fresh sage
1 teaspoon Dijon mustard
1 tablespoon cornmeal
2 cups chopped beet greens or fresh spinach
½ cup chopped apple
2 fully cooked apple chicken sausage links or flavor of your choice (3 ounces each), sliced
¾ cup shredded smoked cheddar cheese

1. In a small bowl, combine the all-purpose flour, ½ cup whole wheat flour, yeast, salt and sugar. Stir in the water, oil and honey; beat just until moistened. Stir in enough remaining whole wheat flour to form a soft dough (dough will be sticky).

2. Turn onto a floured surface; knead until smooth and elastic, about 6-8 minutes. Cover and let rest for 30 minutes.

3. Meanwhile, in a large skillet, saute the onion, 2 teaspoons vinegar, 1 teaspoon syrup, salt and cayenne in oil until onion is tender. Remove from the heat; stir in the sage, mustard and remaining vinegar and syrup.

4. Grease a 12-in. pizza pan; sprinkle with cornmeal. Roll out dough to fit prepared pan; prick thoroughly with a fork. Bake at 450° for 5-8 minutes or until edges are lightly browned.

5. Arrange the onion mixture, beet greens, apple, sausage and cheese over top. Bake 5-7 minutes longer or until crust is golden and cheese is melted.

HAM AND LEEK PIES

Here's my favorite recipe for leftover holiday ham. I like to freeze the individual pies for a quick, comforting meal anytime.
—**BONNY TILLMAN** ACWORTH, GEORGIA

PREP: 40 MIN. **BAKE:** 20 MIN. **MAKES:** 4 SERVINGS

- 4 cups sliced leeks (white portion only)
- ½ pound sliced fresh mushrooms
- 1½ cups sliced fresh carrots
- ¼ cup butter, cubed
- ½ cup all-purpose flour
- 1¼ cups vegetable broth
- 1¼ cups milk
- 1¾ cups diced fully cooked ham
- 2 tablespoons minced fresh parsley
- ¼ to ½ teaspoon ground nutmeg
  Dash pepper
- 1 sheet frozen puff pastry, thawed
- 1 egg, lightly beaten

1. In a large saucepan, saute the leeks, mushrooms and carrots in butter until tender. Stir in flour until blended. Gradually stir in broth and milk. Bring to a boil over medium heat. Cook and stir for 2 minutes or until thickened. Remove from the heat; stir in the ham, parsley, nutmeg and pepper.

2. On a lightly floured surface, roll pastry to ¼-in. thickness. Using a 10-oz. ramekin as a template, cut out four tops from the pastry for pies.

3. Fill four greased 10-oz. ramekins with leek mixture; top with pastry. Cut slits in pastry. Cut decorative shapes out of pastry scraps if desired; arrange over pies. Brush tops with egg.

4. Bake at 425° for 18-22 minutes or until golden brown. Let stand for 5 minutes before serving.

SCALLOP MAC & CHEESE

How do you make ever-popular macaroni and cheese even better? Add tender scallops, fresh mushrooms and toasted bread crumbs. They transform a classic dish into a sensational entree.
—**LAURIE LUFKIN** ESSEX, MASSACHUSETTS

PREP: 35 MIN. **BAKE:** 15 MIN. **MAKES:** 5 SERVINGS

- 2 cups uncooked medium pasta shells
- ½ cup butter, divided
- 1 cup French bread baguette crumbs
- 1 pound bay scallops
- 1 cup sliced fresh mushrooms
- 1 small onion, chopped
- 3 tablespoons all-purpose flour
- ¾ teaspoon dried thyme
- ¼ teaspoon salt
- ⅛ teaspoon pepper
- 2 cups whole milk
- ½ cup white wine or chicken broth
- 2 tablespoons sherry or chicken broth
- 1 cup (4 ounces) shredded Swiss cheese
- 1 cup (4 ounces) shredded sharp cheddar cheese

1. Cook pasta according to package directions. Meanwhile, in a small skillet, melt 4 tablespoons butter. Add bread crumbs; cook and stir until lightly toasted.

2. In a large skillet over medium heat, melt 2 tablespoons butter. Add scallops; cook and stir for 2 minutes or until firm and opaque. Remove and keep warm. Melt remaining butter in the pan; add mushrooms and onion. Cook and stir until tender. Stir in the flour, thyme, salt and pepper until blended.

3. Gradually add the milk, wine and sherry. Bring to a boil; cook and stir for 1-2 minutes or until thickened. Stir in cheeses until melted. Drain pasta; stir pasta and scallops into sauce.

4. Divide among five 10-oz. ramekins or custard cups. Sprinkle with bread crumbs. Place the ramekins on a baking sheet. Bake, uncovered, at 350° for 15-20 minutes or until heated through. Spoon onto plates if desired.

SHEPHERD'S PIE TWICE-BAKED POTATOES

What do you get when you combine classic shepherd's pie with baked potatoes? These main-dish spuds packed with ground beef and two kinds of cheese. Round out the meal with a green salad.
—**CYNDY GERKEN** NAPLES, FLORIDA

PREP: 1¾ HOURS **BAKE:** 25 MIN. **MAKES:** 6 SERVINGS

- 6 large russet potatoes
- 2 tablespoons olive oil
- 1 pound ground beef
- 1 medium onion, chopped
- 1 medium green pepper, chopped
- 1 medium sweet red pepper, chopped
- 4 garlic cloves, minced
- 1 package (16 ounces) frozen mixed vegetables
- 3 tablespoons Worcestershire sauce
- 1 tablespoon tomato paste
- 1 tablespoon steak seasoning
- ¼ teaspoon salt
- ⅛ teaspoon pepper
  Dash cayenne pepper
- 2 teaspoons paprika, divided
- ½ cup butter, cubed
- ¾ cup heavy whipping cream
- ¼ cup sour cream
- 1 cup shredded Monterey Jack cheese
- 1 cup shredded cheddar cheese
- ¼ cup shredded Parmesan cheese
- 2 tablespoons minced chives

TOPPINGS
- 1 teaspoon paprika
- ½ cup shredded cheddar cheese
- 1 tablespoon minced chives

1. Scrub and pierce the potatoes; rub with oil. Bake at 375° for 1 hour or until tender.
2. In a large skillet, cook the beef, onion, peppers and garlic over medium heat until beef is no longer pink; drain. Add the mixed vegetables, Worcestershire sauce, tomato paste, steak seasoning, salt, pepper, cayenne and 1 teaspoon paprika. Cook and stir until vegetables are tender.

3. When cool enough to handle, cut a thin slice off the top of each potato and discard. Scoop out the pulp, leaving thin shells.
4. In a large bowl, mash the pulp with butter. Add the whipping cream, sour cream, cheeses and chives. Mash potatoes until combined. Spoon 1 cup meat mixture into each potato shell; top with ½ cup potato mixture. Sprinkle with remaining paprika.
5. Place on a baking sheet. Bake at 375° for 20 minutes. Sprinkle with cheese; bake 5 minutes longer or until melted. Sprinkle with chives.

LEMON-BASIL TURKEY BREAST

With vegetables and a refreshing blend of lemon and basil, you can transform plain turkey breast into a company-worthy entree. The golden-brown meat is super-moist and tender.
—**SHARON DELANEY-CHRONIS** SOUTH MILWAUKEE, WISCONSIN

PREP: 20 MIN. **BAKE:** 2 HOURS **MAKES:** 12 SERVINGS

- 6 medium carrots
- 3 celery ribs
- 2 medium onions
- 2 cups reduced-sodium chicken broth
- 1 cup water
- 1 cup minced fresh basil
- 2 tablespoons grated lemon peel
- 4 garlic cloves, minced
- ½ teaspoon salt
- ½ teaspoon pepper
- 1 bone-in turkey breast (5 to 6 pounds)
- 2 medium lemons, sliced

1. Cut the carrots and celery into 2-in. lengths; cut onions into wedges. Place in a roasting pan; add broth and water.
2. In a small bowl, combine the basil, lemon peel, garlic, salt and pepper. With fingers, carefully loosen skin from the turkey breast; rub mixture under the skin. Secure skin to underside of breast with toothpicks. Place turkey breast over carrot mixture. Place lemon slices over skin.
3. Bake, uncovered, at 325° for 2 to 2½ hours or until a thermometer reads 170°, basting every 30 minutes. Cover loosely with foil if the turkey browns too quickly. Cover and let stand for 15 minutes before slicing turkey. Serve with vegetables.

PORTOBELLOS
WITH RATATOUILLE

These veggie-stuffed portobello mushrooms prove that a meatless dinner can be hearty and satisfying. Keep the recipe in mind when your summer garden is full of fresh produce.

—**MARIE RIZZIO** INTERLOCHEN, MICHIGAN

PREP: 30 MIN. **BAKE:** 25 MIN. **MAKES:** 4 SERVINGS

- 1 **large onion, chopped**
- 1 **tablespoon plus 1 teaspoon olive oil, divided**
- 5 **garlic cloves, minced, divided**
- 1 **small eggplant, peeled and cubed**
- 2 **medium zucchini, cubed**
- 1 **medium sweet red pepper, chopped**
- ¼ **cup tomato paste**
- 2 **teaspoons red wine vinegar**
- 1 **teaspoon minced fresh thyme or ¼ teaspoon dried thyme**
- ½ **teaspoon salt**
- ⅛ **teaspoon pepper**
  Dash cayenne pepper
- 2 **medium tomatoes, chopped**
- 4 **large portobello mushrooms (4 to 4½ inches)**
- 2 **packages (6 ounces each) fresh baby spinach**
  Minced fresh parsley and shaved Parmesan cheese

1. In a large skillet, saute onion in 1 tablespoon oil until tender. Add 3 garlic cloves; cook 1 minute longer. Stir in the eggplant, zucchini, red pepper, tomato paste, vinegar and seasonings.

2. Transfer to a 15-in. x 10-in. x 1-in. baking pan coated with cooking spray. Bake at 400° for 10 minutes. Stir in the tomatoes; bake 15-20 minutes longer or until vegetables are tender.

3. Meanwhile, remove and discard the stems and gills from the mushrooms. Place the mushrooms, stem side up, on a baking sheet coated with cooking spray; drizzle with remaining oil and sprinkle with remaining garlic. Bake at 400° for 20-25 minutes or until tender, turning once.

4. Place spinach in a large nonstick skillet coated with cooking spray; cook and stir for 4-5 minutes or until wilted.

5. Divide spinach among four plates; top with mushrooms. Fill mushrooms with ratatouille; sprinkle with parsley and cheese.

PAN-FRIED CATFISH WITH
SPICY PECAN GREMOLATA

A citrusy minced herb mix, gremolata makes a wonderful garnish. This well-seasoned version includes glazed pecans and brings an unexpectedly nutty flavor to fried catfish fillets.

—**LAUREEN PITTMAN** RIVERSIDE, CALIFORNIA

PREP: 25 MIN. **COOK:** 10 MIN./BATCH **MAKES:** 4 SERVINGS

- ½ **cup packed fresh parsley sprigs**
- ½ **cup glazed pecans**
- 2 **tablespoons grated lemon peel**
- 1 **tablespoon grated orange peel**
- 1 **garlic clove, halved**
- 1 **teaspoon brown sugar**
- ¼ **teaspoon cayenne pepper**
- 1 **cup buttermilk**
- 1 **cup all-purpose flour**
- 1 **cup cornmeal**
- 2 **teaspoons Cajun seasoning**
- 4 **catfish fillets (6 ounces each)**
- ½ **cup canola oil**

1. Place the first seven ingredients in a food processor. Cover and process until chunky; set aside.

2. Place buttermilk in a shallow bowl. In another shallow bowl, combine the flour, cornmeal and Cajun seasoning. Dip fish in buttermilk, then coat with cornmeal mixture.

3. In a large skillet, cook fillets in oil in batches over medium heat for 4-5 minutes on each side or until fish flakes easily with a fork. Serve with gremolata.

3. Remove the roast; cool slightly. Strain the cooking juices, reserving the vegetables and 1¼ cups juices; skim the fat from reserved juices. Shred the beef with two forks and return to slow cooker. Stir in the reserved vegetables and juices; heat through. Serve with noodles.

GNOCCHI WITH MEAT SAUCE

This popular dish from my mother-in-law is an Italian version of a meat-and-potatoes meal. I recently fixed the saucy gnocchi for friends, and they immediately requested the recipe.
—**KARIN NOLTON** ORTONVILLE, MICHIGAN

PREP: 30 MIN. **COOK:** 15 MIN. **MAKES:** 6 SERVINGS

- ½ **pound lean ground beef (90% lean)**
- 1 **large onion, finely chopped**
- 4 **garlic cloves, minced**
- 2 **cans (15 ounces each) tomato sauce**
- 1 **can (14½ ounces) diced tomatoes**
- 1 **teaspoon dried oregano**
- 1 **teaspoon dried basil**
- ½ **teaspoon dried rosemary, crushed**
- 1 **to 2 teaspoons sugar**
- ½ **teaspoon salt**
- ⅛ **teaspoon pepper**

GNOCCHI
- 2 **cups mashed potato flakes**
- 1½ **cups boiling water**
- 2 **eggs, beaten**
- 1½ **cups all-purpose flour**
- ¼ **teaspoon salt**
   Grated Parmesan cheese, optional

1. In a large saucepan, cook beef, onion and garlic over medium heat until the meat is no longer pink; drain. Stir in tomato sauce, diced tomatoes and seasonings. Bring to a boil. Reduce heat; cover and simmer for 15-20 minutes or until heated through.
2. Place the mashed potato flakes in a large bowl; stir in boiling water until blended. Stir in the eggs. Add the flour and salt all at once; stir just until combined. Divide into fourths; turn each onto a floured surface. Roll into ¾-in.-thick ropes; cut ropes into ¾-in. pieces.
3. In a large saucepan, bring water to a boil. Cook gnocchi, in batches, for 30-60 seconds or until gnocchi float. Remove with a slotted spoon. Place in a large bowl; top with sauce. Gently stir to coat. Sprinkle with cheese.

GET TO KNOW GNOCCHI
Gnocchi are Italian dumplings traditionally made with potatoes and flour or farina. Seasonings and eggs are added before the dough is shaped into long ropes, cut into small pieces and rolled into balls. Sometimes the balls are rolled over the tines of a fork, cheese grater or a special gnocchi board to make small ridges in the dough.

SWEET AND SAVORY PULLED BEEF DINNER

Pull out your slow cooker to make a delicious dinner of pulled beef. The meat is wonderfully versatile—try piling it onto hard rolls for casual party sandwiches or serving it over rice or pasta.
—**PATTY MANOCCHI** GLENVILLE, NEW YORK

PREP: 25 MIN. **COOK:** 6 HOURS **MAKES:** 6 SERVINGS

- 1 **teaspoon salt**
- 1 **teaspoon ground mustard**
- 1 **teaspoon barbecue seasoning**
- 1 **teaspoon paprika**
- 1 **teaspoon chili powder**
- ½ **teaspoon pepper**
- 1 **boneless beef chuck roast (3 pounds)**
- 3 **tablespoons olive oil**
- 1 **large onion, halved and sliced**
- 1 **large sweet red pepper, sliced**

SAUCE
- 1 **can (8 ounces) tomato sauce**
- ⅓ **cup packed brown sugar**
- 3 **tablespoons honey**
- 2 **tablespoons Dijon mustard**
- 2 **tablespoons Worcestershire sauce**
- 2 **tablespoons soy sauce**
- 5 **garlic cloves, minced**
- 4 **teaspoons balsamic vinegar**
- ¾ **teaspoon salt**
   Cooked egg noodles

1. Combine the first six ingredients. Cut the roast in half; rub with seasonings. In a large skillet, brown the beef in oil on all sides. Transfer to a 4- or 5-qt. slow cooker. Top with onion and red pepper.
2. In a small bowl, combine the tomato sauce, brown sugar, honey, mustard, Worcestershire sauce, soy sauce, garlic, vinegar and salt; pour over vegetables. Cover and cook on low for 6-8 hours or until meat is tender.

ST. PADDY'S IRISH BEEF DINNER

Like shepherd's pie? I prepare an Irish-style variation as the star of our St. Patrick's Day spread every March 17. The beefy supper is great any time you're craving something hearty and comforting.
—**LORRAINE CALAND** SHUNIAH, ONTARIO

PREP: 25 MIN. **COOK:** 35 MIN. **MAKES:** 4 SERVINGS

- 2 medium Yukon Gold potatoes
- 2 small parsnips
- ¾ pound lean ground beef (90% lean)
- 1 medium onion, chopped
- 2 cups finely shredded cabbage
- 2 medium carrots, halved and sliced
- 1 teaspoon dried thyme
- 1 teaspoon Worcestershire sauce
- 1 tablespoon all-purpose flour
- ¼ cup tomato paste
- 1 can (14½ ounces) reduced-sodium chicken or beef broth
- ½ cup frozen peas
- ¾ teaspoon salt, divided
- ½ teaspoon pepper, divided
- ¼ cup 2% milk
- 1 tablespoon butter

1. Peel potatoes and parsnips and cut into large pieces; place in a large saucepan and cover with water. Bring to a boil. Reduce heat; cover and cook for 10-15 minutes or until tender. Drain.

2. Meanwhile, in a large skillet, cook the beef and onion over medium heat until the meat is no longer pink; drain. Stir in the cabbage, carrots, thyme and Worcestershire sauce.

3. In a small bowl, combine the flour, tomato paste and broth until smooth. Gradually stir into the meat mixture. Bring to a boil. Reduce heat; cover and simmer for 15-20 minutes or until the vegetables are tender. Stir in the peas, ¼ teaspoon salt and ¼ teaspoon pepper.

4. Drain the potatoes and parsnips; mash with the milk, butter, and remaining salt and pepper. Serve with meat mixture.

BLUEBERRY FRENCH TOAST

This yummy, slow-cooked French toast makes a wonderful menu item for a late breakfast or brunch. Doing most of the prep work the night before saves time in the morning.
—**ELIZABETH LORENZ** PERU, INDIANA

PREP: 30 MIN. + CHILLING **COOK:** 3 HOURS
MAKES: 12 SERVINGS (2 CUPS SYRUP)

- 8 eggs
- ½ cup plain yogurt
- ⅓ cup sour cream
- 1 teaspoon vanilla extract
- ½ teaspoon ground cinnamon
- 1 cup 2% milk
- ⅓ cup maple syrup
- 1 loaf (1 pound) French bread, cubed
- 1½ cups fresh or frozen blueberries
- 12 ounces cream cheese, cubed

BLUEBERRY SYRUP

- 1 cup sugar
- 2 tablespoons cornstarch
- 1 cup cold water
- ¾ cup fresh or frozen blueberries, thawed, divided
- 1 tablespoon lemon juice
- 1 tablespoon butter

1. In a large bowl, whisk eggs, yogurt, sour cream, vanilla and cinnamon. Gradually whisk in milk and syrup until blended.

2. Place half of the bread in a greased 5- or 6-qt. slow cooker; layer with half of the blueberries, cream cheese and egg mixture. Repeat layers. Cover and refrigerate overnight.

3. Remove from the refrigerator 30 minutes before cooking. Cover and cook on low for 3-4 hours or until a knife inserted in French toast comes out clean.

4. For the syrup, in a small saucepan, combine the sugar and cornstarch; stir in water until smooth. Add ¼ cup blueberries. Bring to a boil; cook and stir until the blueberries pop, about 3 minutes. Remove from the heat; stir in the lemon juice, butter and remaining berries. Serve warm with French toast.

FIG & WINE-SAUCED CHICKEN KABOBS

Unusual but delicious, these kabobs bring a bit of sophistication to barbecues. The dried figs add a wonderfully fruity quality.
—**BARBARA WHEELER** ROYAL OAK, MICHIGAN

PREP: 1 HOUR + MARINATING **GRILL:** 15 MIN. **MAKES:** 6 SERVINGS

- 5 small onions, divided
- ½ cup olive oil
- 2 garlic cloves, minced
- 1½ pounds boneless skinless chicken breasts, cut into 1-inch cubes
- 1¼ pounds dried figs
- 2½ cups sweet white wine
- 3 tablespoons orange marmalade
- 2 tablespoons fig preserves
- 2 tablespoons lemon juice
- ½ teaspoon salt
- ¼ teaspoon white pepper
- ½ pound small fresh portobello mushrooms
   Hot cooked rice
   Fresh mint leaves and lemon wedges, optional

1. Grate two onions; place in a large resealable plastic bag. Add the oil, garlic and chicken; seal bag and turn to coat. Refrigerate for 8 hours or overnight.

2. Meanwhile, in a large saucepan, bring figs and wine to a boil. Reduce heat; simmer, uncovered, for 50-60 minutes or until figs are plumped and tender. Remove figs; keep warm. Bring liquid to a boil; cook until reduced to ⅔ cup. Add orange marmalade, fig preserves, lemon juice, salt and pepper. Cook and stir for 5-6 minutes or until slightly thickened.

3. Cut remaining onions into 1-in. pieces. Drain chicken; discard marinade. On six metal or soaked wooden skewers, alternately thread the chicken, onions and mushrooms.

4. Using long-handled tongs, moisten a paper towel with cooking oil and lightly coat the grill rack. Grill kabobs, covered, over medium heat or broil 4 in. from the heat for 10-15 minutes or until juices run clear, turning occasionally.

5. Serve kabobs with rice and reserved figs; drizzle with sauce. Garnish with mint and lemon if desired.

MEDITERRANEAN FRITTATA

Here's an extra-special egg bake for Christmas morning or any time you're craving a breakfast treat. Italian bread, feta cheese and olives give the frittata plenty of Mediterranean flair.
—**GERALDINE EVANS** HERMOSA, SOUTH DAKOTA

PREP: 15 MIN. **BAKE:** 30 MIN. **MAKES:** 6 SERVINGS

- 2 medium onions, halved and thinly sliced
- 2 tablespoons olive oil
- 2 garlic cloves, minced
- ½ cup chopped roasted sweet red peppers, drained
- ½ cup chopped pimiento-stuffed olives
- 3 cups cubed Italian bread
- ½ cup crumbled feta cheese
- 6 eggs, lightly beaten
- ½ cup chicken broth
- ¼ teaspoon pepper

1. In a large skillet, saute onions in oil until tender. Add garlic; cook 1 minute longer. Remove from the heat. Stir in red peppers and olives. Place bread cubes in a greased 9-in. deep-dish pie plate. Top with onion mixture and cheese.

2. In a large bowl, whisk the eggs, broth and pepper; pour over cheese. Bake at 375° for 30-35 minutes or until a knife inserted near the center comes out clean. Let stand for 5 minutes before cutting into wedges.

3. Grill the steaks, covered, over medium heat or broil 3-4 in. from the heat for 5-7 minutes on each side or until meat reaches desired doneness (for medium-rare, a thermometer should read 145°; medium, 160°; well-done, 170°).

4. For herb butter, in a small bowl, beat the butter, parsley and horseradish until blended. Spoon 1 tablespoon herb butter over each steak.

Editor's Note: *Look for herbes de Provence in the spice aisle.*

HOMEMADE MARINATED FLANK STEAK

Just five simple ingredients—lemon juice, olive oil, beef bouillon, ginger and garlic—really enhance flank steak. I marinate thin slices overnight for extra flavor and tenderness.

—JANET WRIGHT PORTAGE, PENNSYLVANIA

PREP: 10 MIN. + MARINATING **GRILL:** 15 MIN. **MAKES:** 5 SERVINGS

- ½ cup lemon juice
- ¼ cup olive oil
- 2 garlic cloves, minced
- 2 teaspoons reduced-sodium beef bouillon granules
- 2 teaspoons minced fresh gingerroot
- 1 beef flank steak (1½ pounds)

1. In a small bowl, combine the lemon juice, oil, garlic, beef bouillon and ginger. Pour ⅓ cup into a large resealable plastic bag; add the flank steak. Seal bag and turn to coat; refrigerate overnight. Cover and refrigerate the remaining marinade for basting.

2. Drain and discard the marinade. Grill steak, covered, over medium heat for 6-8 minutes on each side or until meat reaches desired doneness (for medium-rare, a thermometer should read 145°; medium, 160°; well-done, 170°), basting occasionally with reserved marinade. Let stand 5 minutes before serving. To serve, thinly slice across the grain.

GRILLED RIBEYES WITH HERB BUTTER

This recipe is also great made with filet mignon, T-bones and strip steaks in place of ribeyes. Whatever meat you choose, you won't want to skip the accompanying herb butter!

—JOHN BARANSKI BALDWIN CITY, KANSAS

PREP: 25 MIN. + MARINATING **GRILL:** 10 MIN. **MAKES:** 4 SERVINGS

- ¼ cup olive oil
- ¼ cup dry red wine
- 1 tablespoon minced fresh rosemary or 1 teaspoon dried rosemary, crushed
- 1 tablespoon red wine vinegar
- 1 tablespoon Dijon mustard
- 1 teaspoon coarsely ground pepper
- 1 teaspoon Worcestershire sauce
- 2 garlic cloves, minced
- 4 beef ribeye steaks (¾ pound each)

STEAK SEASONINGS

- 2 teaspoons kosher salt
- 1 teaspoon sugar
- 1 teaspoon herbes de Provence
- 1 teaspoon coarsely ground pepper

HERB BUTTER

- ¼ cup butter, softened
- 1 tablespoon minced fresh parsley
- 1 teaspoon prepared horseradish

1. In a large resealable plastic bag, combine the first eight ingredients. Add the steaks; seal the plastic bag and turn to coat. Refrigerate overnight.

2. Drain and discard marinade. Combine the steak seasonings; sprinkle over steaks.

BREADS, ROLLS & MORE

Mmm! Family and friends are sure to come running when you take a pan of these tender, golden-brown goodies out of the oven. From the heavenly aroma to the scrumptious taste, these fresh-baked treats are impossible to resist.

CARAMEL APPLE MUFFINS

If you like caramel apples, you'll love these ooey-gooey goodies. Serve them for breakfast and save one for your coffee break.

—THERESE PUCKETT SHREVEPORT, LOUISIANA

PREP: 25 MIN. **BAKE:** 20 MIN. **MAKES:** 14 MUFFINS

- 2   cups all-purpose flour
- ¾   cup sugar
- 2   teaspoons baking powder
- 2½ teaspoons ground cinnamon
- ½   teaspoon salt
- 1   egg
- 1   cup 2% milk
- ¼   cup butter, melted
- 2   teaspoons vanilla extract
- ½   cup chopped peeled tart apple
- 12 caramels, chopped

TOPPING
- ½   cup packed brown sugar
- ¼   cup quick-cooking oats
- 3   tablespoons butter, melted
- 1   teaspoon ground cinnamon

1. In a large bowl, combine the flour, sugar, baking powder, cinnamon and salt. In another bowl, whisk the egg, milk, butter and vanilla. Stir into dry ingredients just until moistened. Fold in apple and caramels.

2. Fill paper-lined muffin cups three-fourths full. Combine topping ingredients; sprinkle over batter.

3. Bake at 350° for 20-25 minutes or until a toothpick inserted in the cake portion comes out clean. Cool for 5 minutes before removing from pans to wire racks. Serve warm.

BIG-BATCH YEAST ROLLS

Tender and light, these yeast rolls have just a touch of sweetness. They complement many different types of main courses, and everyone enjoys the made-from-scratch taste.

—ANNA MAYER FORT BRANCH, INDIANA

PREP: 50 MIN. **BAKE:** 15 MIN. + RISING **MAKES:** 3 DOZEN

- 2   packages (¼ ounce each) active dry yeast
- ½   cup warm water (110° to 115°)
- 2½ cups warm 2% milk (110° to 115°)
- ½   cup butter, melted
- ½   cup mashed potato flakes
- 1   cup sugar
- 3   eggs
- 2½ teaspoons salt
- 7   to 7½ cups all-purpose flour
- 1   tablespoon cold water

1. In a large bowl, dissolve yeast in warm water. In another bowl, combine milk and butter; stir in potato flakes. Let stand for 1 minute. Add the milk mixture, sugar, 2 eggs, salt and 3 cups flour to yeast mixture; beat until smooth. Add enough remaining flour to form a soft dough.

2. Turn onto a floured surface; knead until smooth and elastic, about 6-8 minutes. Place in a greased bowl, turning once to grease the top. Cover and let rise in a warm place until doubled, about 1 hour.

3. Punch dough down; divide into 36 pieces. Shape each into a ball. Place 2 in. apart on greased baking sheets. Cover and let rise until doubled, about 30 minutes. Beat remaining egg and cold water; brush over rolls. Bake at 350° for 12-15 minutes or until golden brown.

RASPBERRY-PECAN MINI LOAVES

Dotted with raspberries and pecans, my miniature glazed loaves make yummy gifts during the holiday season or any time at all. With six little breads, you'll have plenty to share.

—KATHLEEN SHOWALTER SHORELINE, WASHINGTON

PREP: 20 MIN. **BAKE:** 25 MIN. + COOLING
MAKES: 6 MINI LOAVES (6 SLICES EACH)

- 2 **cups all-purpose flour**
- ½ **cup sugar**
- 2 **teaspoons baking powder**
- ½ **teaspoon salt**
- ¼ **teaspoon baking soda**
- 2 **eggs**
- ½ **cup vanilla yogurt**
- ⅓ **cup orange juice**
- ¼ **cup unsweetened applesauce**
- ¼ **cup canola oil**
- ½ **teaspoon orange extract**
- 1 **cup chopped pecans, toasted**
- 1 **cup fresh or frozen raspberries**

GLAZE
- 1 **cup confectioners' sugar**
- 4 **to 5 teaspoons orange juice**

1. In a large bowl, combine the flour, sugar, baking powder, salt and baking soda. In a small bowl, whisk the eggs, yogurt, orange juice, applesauce, oil and extract. Stir into dry ingredients just until moistened. Fold in pecans and raspberries.

2. Transfer to six greased 4½-in. x 2½-in. x 1½-in. loaf pans. Bake at 350° for 25-28 minutes or until a toothpick inserted near the center comes out clean. Cool for 10 minutes before removing from pans to wire racks.

3. For glaze, combine confectioners' sugar and enough orange juice to achieve desired consistency. Drizzle over warm loaves.

Editor's Note: *If using frozen raspberries, use without thawing to avoid discoloring the batter.*

FAVORITE IRISH SODA BREAD

My best friend, Rita O'Malley, gave me her wonderful Irish soda bread recipe. It bakes up nice and high, with a golden-brown top and a combination of sweet and savory flavors.

—JAN ALFANO PRESCOTT, ARIZONA

PREP: 20 MIN. **BAKE:** 45 MIN. + COOLING
MAKES: 1 LOAF (12 WEDGES)

- 3 **cups all-purpose flour**
- ⅔ **cup sugar**
- 3 **teaspoons baking powder**
- 1 **teaspoon salt**
- 1 **teaspoon baking soda**
- 1 **cup raisins**
- 2 **eggs, beaten**
- 1½ **cups buttermilk**
- 1 **tablespoon canola oil**

1. In a large bowl, combine the first five ingredients. Stir in raisins. Set aside 1 tablespoon beaten egg. In a bowl, combine the buttermilk, oil and remaining eggs; stir into flour mixture just until moistened (dough will be sticky). Transfer to a greased 9-in. round baking pan; brush top with reserved egg.

2. Bake at 350° for 45-50 minutes or until a toothpick inserted near the center comes out clean. Cool for 10 minutes before removing from pan to a wire rack to cool. Cut into wedges.

CITRUS-RASPBERRY COFFEE CAKE

Refreshing orange and lemon flavors accent the tangy raspberries in this dense coffee cake. A dusting of confectioners' sugar makes this pretty treat even prettier for special occasions.

—PAT HARLOW CATALDO, IDAHO

PREP: 20 MIN. **BAKE:** 55 MIN. + COOLING **MAKES:** 16 SERVINGS

 3 cups all-purpose flour
 2 cups sugar
 3 teaspoons baking powder
 1 teaspoon salt
 4 eggs
 1 cup canola oil
 ½ cup orange juice
 1 teaspoon lemon extract
 2 cups fresh or frozen unsweetened raspberries
 Confectioners' sugar

1. In a large bowl, combine the flour, sugar, baking powder and salt. In another bowl, combine the eggs, oil, orange juice and extract. Stir into dry ingredients just until moistened.
2. Pour half of the batter into a greased and floured 10-in. fluted tube pan. Sprinkle with raspberries. Top with remaining batter. Bake at 350° for 55-65 minutes or until a toothpick inserted near the center comes out clean.
3. Cool in pan for 10 minutes before removing from pan to a wire rack to cool completely. Dust with confectioners' sugar.
Editor's Note: *If using frozen raspberries, use without thawing to avoid discoloring the batter.*

HERB & SUN-DRIED TOMATO MUFFINS

My mom used to serve her herb muffins instead of buns and other breads. Now I whip up a batch when we're having soup or chili.
— BETSY KING DULUTH, MINNESOTA

PREP: 15 MIN. **BAKE:** 20 MIN. **MAKES:** 1 DOZEN

 2 cups all-purpose flour
 2 teaspoons baking powder
 1 teaspoon snipped fresh dill or ¼ teaspoon dill weed
 1 teaspoon minced fresh thyme or ¼ teaspoon dried thyme
 ½ teaspoon baking soda
 ½ teaspoon salt
 ½ teaspoon pepper
 1 egg
 1¼ cups 2% milk
 ¼ cup olive oil
 ½ cup shredded cheddar cheese
 ½ cup oil-packed sun-dried tomatoes, finely chopped

1. In a large bowl, mix the first seven ingredients. In another bowl, whisk the egg, milk and oil. Add to flour mixture; stir just until moistened. Fold in cheese and tomatoes.
2. Fill greased muffin cups three-fourths full. Bake at 375° for 18-20 minutes or until a toothpick inserted in center comes out clean. Cool for 5 minutes before removing from pan to a wire rack. Serve warm.

GOLDEN DANISH TWISTS

These beautiful Danish twists boast a cream-cheese filling, crunchy sliced almonds and a sweet, lemony icing. My family loves them for breakfast on Christmas morning after opening presents.

—**ANNIE DE LA HOZ** DELTA, COLORADO

PREP: 1¼ HOURS + RISING **BAKE:** 15 MIN. **MAKES:** 3 DOZEN

- 2 packages (¼ ounce each) active dry yeast
- ½ cup warm water (110° to 115°)
- 1 cup warm 2% milk (110° to 115°)
- 1 cup canned pumpkin
- 2 eggs
- ¼ cup sugar
- ¼ cup butter, softened
- 3 teaspoons salt
- 6 to 6½ cups all-purpose flour

FILLING
- 2 packages (8 ounces each) cream cheese, softened
- ⅓ cup confectioners' sugar
- ½ cup heavy whipping cream
- 2 teaspoons grated lemon peel
- 1 teaspoon vanilla extract

ICING
- ¼ cup butter, cubed
- 2 tablespoons all-purpose flour
- ¼ cup lemon juice
- 2⅔ cups confectioners' sugar
- 1 tablespoon grated lemon peel
- ¾ cup sliced almonds

1. In a large bowl, dissolve yeast in warm water. Add the milk, pumpkin, eggs, sugar, butter, salt and 3 cups flour; beat until smooth. Stir in enough remaining flour to make a soft dough.

2. Turn the dough onto a floured surface; knead until smooth and elastic, about 6-8 minutes. Place in a greased bowl, turning once to grease the top. Cover and let rise in a warm place until doubled, about 1 hour.

3. Meanwhile, for filling, in a small bowl, beat cream cheese and confectioners' sugar until smooth. Beat in the cream, lemon peel and vanilla.

4. Punch the dough down; transfer to a lightly floured surface. Divide dough in half. Roll one portion into an 18-in. x 12-in. rectangle. Spread half of the filling lengthwise over half of the dough to within ½ in. of the edges. Fold dough over filling; seal edges. Cut into 18 strips. Twist and loosely coil each strip. Tuck end under; pinch to seal. Place on greased baking sheets. Repeat with remaining dough and filling.

5. Cover and let rise until doubled, about 30 minutes. Bake at 375° for 12-15 minutes or until golden brown. Remove to wire racks.

6. For the icing, in a large saucepan, melt butter. Stir in flour until smooth. Stir in lemon juice. Bring to a boil; cook and stir for 2 minutes or until thickened. Remove from the heat. Stir in the confectioners' sugar and lemon peel until blended. Drizzle icing over warm twists. Sprinkle with almonds. Refrigerate leftovers.

EASY YEAST TEST
To test if rising yeast dough has doubled in size, quickly press two fingers into it. If an indentation remains, the dough is ready to be shaped.
—**ANNA JENELL CAMPBELL** TUTTLE, OKLAHOMA

SWIRLED HERB BREAD

With a delicious herb spiral, this savory loaf makes an impressive side for just about any entree. If your main course is spaghetti or lasagna, try sprinkling the bread with Parmesan cheese.

—**KARI BONCHER** GREEN BAY, WISCONSIN

PREP: 30 MIN. + RISING **BAKE:** 35 MIN. + COOLING
MAKES: 2 LOAVES (12 SLICES EACH)

- 5 to 6 cups all-purpose flour
- 2 packages (¼ ounce each) active dry yeast
- 1½ teaspoons salt
- 1 teaspoon sugar
- 1 cup 2% milk
- ¾ cup water
- ½ cup butter, cubed

FILLING

- ½ cup butter, softened
- 2 teaspoons dried basil
- 2 teaspoons dill weed
- 1 teaspoon dried minced onion
- 1 teaspoon garlic powder

1. In a large bowl, combine 3 cups flour, yeast, salt and sugar. In a small saucepan, heat milk, water and butter to 120°-130°. Add to dry ingredients; beat until smooth. Stir in enough remaining flour to form a soft dough (dough will be sticky).

2. Turn onto a floured surface; knead until smooth and elastic, about 6-8 minutes. Place in a greased bowl, turning once to grease the top. Cover and let rise in a warm place until doubled, about 1 hour. Meanwhile, in a small bowl, combine the filling ingredients; set aside.

3. Punch down dough; divide in half. Turn onto a lightly floured surface. Roll each portion into a 12-in. x 8-in. rectangle. Spread the filling over each to within ½ in. of the edges. Roll up jelly-roll style, starting with a short side; pinch the seams to seal and tuck the ends under.

4. Place seam side down in two greased 8-in. x 4-in. loaf pans. Cover and let rise in a warm place until doubled, about 30 minutes.

5. Bake at 375° for 35-40 minutes or until browned. Cool for 10 minutes before removing from pans to wire racks.

JUMBO JALAPENO CHEDDAR ROLLS

When I want to add some excitement to an everyday meal, I whip up a batch of my cheesy, peppery rolls. The cheddar and jalapeno flavors are mild, but everyone loves the zippy taste.

—**LINDA FOREMAN** LOCUST GROVE, OKLAHOMA

PREP: 35 MIN. + RISING **BAKE:** 20 MIN. **MAKES:** 1 DOZEN

- 2 packages (¼ ounce each) active dry yeast
- 2 tablespoons sugar
- 2 cups warm milk (110° to 115°)
- 2 eggs
- 2 teaspoons salt
- 6½ to 7½ cups all-purpose flour
- 2 cups (8 ounces) shredded cheddar cheese
- ¼ cup chopped seeded jalapeno pepper

EGG WASH

- 1 egg
- 2 teaspoons water

1. In a large bowl, dissolve yeast and sugar in warm milk. Add eggs, salt and 4 cups flour. Beat on medium speed for 3 minutes. Add cheese and jalapeno. Stir in enough remaining flour to form a firm dough.

2. Turn onto a floured surface; knead until smooth and elastic, about 6-8 minutes. Place in a greased bowl, turning once to grease the top. Cover and let rise in a warm place until doubled, about 1 hour.

3. Punch the dough down. Turn onto a lightly floured surface; divide into 12 pieces. Shape each into a roll. Place 3-in. apart on lightly greased baking sheets. Cover and let rise until doubled, about 30 minutes.

4. Combine egg and water; brush over rolls. Bake at 375° for 16-20 minutes or until golden brown. Remove from pans to wire racks. Serve warm.

Editor's Note: *Wear disposable gloves when cutting hot peppers; the oils can burn skin. Avoid touching your face.*

HOW HOT IS HOT?

Chili (hot) peppers come in a variety of heat levels:

FIERY Habanero
HOTTER Serrano
HOT Jalapeno
MODERATELY HOT Ancho, Pasilla
MILD Anaheim, Banana, Cubanelle

APPLE CRISP MUFFINS

Wake up your family to a real treat—the aroma and taste of fresh-baked apple muffins. With a creamy maple filling and nutty oat topping, these could even be served for dessert!

—**CONNIE BOLL** CHILTON, WISCONSIN

PREP: 30 MIN. **BAKE:** 20 MIN. **MAKES:** 1 DOZEN

- 2 **cups all-purpose flour**
- ⅓ **cup packed brown sugar**
- 2 **teaspoons baking powder**
- ½ **teaspoon salt**
- ½ **teaspoon ground cinnamon**
- 1 **egg, beaten**
- 1 **cup 2% milk**
- ½ **cup canola oil**
- 2 **cups finely chopped peeled apples**

FILLING

- 1 **package (8 ounces) cream cheese, softened**
- 2 **tablespoons maple syrup**
- 4 **teaspoons grated orange peel**
- ¼ **teaspoon ground nutmeg**

TOPPING

- ¼ **cup all-purpose flour**
- ¼ **cup old-fashioned oats**
- ¼ **cup packed brown sugar**
- ¼ **teaspoon ground cinnamon**
- 3 **tablespoons cold butter**
- ¼ **cup chopped pecans**

1. In a large bowl, combine the flour, sugar, baking powder, salt and cinnamon. In another bowl, combine the egg, milk and oil. Stir into dry ingredients just until moistened. Fold in apples. Fill greased or paper-lined muffin cups three-fourths full.

2. In a small bowl, beat filling ingredients until smooth. Drop by tablespoonfuls into centers of muffins.

3. For topping, in a small bowl, combine the flour, oats, brown sugar and cinnamon. Cut in butter until crumbly. Stir in pecans. Sprinkle over filling. Bake at 400° for 16-20 minutes or until a toothpick inserted in muffin comes out clean. Cool for 5 minutes before removing from pan to wire rack.

APPLE FRITTERS

I've been making these little golden bites for more than 25 years. My family and friends can never get enough, so I'm thankful the fritters are so quick and easy to prepare.

—**MARY SHIVERS** ADA, OKLAHOMA

PREP: 15 MIN. **COOK:** 5 MIN./BATCH **MAKES:** ABOUT 3½ DOZEN

- 3 **cups all-purpose flour**
- ½ **cup sugar**
- 2 **teaspoons baking powder**
- ½ **teaspoon salt**
- 1 **egg, beaten**
- 1 **cup milk**
- ¼ **cup orange juice**
- ¼ **cup butter, melted**
- 1 **teaspoon vanilla extract**
- 1 **teaspoon grated orange peel**
- 1 **cup grated unpeeled apples**
  Oil for deep-fat frying
  Confectioners' sugar

1. In a large bowl, combine the flour, sugar, baking powder and salt. Combine the egg, milk, orange juice, butter, vanilla and orange peel; add to the dry ingredients just until moistened. Fold in the apples.

2. In an electric skillet or deep fryer, heat oil to 375°. Drop the batter by rounded tablespoonfuls, a few at a time, into hot oil. Fry until golden brown, about 1-2 minutes on each side. Drain on paper towels. Dust with confectioners' sugar.

PUMPKIN CHEESECAKE MUFFINS

My mother-in-law came up with wonderful, dessert-like muffins by combining a few of her favorite recipes. With a cream cheese filling and a crunchy praline topping, her fall-flavored goodies are perfect with coffee or tea on a cool autumn morning.
—**LISA POWELSON** SCOTT CITY, KANSAS

PREP: 25 MIN. **BAKE:** 15 MIN. **MAKES:** 2 DOZEN

- 3 cups all-purpose flour
- 2 cups sugar
- 2 teaspoons baking soda
- 2 teaspoons baking powder
- 1 teaspoon salt
- 1 teaspoon ground cinnamon
- 4 eggs
- 1 can (15 ounces) solid-pack pumpkin
- 1½ cups canola oil

CREAM CHEESE FILLING
- 1 package (8 ounces) cream cheese, softened
- ½ cup sugar
- 1 egg
- 1 tablespoon all-purpose flour

PRALINE TOPPING
- ⅔ cup chopped pecans
- ⅓ cup packed brown sugar
- 2 tablespoons sour cream

1. In a large bowl, combine the first six ingredients. In another bowl, whisk the eggs, pumpkin and oil. Stir into dry ingredients just until moistened. Fill greased or paper-lined muffin cups one-third full.

2. For filling, beat the cream cheese, sugar, egg and flour until smooth. Drop by tablespoonfuls into center of each muffin. Top with remaining batter.

3. For topping, in a small bowl, combine the pecans, brown sugar and sour cream; spoon over the batter. Bake at 400° for 15-18 minutes or until a toothpick inserted in the muffin comes out clean. Cool for 5 minutes before removing from pans to wire racks. Serve warm. Refrigerate leftovers.

EASTER BREAD WITH ORANGE BUTTER

I discovered this holiday-worthy bread while looking through my great-aunt's handwritten cookbook. I love a big slice topped with the accompanying orange butter—or even apple butter.
—**SANDI PICHON** SLIDELL, LOUISIANA

PREP: 35 MIN. + RISING **BAKE:** 25 MIN. + COOLING
MAKES: 1 LOAF (32 SLICES)

- 1 envelope (¼ ounce) active dry yeast
- ¾ cup warm water (110° to 115°)
- 3 eggs
- ¼ cup sugar
- ¼ cup canola oil
- 2 teaspoons salt
- 2 teaspoons grated lemon peel
- 4 to 5 cups all-purpose flour
- ½ cup raisins
- 2 teaspoons butter, melted
- ¾ cup butter, softened
- 3 tablespoons orange marmalade

1. In a large bowl, dissolve yeast in warm water. Add the eggs, sugar, oil, salt, lemon peel and 2 cups flour. Beat until smooth. Stir in enough remaining flour to form a soft dough.

2. Turn onto a floured surface. Sprinkle with raisins; knead until smooth and elastic, about 6-8 minutes. Place in a greased bowl, turning once to grease the top. Cover and let rise in a warm place until doubled, about 1 hour.

3. Punch the dough down. Turn onto a lightly floured surface; divide dough into thirds. Shape each into a 20-in. rope. Place ropes on a greased baking sheet and braid; pinch ends to seal and tuck under. Cover and let rise until doubled, about 1 hour.

4. Bake at 350° for 24-28 minutes or until golden brown. Brush with melted butter. Remove from pan to a wire rack to cool. In a small bowl, combine softened butter and orange marmalade; serve with bread.

GARLIC KNOTTED ROLLS

Here are simple yet delicious rolls your guests won't be able to resist. And no one will guess you used frozen bread dough! The garlic and dried minced onion add terrific taste.

—KATHY HARDING RICHMOND, MISSOURI

PREP: 15 MIN. + RISING **BAKE:** 15 MIN. **MAKES:** 10 ROLLS

- 1 loaf (1 pound) frozen bread dough, thawed
- 1½ teaspoons dried minced onion
- 3 tablespoons butter
- 4 garlic cloves, minced
- ⅛ teaspoon salt
- 1 egg, beaten
- 1 teaspoon poppy seeds

1. Pat out the dough on a work surface; sprinkle with minced onion and knead until combined. Divide dough in half. Shape each piece into five balls. To form knots, roll each ball into a 10-in. rope; tie into a knot. Tuck the ends under. Place rolls 2 in. apart on a greased baking sheet.

2. In a small skillet over medium heat, melt butter. Add garlic and salt; cook and stir for 1-2 minutes. Brush over rolls. Cover and let rise until doubled, about 30 minutes.

3. Brush tops with egg; sprinkle with poppy seeds. Bake at 375° for 15-20 minutes or until golden brown.

MINCED GARLIC OPTIONS

Minced garlic that you can buy, garlic that's been finely chopped by hand and garlic that's been put through a press can all be used interchangeably in recipes calling for minced garlic. Choose whichever option is easiest and most convenient for you.

LEMONY POPPY SEED MUFFINS

These jumbo-sized treats always prove popular at brunches and bake sales. For a great Christmas gift, put the muffins in a pretty basket or other container and include a jar of preserves.

—KIMBERLY BAXTER EXETER, RHODE ISLAND

PREP: 25 MIN. **BAKE:** 20 MIN. **MAKES:** 6 JUMBO MUFFINS

- ½ cup butter, softened
- ¾ cup sugar
- 2 eggs
- ¾ cup sour cream
- ¼ cup lemon juice
- 3 teaspoons lemon extract
- 1 teaspoon vanilla extract
- 1 teaspoon grated lemon peel
- 2 cups all-purpose flour
- 1 teaspoon baking powder
- 1 teaspoon baking soda
- ¼ teaspoon salt
- 2 tablespoons poppy seeds

1. In a large bowl, cream butter and sugar until light and fluffy. Add eggs, one at a time, beating well after each addition. Beat in the sour cream, lemon juice, extracts and lemon peel.

2. Combine the flour, baking powder, baking soda and salt; gradually add to creamed mixture just until moistened. Fold in poppy seeds.

3. Fill six greased jumbo muffin pans. Bake at 375° for 20-23 minutes or until a toothpick inserted near the center comes out clean. Remove to a wire rack. Serve warm.

Sensational Scones

At tea time or any time you want a treat, look here! Warm from the oven, these tender and flaky scones are a special indulgence spread with butter, jam, preserves or nothing at all.

SUGAR PLUM SCONES

Dried plums, a bit of grated orange peel and a sprinkling of coarse sugar make these wedges delightfully Christmasy. But they're so good, you'll want to enjoy them year-round.

—JULIE MCQUISTON BRADENTON, FLORIDA

PREP: 20 MIN. **BAKE:** 15 MIN. **MAKES:** 1 DOZEN

- 3 **cups all-purpose flour**
- ½ **cup sugar**
- 3 **teaspoons baking powder**
- ½ **teaspoon salt**
- ½ **cup cold butter**
- 1 **egg**
- 1 **cup buttermilk**
- 1 **cup pitted dried plums, chopped**
- 1 **tablespoon grated orange peel**

TOPPING

- 1 **egg**
- 1 **tablespoon 2% milk**
- 2 **tablespoons coarse sugar**

1. In a large bowl, combine the flour, sugar, baking powder and salt. Cut in butter until mixture resembles coarse crumbs. Whisk egg and buttermilk; stir into crumb mixture just until moistened. Stir in plums and orange peel. Turn onto a floured surface; knead 10 times.

2. Divide dough in half; pat each into a 7-in. circle. Cut each into six wedges. Separate wedges and place on a greased baking sheet. Combine egg and milk; brush over scones. Sprinkle with coarse sugar. Bake at 375° for 15-20 minutes or until golden brown. Serve warm.

ROSEMARY-LEMON SCONES

My wife and I enjoyed a wonderful rosemary-lemon coffee cake while staying at a bed and breakfast many years ago. I decided to try adapting my favorite scone recipe to capture that unusual flavor combination, and we loved the results.

—DAVID BYLAND SHAWNEE, OKLAHOMA

PREP: 20 MIN. **BAKE:** 15 MIN. **MAKES:** 8 SCONES

- 2 **cups all-purpose flour**
- 3 **tablespoons sugar**
- 2 **teaspoons baking powder**
- ½ **teaspoon baking soda**
- ½ **teaspoon salt**
- 5 **tablespoons cold butter**
- 1 **cup (8 ounces) sour cream**
- 1 **egg**
- 2 **teaspoons grated lemon peel**
- 1 **teaspoon minced fresh rosemary**
- 1 **teaspoon coarse sugar**

1. In a large bowl, combine the flour, sugar, baking powder, baking soda and salt. Cut in butter until mixture resembles coarse crumbs. Whisk sour cream and egg; stir into crumb mixture just until moistened. Stir in lemon peel and rosemary. Turn onto a floured surface; knead 10 times.

2. Pat into an 8-in. circle. Cut into eight wedges, but do not separate. Place on an ungreased baking sheet. Sprinkle with coarse sugar. Bake at 400° for 15-18 minutes or until golden brown. Serve warm.

WHOLE WHEAT CRANBERRY SCONES

Plenty of dried cranberries lend a tongue-tingling burst to each bite of these wholesome goodies. With a biscuit-like texture and a topping of cinnamon-sugar, they're perfect alongside a bowl of fresh berries or other fruit at a holiday brunch.

—PATSYE YONCE OVID, NEW YORK

PREP: 20 MIN. **COOK:** 15 MIN. **MAKES:** 16 SCONES

- 1½ **cups all-purpose flour**
- 1½ **cups whole wheat flour**
- ½ **cup sugar**
- 3 **teaspoons baking powder**
- ½ **teaspoon baking soda**
- ½ **teaspoon salt**
- ¼ **teaspoon ground nutmeg**
- ¾ **cup cold butter**
- 1 **egg**
- 1 **cup vanilla yogurt**
- ½ **teaspoon vanilla extract**
- 1 **cup dried cranberries**
- 1 **tablespoon milk**
- 2 **teaspoons cinnamon-sugar**

1. In a large bowl, combine the flours, sugar, baking powder, baking soda, salt and nutmeg; cut in butter until crumbly. In a small bowl, combine the egg, yogurt and vanilla; stir into the dry ingredients just until moistened. Stir in cranberries. Turn onto a floured surface, knead 6-8 times.

2. Divide the dough in half. Transfer each portion to a greased baking sheet. Pat into an 8-in. circle. Cut each circle into 8 wedges, but do not separate. Brush with milk; sprinkle with cinnamon-sugar. Bake at 400° for 15-20 minutes or until golden brown. Serve warm.

MOCHA CHIP HAZELNUT SCONES

Perk up coffee lovers with java-infused scones full of semisweet chocolate chips and toasted hazelnuts. For an even more luscious treat, slather on a chocolate-hazelnut spread.

—SHARON GEROW BELLEVILLE, ONTARIO

PREP: 20 MIN. **BAKE:** 10 MIN./BATCH **MAKES:** 16 SCONES

- 4½ **teaspoons instant coffee granules**
- 1 **cup 2% milk**
- 2½ **cups all-purpose flour**
- ⅔ **cup packed brown sugar**
- 3 **teaspoons baking powder**
- ½ **cup cold butter**
- 1 **cup chopped hazelnuts, toasted**
- ⅔ **cup miniature semisweet chocolate chips**

1. Dissolve the instant coffee granules in milk; set aside.

2. In a large bowl, combine the flour, brown sugar and baking powder. Cut in butter until mixture resembles coarse crumbs. Stir milk mixture into crumb mixture just until moistened. Stir in hazelnuts and chocolate chips. Turn onto a floured surface; knead 10 times.

3. Drop the dough by ¼ cupfuls 2 in. apart onto greased baking sheets. Bake at 400° for 12-15 minutes or until golden brown. Serve warm.

APRICOT TEA BREAD

I received my tea bread recipe from a radio program many years ago. The crumb-topped loaf has been a family favorite ever since.
—LYN ROBITAILLE EAST HARTLAND, CONNECTICUT

PREP: 30 MIN. **BAKE:** 40 MIN. + COOLING
MAKES: 2 LOAVES (12 SLICES EACH)

- ½ cup butter, softened
- 1 cup sugar
- 3 eggs
- 2 teaspoons vanilla extract
- 2 cups all-purpose flour
- 1½ teaspoons baking powder
- 1 teaspoon baking soda
- 1 cup (8 ounces) sour cream
- 1 cup chopped dried apricots
- 1 cup chopped pecans

TOPPING
- ½ cup all-purpose flour
- ¼ cup sugar
- ¼ cup cold butter

1. In a large bowl, cream butter and sugar until light and fluffy. Add the eggs, one at a time, beating well after each addition. Beat in vanilla.

2. Combine the flour, baking powder and baking soda; add to creamed mixture alternately with sour cream, beating well after each addition. Fold in apricots and pecans.

3. Spoon into two greased 8-in. x 4-in. loaf pans. For topping, combine the flour and sugar in a small bowl; cut in butter until mixture resembles coarse crumbs. Sprinkle over batter.

4. Bake at 350° for 40-45 minutes or until a toothpick inserted near the center comes out clean. Cool for 10 minutes before removing from pans to wire racks to cool completely.

MOLASSES-PECAN STICKY BUNS

As much as I like baking, I like watching others enjoy the results even more. These soft, tender buns are loaded with the gooey goodness of molasses and the crunch of pecans.
—SHIRLEY SAYLOR FELTON, PENNSYLVANIA

PREP: 45 MIN. + RISING **BAKE:** 25 MIN. **MAKES:** 12 SERVINGS

- 3½ to 4 cups all-purpose flour
- 3 tablespoons sugar
- 2 packages (¼ ounce each) quick-rise yeast
- 1 teaspoon salt
- 1 cup 2% milk
- ½ cup water
- ¼ cup butter, cubed

FILLING
- ¼ cup butter, softened
- 1½ teaspoons ground cinnamon

TOPPING
- ½ cup butter, cubed
- 1 cup packed brown sugar
- ⅔ cup chopped pecans
- ½ cup molasses

1. In a large bowl, combine 2 cups flour, sugar, yeast and salt. In a small saucepan, heat the milk, water and butter to 120°-130°. Add to dry ingredients; beat just until moistened. Stir in enough remaining flour to form a soft dough (dough will be sticky).

2. Turn onto a floured surface; knead until smooth and elastic, about 6-8 minutes. Cover and let rest for 10 minutes.

3. Roll into a 14-in. x 12-in. rectangle. Spread butter to within ½ in. of edges; sprinkle with cinnamon. Roll up jelly-roll style, starting with a long side; pinch seams to seal. Cut into 12 rolls.

4. In a small saucepan, melt the remaining butter. Stir in brown sugar, pecans and molasses; pour into a greased 13-in. x 9-in. baking dish. Place rolls, cut side down, in dish.

5. Cover and let rise in a warm place until doubled, about 15 minutes. Bake at 375° for 25-30 minutes or until golden brown. Immediately invert onto a serving platter. Serve warm.

ONION DILL BREAD

This savory, golden-brown loaf is crisp on the outside but moist and tender on the inside. Dill weed and onion powder give it some pizzazz without overwhelming your taste buds.
—**CHARLOTTE ELLIOTT** NEENAH, WISCONSIN

PREP: 25 MIN. + RISING **BAKE:** 15 MIN. + COOLING
MAKES: 2 LOAVES (9 SLICES EACH)

- 1½ cups water (70° to 80°)
- 2 tablespoons olive oil, divided
- ¼ cup dried minced onion
- 2 teaspoons sugar
- 1¼ teaspoons salt
- 1 teaspoon dill weed
- ½ teaspoon onion powder
- 3½ cups all-purpose flour
- ¾ cup whole wheat flour
- 1 package (¼ ounce) active dry yeast

1. In bread machine pan, place the water, 1 tablespoon oil, minced onion, sugar, salt, dill, onion powder, flours and yeast in the order suggested by the manufacturer. Select dough setting (check dough after 5 minutes of mixing; add 1 to 2 tablespoons of water or flour if needed).

2. When cycle is completed, turn dough onto a lightly floured surface. Divide dough in half; shape each portion into a 7-in. round loaf. Place on greased baking sheets. Cover and let rise until doubled, about 40 minutes.

3. Bake at 400° for 15-20 minutes or until golden brown. Brush with remaining oil. Remove from pans to wire racks.

PUMPKIN BANANA BREAD

Here's a wonderful homemade gift idea for friends, neighbors and co-workers. Using small loaf pans yields five miniature breads.
—**LINDA WOOD** ROANOKE, VIRGINIA

PREP: 15 MIN. **BAKE:** 35 MIN. + COOLING
MAKES: 5 MINI LOAVES (6 SLICES EACH)

- ½ cup shortening
- 1½ cups sugar
- 2 eggs
- 1 cup mashed ripe bananas (about 2 medium)
- ¾ cup canned pumpkin
- 1 teaspoon vanilla extract
- 1¾ cups all-purpose flour
- 1½ teaspoons baking powder
- ¾ teaspoon baking soda
- ½ teaspoon salt
- ½ cup chopped walnuts or pecans

1. In a large bowl, cream the shortening and sugar. Add eggs, one at a time, beating well after each addition. Beat in bananas, pumpkin and vanilla. Combine the flour, baking power, baking soda and salt; gradually add to creamed mixture. Fold in nuts.

2. Pour into five greased 5¾-in. x 3-in. x 2-in. loaf pans. Bake at 350° for 35-40 minutes or until a toothpick inserted near the center comes out clean. Cool for 10 minutes before removing from pans to wire racks.

RUM RAISIN MUFFINS

We love these rum-flavored, raisin-filled goodies. I think they're best served warm with a hot cup of coffee or cappuccino.
—**LORRAINE CALAND** SHUNIAH, ONTARIO

PREP: 20 MIN. **BAKE:** 15 MIN. **MAKES:** 1 DOZEN

- ½ cup butter, softened
- ¾ cup sugar
- 2 eggs
- 1 teaspoon rum extract
- 1½ cups plus 1 tablespoon all-purpose flour, divided
- 2 teaspoons baking powder
- ½ teaspoon baking soda
- ⅓ cup 2% milk
- 1 cup raisins
- ½ cup chopped pecans
- ¼ cup maple syrup

1. In a large bowl, cream butter and sugar until light and fluffy. Add eggs, one at a time, beating well after each addition. Beat in extract. Combine 1½ cups flour, baking powder and baking soda; add to creamed mixture alternately with milk, beating just until combined. Toss raisins with remaining flour. Fold raisins and pecans into batter.

2. Fill paper-lined muffin cups two-thirds full. Bake at 375° for 15-20 minutes or until a toothpick inserted near the center comes out clean. Immediately brush muffins with maple syrup. Cool for 5 minutes before removing from pans to wire racks. Serve warm.

COOKIES, BARS & CANDIES

Get ready for delights by the dozen! From sugar-sprinkled cutouts and nut-filled clusters to chocolaty brownies and luscious truffles, these taste-tempting treats are the kind your family and friends will want to grab by the handful.

SUPER SPUD BROWNIES

One of my mom's old cookbooks had a recipe for moist, cake-like brownies made with potatoes. Spuds may seem like an unusual ingredient for brownies, but these won first place at a local festival.
—**MARLENE GERER** DENTON, MONTANA

PREP: 15 MIN. **BAKE:** 25 MIN. **MAKES:** 16 SERVINGS

- ¾ cup mashed potatoes
- ½ cup sugar
- ½ cup packed brown sugar
- ½ cup canola oil
- 2 eggs, lightly beaten
- 1 teaspoon vanilla extract
- ½ cup all-purpose flour
- ⅓ cup cocoa powder
- ½ teaspoon baking powder
- ⅛ teaspoon salt
- ½ cup chopped pecans, optional
  Confectioners' sugar

1. In a large bowl, combine the mashed potatoes, sugars, oil, eggs and vanilla. Combine the flour, cocoa, baking powder and salt; gradually add to potato mixture. Fold in pecans if desired. Transfer to a greased 9-in. square baking pan.

2. Bake at 350° for 23-27 minutes or until toothpick inserted near the center comes out clean. Cool on a wire rack. Dust with confectioners' sugar. Cut into bars.

ALMOND CHEESECAKE BARS

My sister-in-law introduced me to her delectable, almond-flavored bars that feature a buttery crust, creamy filling and homemade frosting. I've taken them to countless get-togethers over the years.
—**MARY COUSER** MAPLE PLAIN, MINNESOTA

PREP: 20 MIN. **BAKE:** 35 MIN. + COOLING **MAKES:** 3 DOZEN

- 2 cups all-purpose flour
- 1 cup butter, softened
- ½ cup confectioners' sugar

FILLING

- 1 package (8 ounces) cream cheese, softened
- ½ cup sugar
- 1 teaspoon almond extract
- 2 eggs, lightly beaten

FROSTING

- 1½ cups confectioners' sugar
- ¼ cup butter, softened
- 1 teaspoon almond extract
- 4 to 5 teaspoons milk

1. Combine flour, butter and confectioners' sugar; press onto the bottom of a greased 13-in. x 9-in. baking pan. Bake at 350° for 20-25 minutes or until golden brown.

2. For filling, in a small bowl, beat the cream cheese, sugar and extract until smooth. Add the eggs; beat on low speed just until combined. Pour over the crust. Bake for 15-20 minutes or until center is almost set. Cool on a wire rack.

3. Combine the frosting ingredients until smooth; spread over bars. Store in the refrigerator.

DIAMOND ALMOND BARS

Making a pan of these chewy, nutty treats at Christmastime has been an annual tradition in our family for generations. Be sure to freeze a few dozen to enjoy in the new year, too!

—**LIZ GREEN** TAMWORTH, ONTARIO

PREP: 20 MIN. **BAKE:** 25 MIN. + COOLING **MAKES:** 5 DOZEN

- 1 cup butter, softened
- 1 cup plus 1 tablespoon sugar, divided
- 1 egg, separated
- 1 teaspoon almond extract
- 2 cups all-purpose flour
- ½ cup blanched sliced almonds
- ¼ teaspoon ground cinnamon

1. In a large bowl, cream butter and 1 cup sugar until light and fluffy. Beat in egg yolk. Beat in extract. Gradually add flour to creamed mixture and mix well.

2. Press into a greased 15-in. x 10-in. x 1-in. baking pan. Beat the egg white until foamy; brush over the dough. Top with sliced almonds. Combine the cinnamon and remaining sugar; sprinkle over the top.

3. Bake at 350° for 25-30 minutes or until lightly browned (do not overbake). Cool on a wire rack for 10 minutes. Cut into diamond-shaped bars. Cool completely.

TUMBLEWEEDS

With just a few basic ingredients, easy-to-prepare Tumbleweeds are guaranteed to please fans of sweet-and-salty goodies. Simply melt butterscotch chips and creamy peanut butter, mix in nuts and potato sticks, form little clusters and let them set.

—**PEGGY GRAY** SAVANNAH, TENNESSEE

PREP: 25 MIN. + CHILLING **MAKES:** 5 DOZEN

- 1 package (11 ounces) butterscotch chips
- 2 tablespoons creamy peanut butter
- 1 jar (12 ounces) dry roasted peanuts
- 1 can (4 ounces) potato sticks

1. In a microwave-safe bowl, melt the butterscotch chips and creamy peanut butter; stir until smooth. Stir in the peanuts and potato sticks.

2. Drop by tablespoonfuls onto waxed paper-lined pans. Refrigerate until set. Store in an airtight container.

PICK OF THE PEANUTS

If I want to add extra flair to cookies, candies or bars that call for dry roasted peanuts, I replace those nuts with honey-roasted peanuts. It's an easy substitution and gives some of our favorite recipes a little more flavor and sweetness.

—**JO STEJSKAL** WINONA, MINNESOTA

WHITE CHOCOLATE CRAN-PECAN COOKIES

If you like traditional chocolate chip cookies but want a change of pace, look here! Each delightfully different treat is bursting with tangy dried cranberries, white baking chips and nuts.

—BARB GARRETT JACKSONVILLE, NORTH CAROLINA

PREP: 15 MIN. **BAKE:** 10 MIN./BATCH **MAKES:** ABOUT 2½ DOZEN

- ½ cup butter, softened
- ½ cup sugar
- ½ cup packed brown sugar
- 1 egg
- 1½ teaspoons vanilla extract
- 1½ cups all-purpose flour
- ½ teaspoon baking soda
- 1 cup dried cranberries
- ¾ cup white baking chips
- ½ cup chopped pecans

1. In a large bowl, cream the butter and sugars until light and fluffy. Beat in the egg and vanilla. Combine the flour and baking soda; gradually add to creamed mixture and mix well. Fold in the cranberries, baking chips and pecans.

2. Drop by tablespoonfuls 2 in. apart onto ungreased baking sheets. Bake at 375° for 8-10 minutes or until lightly browned. Remove to wire racks.

TOFFEE CANDY

When you're choosing what candies to make for Christmastime, consider this classic, crunchy toffee covered with milk chocolate and finished off with a generous sprinkling of chopped pecans. It always proves popular on my holiday treat platter and is great for packing into festive gift boxes or tins.

—JANICE CRANOR BARTLESVILLE, OKLAHOMA

PREP: 10 MIN. **COOK:** 30 MIN. + COOLING
MAKES: ABOUT 2½ POUNDS

- 2 teaspoons plus 2 cups butter, divided
- 2 cups sugar
- ¼ cup water
- 1 cup milk chocolate chips
- 1½ cups finely chopped pecans

1. Grease a 15-in. x 10-in. x 1-in. pan with 2 teaspoons butter; set aside. In a large heavy saucepan, melt the remaining butter. Add sugar and water; cook and stir over medium heat until a candy thermometer reads 300° (hard-crack stage).

2. Quickly pour into the prepared pan. Immediately sprinkle with chocolate chips. Allow chocolate chips to soften for a few minutes, then spread over the toffee. Sprinkle with pecans. Let stand until set, about 1 hour.

3. Break the candy into bite-size pieces. Store in an airtight container.

HAZELNUT CRINKLE COOKIES

I enjoy trying new recipes and have plenty of willing "taste testers" around the house. When I baked these sugar-dusted goodies, my family's response was unanimous—an enthusiastic thumbs-up!
—**JANEL ANDREWS** JEROME, IDAHO

PREP: 30 MIN. + CHILLING **BAKE:** 10 MIN./BATCH **MAKES:** 7 DOZEN

> 1 jar (13 ounces) Nutella
> ¼ cup shortening
> 1⅓ cups sugar
> 2 eggs
> 1 teaspoon vanilla extract
> 3 cups all-purpose flour
> 2 teaspoons baking powder
> ½ teaspoon salt
> ⅓ cup 2% milk
> 2½ cups chopped hazelnuts, toasted, divided
> ½ cup confectioners' sugar

1. In a large bowl, cream the Nutella, shortening and sugar until light and fluffy, about 4 minutes. Beat in eggs and vanilla. Combine the flour, baking powder and salt; add to the creamed mixture alternately with milk, mixing well after each addition. Fold in ½ cup hazelnuts. Cover and refrigerate for 30 minutes or until firm.

2. Finely chop the remaining hazelnuts. Place hazelnuts and confectioners' sugar in separate shallow bowls. Roll dough into 1-in. balls; roll in hazelnuts, then sugar.

3. Place 1 in. apart on ungreased baking sheets. Bake at 375° for 10-12 minutes or until set and the surface is cracked. Cool for 1 minute before removing from pans to wire racks.

GLAZED GINGER BARS

I can't imagine the holidays without a pan of ginger bars. The spicy flavor and heavenly aroma are just right for the season, and a light orange glaze adds the perfect amount of sweetness.
—**DARLENE BRENDEN** SALEM, OREGON

PREP: 25 MIN. **BAKE:** 20 MIN. + COOLING **MAKES:** 32 BARS

> ⅔ cup butter, softened
> ¾ cup packed brown sugar
> ½ cup molasses
> 1 egg
> 2 cups all-purpose flour
> 2 teaspoons ground ginger
> ½ teaspoon baking soda
> ½ teaspoon baking powder
> ½ teaspoon ground cinnamon
> ¼ teaspoon salt
> ½ cup raisins
> **ORANGE GLAZE**
> 1 cup confectioners' sugar
> 5 teaspoons orange juice
> 4 teaspoons butter, melted
> ¾ teaspoon vanilla extract
> ½ teaspoon grated orange peel

1. In a large bowl, cream the butter and brown sugar until light and fluffy. Beat in molasses and egg. Combine the flour, ginger, baking soda, baking powder, cinnamon and salt; add to creamed mixture and mix well. Stir in raisins.

2. Spread into a greased 13-in. x 9-in. baking pan. Bake at 350° for 20-25 minutes or until a toothpick inserted near the center comes out clean.

3. Combine the orange glaze ingredients until smooth; spread over warm bars. Cool completely on a wire rack before cutting into bars.

SO-EASY TRUFFLES

Expect these creamy truffles to disappear in a flash. You may even need to hide them if you make them ahead for a special event!
—**DENISE KUTCHKO** ODESSA, MISSOURI

PREP: 45 MIN. **MAKES:** 4 DOZEN

- 1 **package (15½ ounces) Oreo cookies**
- 1 **package (8 ounces) cream cheese, cubed**
- 1 **cup chocolate wafer crumbs**

1. Place the cookies in a food processor; cover and process until finely crushed. Add the cream cheese; process until blended. Roll into 1-in. balls. Roll in the wafer crumbs. Store in an airtight container in the refrigerator.

Peanut Butter Truffles: *Substitute a 16-oz. package of peanut butter cream-filled sandwich cookies for the chocolate sandwich cookies. Omit the chocolate crumbs. Melt 12 ounces of milk chocolate candy coating; stir until smooth. Dip the balls in the chocolate; place on waxed paper until set. Store in the refrigerator.* **Yield:** *4 dozen.*

Vanilla Cookie Truffles: *Substitute a 16-oz. package of vanilla cream-filled sandwich cookies for the chocolate sandwich cookies. Melt 12 ounces of milk chocolate candy coating; stir until smooth. Dip balls in chocolate; sprinkle with ¼ cup chocolate crumbs. Place on waxed paper until set. Store in the refrigerator.* **Yield:** *4 dozen.*

TAKING A DIP

Dipping truffles or other round candies into melted chocolate, lifting them out and placing them on waxed paper can be tricky. To make the process easier, I hold the candy with a toothpick.

—**JILL LANGHAM** ALBUQUERQUE, NEW MEXICO

MOCHA LOGS

My mother liked to bake her mocha-flavored, log-shaped cookies for Christmas when I was a child. Now I enjoy whipping up batches of my own. They're wonderful to share with family and friends.
—**GAYLE TARKOWSKI** TRAVERSE CITY, MICHIGAN

PREP: 50 MIN. **BAKE:** 10 MIN./BATCH + COOLING
MAKES: 12½ DOZEN

- 1 **cup butter, softened**
- 2 **tablespoons instant coffee granules**
- ¾ **cup sugar**
- 1 **egg**
- 1 **teaspoon vanilla extract**
- 2¼ **cups all-purpose flour**
- ½ **teaspoon salt**
- ¼ **teaspoon baking powder**
- 1 **cup (6 ounces) semisweet chocolate chips**
- 1½ **teaspoons shortening**
- 1 **cup chopped walnuts**

1. In a small bowl, beat butter and coffee granules for 1 minute. Add the sugar; beat until light and fluffy. Beat in egg and vanilla. Combine the flour, salt and baking powder; gradually add to the creamed mixture and mix well.
2. Roll dough into ½-in.-thick logs; cut into 2-in. pieces. Place on ungreased baking sheets. Or use a cookie press fitted with a star-shaped disk to press dough into 2-in. logs 1 in. apart on baking sheets.
3. Bake at 375° for 8-12 minutes or until lightly browned. Cool for 2 minutes before removing to wire racks to cool completely.
4. In a microwave, melt chocolate chips and shortening; stir until smooth. Dip ends of cookies in chocolate; allow excess to drip off. Sprinkle with walnuts. Place on waxed paper; let stand until set. Store in an airtight container.

CASHEW CLUSTERS

When we have bake sales at the community college where I work, I bring my nut-filled clusters. They always sell out quickly.

—**BETSY GRANTIER** CHARLOTTESVILLE, VIRGINIA

PREP: 20 MIN. + STANDING **MAKES:** 6 DOZEN

- 1 pound white candy coating, coarsely chopped
- 1 cup (6 ounces) semisweet chocolate chips
- 4 ounces German sweet chocolate, chopped
- 1/3 cup milk chocolate chips
- 1 can (9¾ ounces) salted whole cashews
- 1 can (9¼ ounces) salted cashew halves and pieces

1. In a large microwave-safe bowl, combine the first four ingredients. Cover and microwave at 50% power until melted, stirring every 30 seconds.

2. Stir in cashews. Drop by tablespoonfuls onto waxed paper-lined pans. Let stand until set. Store in an airtight container.

Editor's Note: *This recipe was tested in a 1,100-watt microwave.*

WHITE CHOCOLATE RASPBERRY TRUFFLES

These no-bake goodies are simply heavenly! I love to serve them on a fancy platter for an after-dinner treat.

—**MOLLY SEIDEL** EDGEWOOD, NEW MEXICO

PREP: 20 MIN. + CHILLING **MAKES:** ABOUT 3½ DOZEN

- 1 package (8 ounces) cream cheese, softened
- 1 cup white baking chips, melted
- ¾ cup crushed vanilla wafers (about 25 wafers)
- ¼ cup seedless raspberry preserves
- ⅔ cup finely chopped almonds, toasted

1. In a small bowl, beat cream cheese until smooth. Beat in the melted chips, wafer crumbs and preserves. Cover and refrigerate for 2 hours or until easy to handle.

2. Shape into 1-in. balls; roll in almonds. Store in an airtight container in the refrigerator.

MOLASSES FUDGE

The combination of molasses, cinnamon and other spices in this out-of-the-ordinary fudge reminds many people of gingerbread. Each decadent bite is loaded with old-fashioned appeal.

—**BECKY BURCH** MARCELINE, MISSOURI

PREP: 25 MIN. **COOK:** 20 MIN. + COOLING
MAKES: ABOUT 4 DOZEN

- 1 teaspoon plus 2 tablespoons butter, divided
- 1 cup sugar
- 1 cup packed brown sugar
- ½ cup half-and-half cream
- 2 tablespoons molasses
- ½ teaspoon ground cinnamon
- ¼ teaspoon ground nutmeg
- ⅛ teaspoon ground cloves
- 1½ teaspoons vanilla extract
- ½ cup coarsely chopped walnuts

1. Line a 9-in. x 5-in. loaf pan with foil. Grease the foil with ½ teaspoon butter; set aside.

2. Grease the sides of a large heavy saucepan with ½ teaspoon butter. Add the sugars, cream, molasses and spices. Cook and stir over medium heat until sugar is dissolved and mixture comes to a boil. Cook over medium-low heat until a candy thermometer reads 240° (soft-ball stage), stirring often.

3. Remove from the heat. Add vanilla and remaining butter (do not stir). Cool, without stirring, to 110°, about 55 minutes.

4. Remove thermometer; beat vigorously with a wooden spoon until mixture begins to thicken; add walnuts. Beat until fudge is very thick and mixture begins to lose its gloss, about 10 minutes.

5. Quickly pour into prepared pan. While warm, score into 1-in. squares. When fudge is firm, use foil to lift candy out of pan; cut into squares. Store in an airtight container.

Editor's Note: *We recommend that you test your candy thermometer before each use by bringing water to a boil; the thermometer should read 212°. Adjust your recipe temperature up or down based on your test.*

CRISPY PEANUT BUTTER BALLS

During the Christmas season, I make more than 40 different kinds of cookies and candies to share with friends and family. Chocolaty peanut butter balls are one of my most popular creations.

—**LIZ DAVID** ST. CATHARINES, ONTARIO

PREP: 40 MIN. + CHILLING **MAKES:** 6 DOZEN

> 2 **cups creamy peanut butter**
> ½ **cup butter, softened**
> 3¾ **cups confectioners' sugar**
> 3 **cups crisp rice cereal**
> 4 **cups (24 ounces) semisweet chocolate chips**
> ¼ **cup plus 1 teaspoon shortening, divided**
> ⅓ **cup white baking chips**

1. In a large bowl, beat peanut butter and butter until blended; gradually beat in the confectioners' sugar until smooth. Stir in cereal. Shape into 1-in. balls. Refrigerate until chilled.

2. In a microwave, melt chocolate chips and ¼ cup shortening; stir until smooth. Dip balls into chocolate; allow excess to drip off. Place on a waxed paper-lined pan. Let stand until set.

3. In a microwave, melt the white baking chips and remaining shortening. Stir until smooth. Drizzle over candies. Refrigerate until set.

Editor's Note: *Reduced-fat peanut butter is not recommended for this recipe.*

SUCCESSFUL MELTING

It's best to melt chocolate slowly to avoid scorching. When microwaving, keep in mind that chocolate chips and chunks may appear formed and unmelted after heating but will be fluid upon stirring.

CARAMEL-NUT CANDY BARS

As a busy mother of six, I appreciate any recipe that's quick, easy and family-pleasing. These Snickers-like bars fit that description perfectly! My children absolutely love them.

—**SHERALYN YLIOJA** LETHBRIDGE, ALBERTA

PREP: 25 MIN. + CHILLING **MAKES:** 2¼ POUNDS

> 1½ **teaspoons plus ¼ cup butter, softened, divided**
> 2 **packages (11½ ounces each) milk chocolate chips**
> ¼ **cup shortening**
> 1 **package (14 ounces) caramels**
> 5 **teaspoons water**
> 1 **cup chopped pecans**

1. Line a 13-in. x 9-in. pan with foil and grease the foil with 1½ teaspoons butter; set aside. In a microwave, melt milk chocolate chips and shortening at 70% power for 1 minute; stir. Microwave at additional 10- to 20-second intervals, stirring until smooth.

2. Spread half of the mixture into prepared pan. Refrigerate for 15 minutes or until firm. Set remaining chocolate mixture aside.

3. In a large microwave-safe bowl, melt the caramels, water and remaining butter; stir until smooth. Stir in pecans. Spread over chocolate layer.

4. Heat reserved chocolate mixture if necessary to achieve spreading consistency; spread over caramel layer. Cover and refrigerate for 1 hour or until firm.

5. Using foil, lift candy out of pan. Gently peel off foil; cut candy into 1½-in. x 1-in. bars. Store in the refrigerator.

Editor's Note: *This recipe was tested in a 1,100-watt microwave.*

CHOCOLATE MEXICAN WEDDING CAKES

Here's a yummy twist on a traditional favorite. Sometimes I add miniature chocolate chips to the dough and, after baking, dip the cooled wedding cakes in melted almond bark.
—**JOANNE VALKEMA** FREEPORT, ILLINOIS

PREP: 20 MIN. **BAKE:** 15 MIN./BATCH **MAKES:** ABOUT 3½ DOZEN

- 1 **cup butter, softened**
- 1¾ **cups confectioners' sugar, divided**
- 1 **teaspoon vanilla extract**
- 1½ **cups all-purpose flour**
- ¼ **cup cornstarch**
- ¼ **cup baking cocoa**
- ½ **teaspoon salt**
- 1¼ **cups finely chopped pecans or almonds**
- ½ **teaspoon ground cinnamon**

1. In a large bowl, cream the butter and 1 cup confectioners' sugar until light and fluffy. Beat in the vanilla. Combine the flour, cornstarch, cocoa and salt; gradually add to the creamed mixture and mix well. Stir in nuts.

2. Shape tablespoonfuls of dough into 1-in. balls. Place 2 in. apart on ungreased baking sheets. Bake at 325° for 12-14 minutes or until set.

3. In a small bowl, combine the cinnamon and remaining confectioners' sugar. Roll warm cookies in sugar mixture; cool on wire racks. Store in an airtight container.

CRANBERRY-CASHEW DROP COOKIES

These memorable goodies have a wonderful, chunky combination of ingredients that both adults and kids like. Don't forget to save a few to enjoy during your afternoon coffee break.
—**MONICA MCGILVRAY** MUKWONAGO, WISCONSIN

PREP: 20 MIN. **BAKE:** 10 MIN./BATCH **MAKES:** 4½ DOZEN

- 1 **cup butter, softened**
- 1 **cup packed brown sugar**
- ½ **cup sugar**
- 2 **eggs**
- 1 **teaspoon vanilla extract**
- 2¼ **cups all-purpose flour**
- 1 **teaspoon baking soda**
- 1 **teaspoon salt**
- 1 **package (10 to 12 ounces) white baking chips**
- 1 **cup chopped cashews**
- 1 **cup dried cranberries**

1. In a large bowl, cream the butter, brown sugar and sugar until light and fluffy. Beat in the eggs and vanilla. Combine the flour, baking soda and salt; gradually add to the creamed mixture and mix well. Stir in the white baking chips, cashews and dried cranberries.

2. Drop by rounded tablespoonfuls 2 in. apart onto ungreased baking sheets. Bake at 350° for 9-11 minutes or until golden brown. Remove to wire racks to cool.

Love that Lemon!

Just a twist of tangy, refreshing lemon can elevate a recipe from ordinary to amazing.
Try the delightfully citrusy recipes here for a tongue-tingling burst of flavor you'll crave.

LEMON THINS

These sugar-dusted thins feature a pleasingly tart taste and crisp texture. For an easy but elegant dessert, add a few to individual bowls filled with scoops of chocolate or vanilla ice cream.

—**JUDY WILSON** SUN CITY WEST, ARIZONA

PREP: 35 MIN. + CHILLING **BAKE:** 10 MIN./BATCH + COOLING
MAKES: 4½ DOZEN

- ⅓ cup butter, softened
- ⅓ cup shortening
- 1 cup sugar
- 2 tablespoons lemon juice
- 2 teaspoons grated lemon peel
- ½ teaspoon lemon extract
- ½ teaspoon vanilla extract
- 1½ cups all-purpose flour
- 1½ teaspoons baking powder
- ½ teaspoon baking soda
- ¼ teaspoon salt
- 2 tablespoons confectioners' sugar

1. In a large bowl, cream the butter, shortening and sugar until light and fluffy. Beat in the lemon juice, lemon peel and extracts.
2. Combine the flour, baking powder, baking soda and salt; gradually add to the creamed mixture and mix well. Shape into a 12-in. roll; wrap in plastic wrap. Refrigerate for at least 2 hours or until firm.
3. Unwrap dough; cut into ¼-in. slices. Place 2 in. apart on ungreased baking sheets.
4. Bake at 350° for 8-9 minutes or until the edges are lightly browned. Cool for 1-2 minutes before removing from pans to wire racks to cool completely. Dust with confectioners' sugar.

EASY LEMON CURD BARS

A cup of tea looks lonely without something sweet to eat beside it. My simple citrus bars make a nice accompaniment. I especially like the addition of coconut and toasted almonds.

—**DONNA HARDIN** NEW VIRGINIA, IOWA

PREP: 30 MIN. **BAKE:** 20 MIN. + COOLING **MAKES:** 2 DOZEN

- 1 cup butter, softened
- 1 cup sugar
- 2 cups all-purpose flour
- ½ teaspoon baking soda
- 1 jar (10 ounces) lemon curd
- ⅔ cup flaked coconut
- ½ cup chopped almonds, toasted

1. In a large bowl, cream butter and sugar until light and fluffy. Combine the flour and baking soda; gradually add to creamed mixture and mix well.
2. Set aside 1 cup mixture for topping; press remaining mixture onto the bottom of a greased 13-in. x 9-in. baking dish. Bake at 350° for 12-15 minutes or until edges are lightly browned. Cool for 10 minutes.
3. Spread lemon curd over crust. In a small bowl, combine the coconut, almonds and reserved topping mixture; sprinkle over lemon curd.
4. Bake for 18-22 minutes or until golden brown. Cool completely on a wire rack. Cut into bars.

GINGERBREAD COOKIES WITH LEMON FROSTING

When I topped off my little gingerbread rounds with a lemony cream-cheese frosting, I knew I'd found a winning combination. The cardamom and allspice lend a hint of chai tea.

—**AYSHA SCHURMAN** AMMON, IDAHO

PREP: 25 MIN. **BAKE:** 10 MIN./BATCH + COOLING
MAKES: 4 DOZEN

- ½ cup butter, softened
- ¾ cup packed brown sugar
- 2 eggs
- ¼ cup molasses
- 3 cups all-purpose flour
- 1 tablespoon ground ginger
- 2 teaspoons baking soda
- 1 teaspoon each ground cardamom, cinnamon and allspice
- 1 teaspoon grated lemon peel
- ½ teaspoon salt

FROSTING

- 4 ounces cream cheese, softened
- 2½ cups confectioners' sugar
- 2 tablespoons lemon juice
- 1 tablespoon grated lemon peel
- 1 teaspoon vanilla extract

1. In a large bowl, cream the butter and brown sugar until light and fluffy. Beat in eggs and molasses. Combine the flour, ginger, baking soda, cardamom, cinnamon, allspice, lemon peel and salt; gradually add to creamed mixture and mix well.

2. Shape into 1-in. balls; place 2 in. apart on ungreased baking sheets. Bake at 350° for 8-10 minutes or until tops are cracked. Cool for 2 minutes before removing from pans to wire racks to cool completely.

3. In a small bowl, beat the cream cheese until fluffy. Add the confectioners' sugar, lemon juice, peel and vanilla; beat until smooth. Frost cookies. Store in an airtight container in the refrigerator.

LEMON STARS

Each bite of these crunchy, sugar-sprinkled cutouts has a citrusy zing. The yellow stars are festive for the Christmas season, but you could also decorate them to fit the Fourth of July.

—**JACQUELINE HILL** NORWALK, OHIO

PREP: 35 MIN. + CHILLING **BAKE:** 10 MIN./BATCH + COOLING
MAKES: 9 DOZEN

- ½ cup butter-flavored shortening
- 1 cup sugar
- 1 egg
- 1½ teaspoons lemon extract
- ½ cup sour cream
- 1 teaspoon grated lemon peel
- 2¾ cups all-purpose flour
- ½ teaspoon baking soda
- ½ teaspoon salt

FROSTING

- 1½ cups confectioners' sugar
- 6 tablespoons butter
- ¾ teaspoon lemon extract
- 3 drops yellow food coloring, optional
- 3 to 4 tablespoons 2% milk
  Yellow colored sugar, optional

1. In a large bowl, cream the shortening and sugar until light and fluffy. Beat in egg and extract. Stir in sour cream and peel. Combine flour, baking soda and salt; gradually add to creamed mixture and mix well. Divide dough into three balls; cover and refrigerate for 3 hours or until easy to handle.

2. Remove one portion of dough from the refrigerator at a time. On a lightly floured surface, roll out dough to ¼-in. thickness. Cut with a floured 2-in. star cookie cutter. Place 1 in. apart on ungreased baking sheets.

3. Bake at 375° for 6-8 minutes or until the edges are lightly browned. Remove to wire racks to cool.

4. For the frosting, in a small bowl, combine the confectioners' sugar, butter, extract, food coloring if desired and enough milk to achieve spreading consistency. Frost cookies; sprinkle with colored sugar if desired.

MAPLE PECAN BARS

Baking pecan bars always gets me reminiscing about my Grandma Marie, who made a similar recipe. I bring a pan of my bars whenever we have an office cookie exchange.
—**AMANDA SPEARING** NEWTON, IOWA

PREP: 30 MIN. **BAKE:** 20 MIN. + COOLING **MAKES:** 5 DOZEN

> 3 **cups all-purpose flour**
> ¾ **cup confectioners' sugar**
> 1½ **cups cold butter**
> **TOPPING**
> 1½ **cups packed brown sugar**
> 1 **cup butter, cubed**
> ½ **cup maple syrup**
> 2 **teaspoons ground cinnamon**
> ¼ **teaspoon salt**
> 4 **cups coarsely chopped pecans**
> 2 **tablespoons plus 1 teaspoon heavy whipping cream**
> ¾ **teaspoon vanilla extract**

1. In a large bowl, combine flour and confectioners' sugar. Cut in the butter until crumbly. Press into a greased 15-in. x 10-in. x 1-in. baking pan. Bake at 350° for 12-15 minutes or until edges are lightly browned.

2. Meanwhile, in a large heavy saucepan, combine the brown sugar, butter, syrup, cinnamon and salt. Bring to a boil. Cook and stir over low heat until butter is melted. Stir in the pecans, cream and vanilla. Remove from the heat; spread over crust.

3. Bake 20-25 minutes longer or until bubbly. Cool on a wire rack. Cut into bars.

ACORN TREATS

My co-workers went nutty over these little autumn treats. They'e so simple to create—just spread melted chocolate on the bottom of a chocolate kiss, attach a Nutter Butter Bite and pipe on a stem.
—**JANE STASIK** GREENDALE, WISCONSIN

PREP: 35 MIN. + CHILLING **MAKES:** 4 DOZEN

> ½ **cup semisweet chocolate chips**
> 48 **milk chocolate kisses**
> 48 **Nutter Butter Bites**

1. In a microwave, melt the chocolate chips; stir until smooth. Spread the flat side of each kiss with a small amount of melted chocolate; immediately attach each to a cookie.

2. Cut a small hole in the corner of a pastry or plastic bag; insert a small round tip. Fill with remaining melted chocolate. Pipe a stem onto each acorn. Place on waxed paper-lined baking sheets; refrigerate until set. Store in an airtight container.

PASTRY BAG POINTER

To easily fill a pastry bag, secure the frosting tip on the bag and place the bag's tip in a tall empty glass. Fold the bag's wide opening halfway over the glass, then transfer your filling to the bag. When it's three-fourths full, put the bag's sides up over the filling, lift it out of the glass and twist the open end to close.

SOFT ORANGE MARMALADE COOKIES

These soft goodies are a family favorite. The marmalade keeps them nice and tender, and the frosting is a pretty finishing touch.
—**MARGARET PETERSON** FOREST CITY, IOWA

PREP: 40 MIN. **BAKE:** 10 MIN./BATCH **MAKES:** 6½ DOZEN

- ½ cup shortening
- 1 cup sugar
- 2 eggs
- 1 cup (8 ounces) sour cream
- ½ cup orange marmalade
- 4 cups all-purpose flour
- 2 teaspoons baking powder
- 1 teaspoon baking soda
- ½ teaspoon salt

FROSTING
- ½ cup butter, softened
- ¼ cup orange marmalade
- 3 cups confectioners' sugar

1. In a large bowl, cream the shortening and sugar until light and fluffy. Add the eggs, one at a time, beating well after each addition. Combine the sour cream and orange marmalade; set aside. Combine the flour, baking powder, baking soda and salt; add to the creamed mixture alternately with the sour cream mixture and mix well.

2. Drop by tablespoonfuls 2 in. apart onto greased baking sheets. Bake at 375° for 10-12 minutes or until lightly browned. Remove to wire racks to cool completely.

3. For the frosting, in a small bowl, combine the butter and orange marmalade. Gradually beat in confectioners' sugar until blended. Frost cookies.

ITALIAN PIGNOLI COOKIES

Cookies are the crown jewels of Italian confections. I can't let a holiday or other special occasion go by without serving a batch of traditional pignoli rounds coated with pine nuts.
—**MARIA REGAKIS** SOMERVILLE, MASSACHUSETTS

PREP: 30 MIN. **BAKE:** 15 MIN./BATCH **MAKES:** 2½ DOZEN

- 1¼ cups (12 ounces) almond paste
- ½ cup sugar
- 4 egg whites, divided
- 1 cup confectioners' sugar
- 1½ cups pine nuts

1. In a small bowl, beat almond paste and sugar until crumbly. Beat in 2 egg whites. Gradually add confectioners' sugar; mix well.

2. Whisk the remaining egg whites in a shallow bowl. Place the pine nuts in another shallow bowl. Shape dough into 1-in. balls. Roll in egg whites and coat with pine nuts. Place 2 in. apart on parchment paper-lined baking sheets. Flatten slightly.

3. Bake at 325° for 15-18 minutes or until lightly browned. Cool for 1 minute before removing from pans to wire racks. Store in an airtight container.

NO-BAKE COOKIE BALLS

Here's a great option when you're short on time or don't want to heat up the house by turning on the oven. I often make these little balls a day or two in advance to let the flavors blend.
—**CARMELETTA DAILEY** WINFIELD, TEXAS

PREP: 20 MIN. + STANDING **MAKES:** 5 DOZEN

- 1 cup (6 ounces) semisweet chocolate chips
- 3 cups confectioners' sugar
- 1¾ cups crushed vanilla wafers (about 55 wafers)
- 1 cup chopped walnuts, toasted
- ⅓ cup orange juice
- 3 tablespoons light corn syrup
  Additional confectioners' sugar

1. In a large microwave-safe bowl, melt chocolate chips; stir until smooth. Stir in the confectioners' sugar, vanilla wafers, walnuts, orange juice and corn syrup.
2. Roll into 1-in. balls; roll in additional confectioners' sugar. Store in an airtight container.

RICH PEANUT CLUSTERS

It's cheaper to make these bite-size morsels than it is to buy them. Best of all, everyone agrees that the homemade ones taste better!
—**JANICE GARVERT** PLAINVILLE, KANSAS

PREP: 20 MIN. + CHILLING **MAKES:** ABOUT 15 DOZEN

- 2 packages (12 ounces each) semisweet chocolate chips
- 2 packages (10 to 12 ounces each) vanilla or white chips
- 1 tablespoon shortening
- 1 teaspoon vanilla extract
- ½ teaspoon butter, softened
- 2 cans (12 ounces each) salted peanuts

1. In a microwave, melt chips and shortening; stir until smooth. Stir in vanilla and butter. Add peanuts; mix well.
2. Drop by teaspoonfuls onto waxed paper-lined pans. Refrigerate until set. Store in an airtight container.

CRISPY STAR POPS

My patriotic pops always go over well at our annual Fourth of July get-together. Serve them as an after-picnic dessert, or slip them into cellophane bags, tie on ribbons and give them as favors.
—**COLLEEN STURMA** MILWAUKEE, WISCONSIN

PREP: 30 MIN. **COOK:** 15 MIN. + COOLING **MAKES:** 15 POPS

- 8 cups miniature marshmallows
- 6 tablespoons butter, cubed
- 12 cups Rice Krispies
- 12 Popsicle sticks
- 1 cup white baking chips
- ½ teaspoon shortening
  Red, white and blue sprinkles

1. In a Dutch oven, heat the marshmallows and butter until melted. Remove from the heat; stir in cereal and mix well. Press into a greased 15-in. x 10-in. x 1-in. baking pan. Cut with a 3-in. star-shaped cookie cutter. Insert a Popsicle stick into the side of each star; place on waxed paper.
2. In a microwave, melt white chips and shortening; stir until smooth. Spread over stars. Decorate with sprinkles.

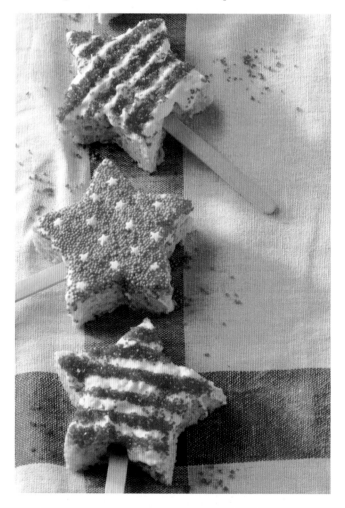

CITRUS ALMOND COOKIES

These frosted goodies were a "must" during the holiday season in my Italian mom's family. I think the combination of milk chocolate, toasted almonds, lemon and orange is cookie perfection.
—**CHERIE DONOHUE** HAPPY VALLEY, OREGON

PREP: 15 MIN. + CHILLING **BAKE:** 15 MIN./BATCH + COOLING
MAKES: 6 DOZEN

- 4 **cups unblanched almonds, toasted**
- 1 **cup sugar**
- 5 **milk chocolate candy bars (1.55 ounces each), chopped**
- ½ **teaspoon ground cinnamon**
- 2 **eggs**
- 4 **teaspoons grated orange peel**
- 1 **tablespoon orange juice**
- 2 **teaspoons grated lemon peel**
- 2 **teaspoons vanilla extract**
- 1 **teaspoon lemon extract**

FROSTING
- 1 **cup confectioners' sugar**
- ½ **teaspoon lemon extract**
- ½ **teaspoon vanilla extract**
- 2 **to 4 teaspoons water**

1. Place almonds in a food processor; cover and process until chopped. In a large bowl, combine the almonds, sugar, chocolate and cinnamon; set aside.
2. In a small bowl, beat eggs, orange peel, orange juice, lemon peel and extracts until combined. Gradually add to almond mixture and mix well. Cover and refrigerate for 2 hours or until easy to handle.
3. Roll into 1-in. balls. Place 2 in. apart on parchment paper-lined baking sheets. Bake at 325° for 12-15 minutes or until the bottoms are lightly browned. Remove to wire racks to cool.

4. Meanwhile, in a small bowl, combine confectioners' sugar, extracts and enough water to achieve spreading consistency. Spread the frosting over the cooled cookies. Store in airtight containers.

CHOCOLATE PECAN TASSIES

Chocolaty tassies are a popular offering on our Christmas Eve buffet. They've been called "sinful" by guests and never last long.
—**LORAINE MEYER** BEND, OREGON

PREP: 35 MIN. + CHILLING **BAKE:** 25 MIN./BATCH + COOLING
MAKES: 2½ DOZEN

- ½ **cup butter, softened**
- 1 **package (3 ounces) cream cheese, softened**
- 1 **cup all-purpose flour**

FILLING
- 1 **egg**
- 1 **tablespoon butter, melted and cooled**
- 1 **teaspoon vanilla extract**
- ⅔ **cup packed brown sugar**
   Dash salt
- 60 **miniature milk chocolate kisses**
- 5 **tablespoons chopped pecans**

1. In a small bowl, beat butter and cream cheese until smooth. Add flour; mix well. Cover and refrigerate for 1 hour or until easy to handle.
2. In a small bowl, whisk egg, butter, vanilla, brown sugar and salt until smooth; set aside. Shape dough into thirty 1-in. balls; press onto the bottom and up the sides of greased miniature muffin cups.
3. Place a chocolate kiss in each cup. Fill each with 1 teaspoon brown sugar mixture; sprinkle with ½ teaspoon pecans.
4. Bake at 325° for 24-26 minutes or until set. Lightly press a second chocolate kiss into the center of each cookie. Cool for 10 minutes before removing from the pans to wire racks to cool completely. Store in an airtight container.

DECADENT DESSERTS

It's so easy to treat family and friends to the luscious cheesecakes, home-style pies, rich puddings, fruit crisps, layer cakes and other special sweets in this chapter. The only hard part? Choosing which one to make first!

CHERRY POUND CAKE

Here's a classic pound cake with the surprise of bright red cherries tucked inside. Spread with a pretty cream cheese frosting dotted with even more cherries, it's a real showstopper.
—**EVVA FOLTZ HANES** CLEMMONS, NORTH CAROLINA

PREP: 25 MIN. **BAKE:** 1¼ HOURS + COOLING **MAKES:** 12 SERVINGS

- 1 jar (10 ounces) maraschino cherries, divided
- 1 cup butter, softened
- ½ cup shortening
- 3 cups sugar
- 6 eggs
- 1 teaspoon vanilla extract
- ¾ cup 2% milk
- 3¾ cups all-purpose flour

FROSTING
- 1 package (3 ounces) cream cheese, softened
- ¼ cup butter, softened
- 3¾ cups confectioners' sugar
- ½ teaspoon vanilla extract
- ½ cup flaked coconut
- ¼ cup chopped walnuts
  Additional coconut, optional

1. Drain and chop the maraschino cherries, reserving the juice; set aside.

2. In a large bowl, cream the butter, shortening and sugar until light and fluffy. Add eggs, one at a time, beating well after each addition. Beat in the vanilla. Combine milk and ¼ cup reserved cherry juice; add to the creamed mixture alternately with flour, beating well after each addition. Fold in ½ cup cherries.

3. Transfer to a greased and floured 10-in. tube pan. Bake at 325° for 1¼ to 1½ hours or until a toothpick inserted near the center comes out clean. Cool for 10 minutes before removing from pan to a wire rack to cool completely.

4. In a large bowl, beat the cream cheese and butter until fluffy. Add confectioners' sugar, vanilla and enough reserved cherry juice to achieve spreading consistency. Fold in the coconut and remaining chopped cherries. Frost cake. Sprinkle with walnuts and additional coconut if desired.

GINGERED CRANBERRY PEAR CRISP

This comforting crisp served in individual ramekins is always a hit with guests. Be prepared to share the recipe!
—**VIRGINIA MIRACLE** MENASHA, WISCONSIN

PREP: 25 MIN. **BAKE:** 25 MIN. **MAKES:** 6 SERVINGS

- ½ cup sugar
- 2 tablespoons all-purpose flour
- 2 tablespoons lemon juice
- 4 cups sliced peeled fresh pears
- 1½ cups fresh or frozen cranberries
- 3 tablespoons finely chopped crystallized ginger

TOPPING
- ¾ cup packed brown sugar
- ¾ cup old-fashioned oats
- ⅔ cup all-purpose flour
- 6 tablespoons cold butter

1. In a large bowl, combine sugar and flour; stir in lemon juice. Add the pears, cranberries and ginger; toss to coat. Divide among six greased 10-oz. ramekins or custard cups.

2. In a small bowl, combine the brown sugar, oats and flour; cut in butter until mixture resembles coarse crumbs. Sprinkle over fruit.

3. Bake at 400° for 25-30 minutes or until the topping is golden brown. Serve warm.

EGGNOG SWEET POTATO PIE

Baking pies is like therapy to me. I prepare my sweet potato pie for special events and holiday celebrations. Flavored with eggnog, the soft filling goes perfectly with the crunchy pecans.
—**SARAH SPAUGH** WINSTON-SALEM, NORTH CAROLINA

PREP: 25 MIN. **BAKE:** 55 MIN. + COOLING **MAKES:** 8 SERVINGS

- ¼ cup caramel ice cream topping
- 1 unbaked pastry shell (9 inches)
- 2 cups mashed sweet potatoes
- ¾ cup eggnog
- 1 egg, lightly beaten
- 2 tablespoons butter, melted
- ½ teaspoon vanilla extract
- ½ cup sugar
- ½ cup packed brown sugar
- ¾ teaspoon ground cinnamon

TOPPING
- ½ cup flaked coconut
- ⅓ cup all-purpose flour
- ¼ cup packed brown sugar
- ⅓ cup cold butter, cubed
- ¼ cup chopped pecans

1. Carefully spread the caramel topping over the bottom of the pastry shell; set aside. In a small bowl, combine sweet potatoes, eggnog, egg, butter and vanilla. Stir in the sugars and cinnamon. Carefully spoon over caramel layer.

2. Bake at 400° for 15 minutes. Reduce the heat to 350°; bake 30 minutes longer.

3. Meanwhile, in a small bowl, combine the coconut, flour and brown sugar. Cut in butter until crumbly; stir in pecans. Sprinkle over pie.

4. Bake for 10-15 minutes or until a knife inserted near the center comes out clean and the topping is golden brown (cover edges with foil if necessary to prevent overbrowning). Cool on a wire rack. Store in the refrigerator.

Editor's Note: *This recipe was tested with commercially prepared eggnog.*

LOW-FAT KEY LIME PIE

Escape to paradise with this easy, creamy treat. Sugar-free gelatin, a reduced-fat crust and fat-free whipped topping make it lighter.
—**FRANCES VANFOSSAN** WARREN, MICHIGAN

PREP: 20 MIN. + CHILLING **MAKES:** 8 SERVINGS

- 1 package (.3 ounce) sugar-free lime gelatin
- ¼ cup boiling water
- 2 cartons (6 ounces each) key lime yogurt
- 1 carton (8 ounces) frozen fat-free whipped topping, thawed
- 1 reduced-fat graham cracker crust (8 inches)

1. In a large bowl, dissolve the gelatin in boiling water. Whisk in the yogurt. Fold in the whipped topping. Pour into the graham cracker crust.

2. Cover and refrigerate pie for at least 2 hours or until set.

SWEET CORN CREME BRULEE

The starch in corn acts as a natural thickener for my creme brulee and lends added sweetness. Garnish it with raspberries and mint leaves for an extra-special presentation.

—MARYANNE JENSEN-GOWAN PELHAM, NEW HAMPSHIRE

PREP: 25 MIN. **BAKE:** 45 MIN. + CHILLING **MAKES:** 6 SERVINGS

1½ cups frozen corn, thawed
4½ teaspoons butter
 3 cups heavy whipping cream
 1 cup 2% milk
 8 egg yolks
1¼ cups plus 2 tablespoons sugar, divided
 2 tablespoons vanilla extract
    Fresh raspberries and mint leaves

1. In a large saucepan, saute corn in butter until tender. Reduce heat. Add cream and milk; heat until bubbles form around sides of pan. Cool slightly. Transfer to a blender; cover and process until smooth. Strain and discard corn pulp. Return to pan.
2. In a small bowl, whisk egg yolks and 1¼ cups sugar. Stir a small amount of hot cream into egg mixture. Return all to the pan, stirring constantly. Stir in vanilla.
3. Transfer to six 6-oz. ramekins. Place in a baking pan; add 1 in. of boiling water to the pan. Bake, uncovered, at 325° for 40-45 minutes or until centers are just set (mixture will jiggle). Remove ramekins from water bath; cool for 10 minutes. Cover and refrigerate for at least 4 hours.
4. If using a creme brulee torch, sprinkle custards with remaining sugar. Heat sugar with the torch until caramelized. Serve immediately.
5. If broiling the custards, place ramekins on a baking sheet; let stand at room temperature for 15 minutes. Sprinkle with sugar. Broil 8 in. from the heat for 4-7 minutes or until sugar is caramelized. Refrigerate for 1-2 hours or until firm.
6. Garnish servings with raspberries and mint leaves.

CRANBERRY-PUMPKIN BREAD PUDDING

Your family and friends are sure to request a second scoop of this autumn comfort food. It's wonderful not only for dessert, but also for breakfast or brunch with a dollop of yogurt.

—LISA VARNER EL PASO, TEXAS

PREP: 15 MIN. **BAKE:** 35 MIN.
MAKES: 9 SERVINGS (1⅓ CUPS SAUCE)

 3 eggs
1½ cups 2% milk
 1 can (15 ounces) solid-pack pumpkin, divided
 ½ cup packed brown sugar
 1 teaspoon vanilla extract
 ¾ teaspoon pumpkin pie spice
 5 cups cubed day-old bread
 ½ cup dried cranberries
 ½ cup fat-free caramel ice cream topping
 ¼ cup chopped walnuts

1. In a large bowl, combine eggs, milk, 1 cup pumpkin, brown sugar, vanilla and pumpkin pie spice. Stir in the bread cubes and dried cranberries.
2. Transfer to an 8-in. square baking dish coated with cooking spray. Cover and bake at 350° for 25 minutes. Uncover and bake 10-15 minutes longer or until a knife inserted near the center comes out clean.
3. Meanwhile, in a small saucepan, combine the caramel ice cream topping and remaining pumpkin. Cook and stir over medium heat until heated through. Stir in the walnuts. Serve with pudding.

PUMPKIN FLANS

When I wanted a recipe that was both luscious and light, I started experimenting in the kitchen and came up with these silky flans. A sprinkling of cinnamon is the perfect finishing touch.

—CHARLES INSLER SILVER SPRING, MARYLAND

PREP: 45 MIN. **BAKE:** 30 MIN. + CHILLING **MAKES:** 6 SERVINGS

 1 cup sugar, divided
 ¼ cup water
1½ cups fat-free evaporated milk
 3 eggs
 1 egg white
 ¼ teaspoon salt
 ¼ teaspoon each ground cinnamon, cloves and ginger
 1 cup canned pumpkin
 1 teaspoon vanilla extract
    Additional ground cinnamon, optional

1. In a small heavy skillet over medium-low heat, combine ⅓ cup sugar and water. Cook, stirring occasionally, until the sugar begins to melt. Cook without stirring until amber, about 20 minutes. Quickly pour into six ungreased 6-oz. ramekins or custard cups, tilting to coat the bottom of the dishes. Let stand for 10 minutes.
2. In a small saucepan, heat the milk until bubbles form around sides of saucepan. In a small bowl, whisk the eggs, egg white, salt,

spices and remaining sugar. Remove milk from the heat; stir a small amount of hot milk into egg mixture. Return all to the pan, stirring constantly. Stir in pumpkin and vanilla. Slowly pour into prepared ramekins.

3. Place in a baking pan; add ¾ in. of boiling water to pan. Bake, uncovered, at 325° for 30-35 minutes or until centers are just set (mixture will jiggle). Remove ramekins from water bath; cool for 10 minutes. Cover and refrigerate for at least 4 hours.

4. Carefully run a knife around edge of pans to loosen; invert each dish onto a rimmed serving dish. Sprinkle with additional cinnamon if desired. Serve immediately.

PUMPKIN-CITRUS BUNDT CAKE

I was determined to create a healthier version of a spiced pumpkin cake. Judging by the response from my taste testers, I succeeded! Even a picky 4-year-old asked for another slice.
—**KRISTA FRANK** RHODODENDRON, OREGON

PREP: 20 MIN. **BAKE:** 55 MIN. + COOLING **MAKES:** 14 SERVINGS

- 2 **cups canned pumpkin**
- 1⅓ **cups sugar**
- 1¼ **cups fat-free milk**
- 2 **eggs**
- ½ **cup orange juice**
- ⅓ **cup canola oil**
- 1½ **teaspoons maple flavoring**
- 1½ **teaspoons vanilla extract**
- 1½ **cups all-purpose flour**
- 1½ **cups whole wheat flour**
- ¼ **cup ground flaxseed**
- 2 **tablespoons grated orange peel**
- 4 **teaspoons baking powder**
- 1 **tablespoon cornstarch**
- 1 **tablespoon poppy seeds**
- 2 **teaspoons pumpkin pie spice**
- 1 **teaspoon salt**
- ½ **teaspoon baking soda**

GLAZE
- 1 **cup confectioners' sugar**
- 1 **teaspoon grated orange peel**
- 1 **to 2 tablespoons orange juice**

1. In a large bowl, beat pumpkin, sugar, milk, eggs, orange juice, oil, maple flavoring and vanilla until well blended. Combine the flours, flaxseed, orange peel, baking powder, cornstarch, poppy seeds, pie spice, salt and baking soda; gradually beat into the pumpkin mixture until blended.

2. Transfer to a greased and floured 10-in. fluted tube pan. Bake at 350° for 55-60 minutes or until a toothpick inserted near the center comes out clean. Cool for 10 minutes before removing from pan to a wire rack to cool completely.

3. In a small bowl, whisk the confectioners' sugar, orange peel and enough orange juice to achieve the desired consistency. Drizzle over cake.

 ## CORN ICE CREAM

This recipe sounds strange, but don't let that stop you from giving it a try! Made with a can of cream-style corn, the unusual but yummy ice cream is sweetly flavored with vanilla and maple syrup.

—**DIANA BURRINK** CRETE, ILLINOIS

PREP: 40 MIN. + CHILLING **PROCESS:** 15 MIN. + FREEZING
MAKES: 4 CUPS

- 2 cups 2% milk
- ¾ cup sugar
- ½ cup maple syrup
- 4 egg yolks, lightly beaten
- 1 can (14¾ ounces) cream-style corn
- 1 teaspoon vanilla extract

1. In a large heavy saucepan, heat milk, sugar and maple syrup until bubbles form around the sides of the pan. Whisk a small amount of the hot mixture into the egg yolks. Return all to pan, whisking constantly.
2. Cook and stir over low heat until the mixture reaches 160°. Quickly transfer mixture to a bowl; place in ice water and stir for 2 minutes. Stir in the corn and vanilla. Press waxed paper onto surface of custard. Refrigerate for several hours or overnight.
3. Strain the custard, discarding corn. Fill cylinder of ice cream freezer two-thirds full; freeze according to the manufacturer's directions. When the ice cream is frozen, transfer to a freezer container; freeze for 2-4 hours before serving.

LIGHTER ICE CREAM

To lighten up my favorite homemade ice cream recipes, I substitute half-and-half cream or skim milk for the full-fat versions.

—**JENNIFER PLEAKE** OMAHA, NEBRASKA

CRANBERRY-PECAN PEAR PIE

Here's a colorful, popular fruit pie for fall and winter celebrations. I always make two because one is never enough!
—**FRANCES BENTHIN** SCIO, OREGON

PREP: 30 MIN. **BAKE:** 55 MIN. + COOLING **MAKES:** 8 SERVINGS

- 2 cups all-purpose flour
- ½ teaspoon salt
- ¾ cup cold butter, cubed
- 6 tablespoons cold water

FILLING

- 4 cups sliced peeled fresh pears (about 5 medium)
- ½ cup chopped dried cranberries
- ½ cup chopped pecans
- ½ cup honey
- ¼ cup butter, melted
- 3 tablespoons cornstarch
- 2 tablespoons grated lemon peel
- 1 teaspoon ground cinnamon
- 1 tablespoon milk
- 1½ teaspoons sugar

1. In a large bowl, combine the flour and salt. Cut in the butter until crumbly. Gradually add the water, tossing with a fork until the dough forms a ball. Roll out half of the pastry to fit a 9-in. pie plate; transfer pastry to pie plate.
2. In a large bowl, combine the pears, dried cranberries, pecans, honey, butter, cornstarch, lemon peel and cinnamon; pour into the crust. Roll out the remaining pastry; make a lattice crust. Trim, seal and flute edges. Brush with milk; sprinkle with sugar.
3. Bake at 400° for 15 minutes. Reduce the heat to 350°; bake 40-50 minutes longer or until crust is golden brown and filling is bubbly. Cool on a wire rack.

CITRUS SOUR CREAM PIE

My fruit-topped cream pie is easy to prepare using the microwave. I like the burst of citrus as a refreshing ending to heavy meals.

—**KALLEE KRONG-MCCREERY** ESCONDIDO, CALIFORNIA

PREP: 20 MIN. + CHILLING **MAKES:** 8 SERVINGS

- ⅔ **cup sugar**
- 3 **tablespoons cornstarch**
- 2 **egg yolks, beaten**
- ¾ **cup orange juice**
- ⅔ **cup 2% milk**
- 2 **tablespoons lemon juice**
- 1 **cup sour cream**
- 1 **graham cracker crust (9 inches)**

TOPPING

- 1 **cup heavy whipping cream**
- 2 **tablespoons confectioners' sugar**
- ¼ **teaspoon vanilla extract**
  - **Grated orange peel**
  - **Optional fruit toppings: mandarin oranges, sliced fresh strawberries and sliced kiwifruit**

1. In a large microwave-safe bowl, combine the sugar and cornstarch. In a small bowl, combine the egg yolks, orange juice, milk and lemon juice; stir into sugar mixture until smooth.
2. Microwave on high for 5-7 minutes or just until the mixture reaches 160°, stirring every minute. Cool to room temperature; press plastic wrap onto the surface of the custard. Refrigerate until chilled.
3. Fold in sour cream; pour filling into crust. Cover and chill for at least 4 hours or overnight.
4. Just before serving, in a large bowl, beat cream until it begins to thicken. Add confectioners' sugar and vanilla; beat until stiff peaks form. Spread over pie. Sprinkle with orange peel; top with fruit if desired.
Editor's Note: *This recipe was tested in a 1,100-watt microwave.*

BUTTER PECAN CHEESECAKE

As soon as autumn rolls around, I start to develop cravings for this rich, creamy, pecan-filled cheesecake. You'll want to put it on your list of favorite desserts for the holidays.

—**LAURA SYLVESTER** MECHANICSVILLE, VIRGINIA

PREP: 30 MIN. **BAKE:** 70 MIN. + CHILLING **MAKES:** 16 SERVINGS

- 1½ **cups graham cracker crumbs**
- ½ **cup finely chopped pecans**
- ⅓ **cup sugar**
- ⅓ **cup butter, melted**

FILLING

- 3 **packages (8 ounces each) cream cheese, softened**
- 1½ **cups sugar**
- 2 **cups (16 ounces) sour cream**
- 1 **teaspoon vanilla extract**
- ½ **teaspoon butter flavoring**
- 3 **eggs, lightly beaten**
- 1 **cup finely chopped pecans**

1. In a large bowl, combine the cracker crumbs, pecans, sugar and butter; set aside ⅓ cup for topping. Press remaining crumb mixture onto the bottom and 1 in. up the sides of a greased 9-in. springform pan.
2. Place springform pan on a double thickness of heavy-duty foil (about 18 in. square). Securely wrap foil around pan.
3. In a large bowl, beat cream cheese and sugar until smooth. Beat in the sour cream, vanilla and butter flavoring. Add eggs; beat on low speed just until combined. Fold in the pecans. Pour into the crust; sprinkle with the reserved crumb mixture. Place the springform pan in a large baking pan; add 1 in. of hot water to the larger pan.
4. Bake at 325° for 70-80 minutes or until center is almost set. Remove springform pan from water bath. Cool on a wire rack for 10 minutes. Carefully run a knife around edge of pan to loosen; cool 1 hour longer. Refrigerate overnight. Remove sides of pan.

A Harvest of Apples

Whether you prefer Granny Smith, McIntosh, Red Delicious, Rome or other varieties, ever-popular apples are wonderfully versatile. See for yourself with the appealing recipes here!

APPLE RAISIN CRUNCH

Warm up your family on chilly days with this fresh-baked favorite. If you like, replace the cheddar cheese slices with a scoop of vanilla ice cream or a dollop of whipped cream.

—MARY ANN MARINO WEST PITTSBURGH, PENNSYLVANIA

PREP: 20 MIN. **BAKE:** 55 MIN. **MAKES:** 6 SERVINGS

- ⅔ cup sugar
- ¾ teaspoon ground cinnamon
- ⅛ to ¼ teaspoon ground nutmeg
- 6 cups thinly sliced peeled tart apples
- ¼ cup raisins
- 1½ teaspoons grated lemon peel
- ⅔ cup biscuit/baking mix
- ¼ cup packed brown sugar
- ⅓ cup butter, melted
  Cheddar cheese slices

1. In a large bowl, combine sugar, cinnamon and nutmeg. Add apples, raisins and lemon peel; toss to coat. Transfer to a greased 8-in. square baking dish.

2. In a small bowl, combine the baking mix and brown sugar. Sprinkle over the apples; drizzle with butter. Bake at 350° for 55-60 minutes or until golden brown. Serve with cheese slices.

APPLE BETTY WITH ALMOND CREAM

Here's an old-fashioned treat I often prepare for friends during the peak of apple season. I always serve a fast meal of soup and bread, so it doesn't take too long to get to dessert!

—LIBBY WALP CHICAGO, ILLINOIS

PREP: 15 MIN. **COOK:** 3 HOURS **MAKES:** 8 SERVINGS

- 3 pounds tart apples, peeled and sliced
- 10 slices cinnamon-raisin bread, cubed
- ¾ cup packed brown sugar
- ½ cup butter, melted
- 1 teaspoon almond extract
- ½ teaspoon ground cinnamon
- ¼ teaspoon ground cardamom
- ⅛ teaspoon salt
WHIPPED CREAM
- 1 cup heavy whipping cream
- 2 tablespoons sugar
- 1 teaspoon grated lemon peel
- ½ teaspoon almond extract

1. Place apples in an ungreased 4- or 5-qt. slow cooker. In a large bowl, combine bread, brown sugar, butter, extract, cinnamon, cardamom and salt; spoon over apples. Cover and cook on low for 3-4 hours or until apples are tender.

2. In a small bowl, beat cream until it begins to thicken. Add the sugar, lemon peel and extract; beat until soft peaks form. Serve with apple mixture.

5. Carefully slip phyllo apples out of ramekins and onto dessert plates. Top with ice cream; drizzle with sauce. Serve immediately.

Editor's Note: *This recipe was tested in a 1,100-watt microwave.*

CARAMEL APPLE CAKE POPS

For fun fall goodies, mix crumbled spice cake and chopped apples with brown-sugar frosting to form balls. Then simply dip them in caramel coating and roll them in peanuts.

—TASTE OF HOME TEST KITCHEN

PREP: 1 HOUR + FREEZING **BAKE:** 25 MIN. + COOLING
MAKES: 39 CAKE POPS

- 1 package spice cake mix (regular size)
- 1½ cups finely chopped peeled tart apples
- ¼ cup packed brown sugar
- 2 tablespoons plus 2 teaspoons heavy whipping cream
- 2 tablespoons butter
- ½ cup confectioners' sugar
- 2 packages (11 ounces each) Kraft caramel bits
- ¼ cup water
- 39 lollipop sticks
- 1 cup finely chopped salted peanuts

1. Prepare the cake mix batter according to package directions, adding apples after mixing. Pour into two greased and floured 9-in. round baking pans. Bake according to package directions. Cool completely.

2. In a small saucepan, combine the brown sugar, cream and butter. Bring to a boil over medium heat, stirring constantly. Remove from the heat; cool for 5 minutes. Gradually beat in the confectioners' sugar until smooth.

3. Crumble one cake layer into a large bowl. (Save remaining cake for another use.) Add the brown sugar mixture; mix well. Shape into 1-in. balls. Arrange on waxed paper-lined baking sheets. Freeze for at least 2 hours or until firm.

4. In a large saucepan, combine caramel bits and water. Cook and stir over medium-low heat until smooth. Dip the ends of lollipop sticks into caramel and insert into cake balls. Dip balls in caramel; roll bottoms in peanuts. Let stand until set. Store in an airtight container in the refrigerator.

PHYLLO APPLES WITH RUM RAISIN SAUCE

Craving something a little bit different? Flaky phyllo dough creates a bowl-like base for the tender fruit and delectable sauce in these individual-size delights. You'll love them!

—MARIE RIZZIO INTERLOCHEN, MICHIGAN

PREP: 35 MIN. **BAKE:** 20 MIN. **MAKES:** 6 SERVINGS

- 6 small apples, peeled and cored
- 4 sheets phyllo dough (14 inches x 9 inches)
- ¼ cup butter, melted
- ⅓ cup slivered almonds, toasted
- ¼ cup sugar
- 1 teaspoon ground cinnamon
- 1 tablespoon cornstarch
- ⅓ cup cold water
- ½ cup packed brown sugar
- ⅓ cup raisins
- 1 tablespoon rum
- 3 cups vanilla ice cream

1. Cut the apples into wedges three-fourths of the way down, leaving the bottoms intact; place in an 11-in. x 7-in. baking dish. Microwave, uncovered, on high for 5 minutes or just until apples begin to soften.

2. Grease six 4-oz. ramekins; set aside. Brush one sheet phyllo dough with butter; layer with remaining sheets and butter. Cut the stack lengthwise into six strips and widthwise into thirds, creating eighteen strips. Layer three strips in a greased 4-oz. ramekin, allowing ends to hang over the edge. Top with an apple. Repeat.

3. Fill the apples with almonds. Combine sugar and cinnamon; sprinkle over the apples. Place ramekins in a 15-in. x 10-in. x 1-in. baking pan. Bake at 375° for 18-22 minutes or until golden brown. Cool slightly.

4. In a small heavy saucepan, combine cornstarch and water until smooth. Stir in the brown sugar and raisins. Cook and stir over medium heat until thickened and bubbly. Remove from the heat; stir in rum.

CHOCOLATE ESPRESSO-NUT TORTE

Chocolate and nuts—two of my favorite foods— come together wonderfully in this espresso-flavored dessert. For an even sweeter treat, finish each serving with a dollop of whipped cream.

—THOMAS FAGLON SOMERSET, NEW JERSEY

PREP: 40 MIN. **BAKE:** 35 MIN. + CHILLING **MAKES:** 14 SERVINGS

- 5 **eggs, separated**
- 1 **teaspoon baking cocoa**
- 1 **cup hazelnuts, toasted and skins removed**
- 3 **tablespoons dark brown sugar**
- ½ **cup butter, softened**
- ⅔ **cup sugar**
- 6 **ounces bittersweet chocolate, melted and cooled**
- 1 **teaspoon instant espresso powder**
- 1 **teaspoon almond extract**
- ¼ **teaspoon salt**

GANACHE
- 6 **ounces bittersweet chocolate, chopped**
- ½ **cup heavy whipping cream**
- ½ **cup finely chopped almonds, toasted**

1. Place the egg whites in a large bowl; let stand at room temperature for 30 minutes. Line the bottom of a greased 9-in. springform pan with waxed paper; grease the paper and dust with cocoa. Set aside.

2. Place hazelnuts and brown sugar in a food processor; cover and process until ground. In a large bowl, cream the butter and sugar until light and fluffy, about 5 minutes. Add egg yolks, one at a time, beating well after each addition. Beat in the melted chocolate, espresso powder, extract and salt. Gradually add the hazelnut mixture.

3. In a large bowl with clean beaters, beat egg whites until stiff peaks form. Fold into batter. Spread into prepared pan. Place pan on a baking sheet.

4. Bake at 375° for 35-40 minutes or until a toothpick inserted near the center comes out with a few moist crumbs. Cool on a wire rack to room temperature. Remove sides of pan and invert onto a serving plate.

5. Place chocolate in a small bowl. In a small saucepan, bring cream just to a boil. Pour over chocolate; whisk until smooth. Cool, stirring occasionally, to room temperature or until the ganache reaches a spreading consistency, about 30 minutes.

6. Spread ganache over top and sides of cake; press almonds onto sides. Cover and refrigerate for 30 minutes or until set.

HOW TO TOAST NUTS

Spread nuts in a 15-in. x 10-in. x 1-in. baking pan and bake them at 350° for 5-10 minutes or until lightly browned, stirring occasionally. Or, spread nuts in a dry nonstick skillet and heat them over low heat until lightly browned, stirring occasionally.

PEANUT & BANANA CUPCAKES

Want goodies that will wow the crowd at a potluck or party? Made-from-scratch banana cupcakes topped off with a creamy homemade frosting are guaranteed to do just that.

—**MARY ANN LEE** CLIFTON PARK, NEW YORK

PREP: 25 MIN. **BAKE:** 20 MIN. + COOLING **MAKES:** 1½ DOZEN

- ½ cup butter, softened
- 1 cup sugar
- 2 eggs
- 1¼ cups mashed ripe bananas (2-3 medium)
- ¼ cup buttermilk
- 2 teaspoons vanilla extract
- 2 cups cake flour
- 1½ teaspoons baking powder
- ¼ teaspoon baking soda
- ⅛ teaspoon salt
- 1 cup chopped lightly salted dry roasted peanuts

FROSTING

- 2 cups confectioners' sugar
- 1 cup creamy peanut butter
- ½ cup butter, softened
- 2 teaspoons vanilla extract
- 3 to 4 tablespoons 2% milk
- 1 cup chopped lightly salted dry roasted peanuts

1. In a large bowl, cream butter and sugar until light and fluffy. Add the eggs, one at a time, beating well after each addition. Combine the bananas, buttermilk and vanilla. Combine the flour, baking powder, baking soda and salt; gradually add to the creamed mixture alternately with banana mixture, mixing well after each addition. Stir in peanuts.

2. Fill paper-lined muffin cups two-thirds full. Bake at 350° for 18-22 minutes or until a toothpick inserted near the center comes out clean. Cool for 10 minutes before removing from pans to wire racks to cool completely.

3. In a large bowl, beat the confectioners' sugar, peanut butter and butter until fluffy. Beat in vanilla and enough milk to achieve desired consistency. Pipe frosting over cupcakes. Sprinkle with peanuts. Store in the refrigerator.

PEANUT MERINGUES

I live in the peanut capital of the world, and this recipe gets many compliments. The meringue is crisp on the outside and tender on the inside, creating the perfect base for a scoop of ice cream.

—**CLARA GIBERSON** DOTHAN, ALABAMA

PREP: 20 MIN. **BAKE:** 1 HOUR + STANDING **MAKES:** 8 SERVINGS

- 4 egg whites
- ¼ teaspoon cream of tartar
- ¼ teaspoon vanilla extract
- ⅛ teaspoon salt
- 1 cup sugar
- ½ cup finely chopped roasted peanuts
  Ice cream of your choice

1. In a large bowl, beat egg whites, cream of tartar, vanilla and salt on medium speed until soft peaks form. Gradually beat in sugar, 1 tablespoon at a time, on high until stiff peaks form. Fold in peanuts.

2. Drop eight mounds onto a parchment paper-lined baking sheet. Shape into 3-in. cups with the back of a spoon. Bake at 250° for 1 hour or until set and dry. Turn the oven off; leave the meringues in the oven for 1 hour. To serve, fill the meringues with ice cream.

PLUM CRISP

The women in my church group love this yummy crisp. Featuring fresh plums and a crunchy oat topping, it's a lighter alternative to classic fruit pie but tastes like an indulgence.
—**DEIDRE KOBEL** BOULDER, COLORADO

PREP: 25 MIN. + STANDING   **BAKE:** 40 MIN.   **MAKES:** 8 SERVINGS

- ¾ cup old-fashioned oats
- ⅓ cup all-purpose flour
- ¼ cup plus 2 tablespoons sugar, divided
- ¼ cup packed brown sugar
- ¼ teaspoon salt
- ¼ teaspoon ground cinnamon
- ¼ teaspoon ground nutmeg
- 3 tablespoons butter, softened
- ¼ cup chopped walnuts
- 5 cups sliced fresh plums (about 2 pounds)
- 1 tablespoon quick-cooking tapioca
- 2 teaspoons lemon juice

1. In a small bowl, combine the oats, flour, ¼ cup sugar, brown sugar, salt, cinnamon and nutmeg. With clean hands, work the butter into the sugar mixture until well combined. Add nuts; toss to combine. Refrigerate for 15 minutes.

2. Meanwhile, in a large bowl, combine the plums, tapioca, lemon juice and remaining sugar. Transfer to a greased 9-in. pie plate. Let stand for 15 minutes. Sprinkle the topping over the plum mixture.

3. Bake at 375° for 40-45 minutes or until the topping is golden brown and plums are tender. Serve warm.

SUMMER BREEZE FRUIT TARTLETS

For a healthier variation of tartlets, I substitute convenient baked wonton wrappers for the usual pastry shells. Refreshing mango, blueberries and strawberries fill each little cup.
—**FRAN FEHLING** STATEN ISLAND, NEW YORK

PREP/TOTAL TIME: 25 MIN.   **MAKES:** 1 DOZEN

- 1 medium mango, peeled and chopped
- 1 cup sliced fresh strawberries
- ½ cup fresh blueberries
- 12 wonton wrappers
  Cooking spray
- ¼ cup apple jelly
- 2 tablespoons sugar
- ½ teaspoon ground cinnamon

1. In a small bowl, combine the mango, strawberries and blueberries.

2. Press wonton wrappers into miniature muffin cups coated with cooking spray; spritz each wrapper with additional cooking spray. Bake at 350° for 7-9 minutes or until lightly browned.

3. In a small saucepan, combine the jelly, sugar and cinnamon. Cook and stir over medium heat until sugar is dissolved. Spoon fruit into cups; brush with jelly mixture.

ZUCCHINI CHOCOLATE CAKE

Wondering what to do with your excess of garden zucchini? Here's the perfect solution—a moist, chocolaty cake!
—**WEDA MOSELLIE** PHILLIPSBURG, NEW JERSEY

PREP: 25 MIN.   **BAKE:** 45 MIN. + COOLING   **MAKES:** 15 SERVINGS

- ½ cup butter, softened
- 1¾ cups sugar
- ½ cup canola oil
- 2 eggs
- 1 teaspoon vanilla extract
- 1 cup 2% milk
- ½ cup buttermilk
- 2½ cups all-purpose flour
- ¼ cup baking cocoa
- 1 teaspoon baking soda
- ½ teaspoon baking powder
- ½ teaspoon salt
- 2 cups shredded zucchini
- ½ cup semisweet chocolate chips
  Confectioners' sugar

1. In a large bowl, beat the butter, sugar and oil until smooth. Add eggs, one at a time, beating well after each addition. Beat in the vanilla. Combine the milk and buttermilk. Combine the flour, cocoa, baking soda, baking powder and salt; add to batter alternately with milk mixture, beating well after each addition. Fold in zucchini.

2. Transfer to a greased 13-in. x 9-in. baking pan. Sprinkle with the chocolate chips. Bake at 325° for 45-50 minutes or until a toothpick inserted near the center comes out clean. Cool on a wire rack. Dust with confectioners' sugar.

ORANGE CHEESECAKE DESSERT

I think of this as my Dreamsicle cheesecake because the flavors remind me of my favorite childhood treat. The accompanying raspberry syrup is just the right finishing touch.
—**PATRICIA HARMON** BADEN, PENNSYLVANIA

PREP: 30 MIN. **BAKE:** 35 MIN. + CHILLING **MAKES:** 18 SERVINGS

- 1¾ cups shortbread cookie crumbs (about 22 cookies)
- ⅔ cup sliced almonds, finely chopped
- 2 tablespoons plus 1 cup sugar, divided
- ⅓ cup butter, melted
- 4 packages (8 ounces each) cream cheese, softened
- ½ cup thawed orange juice concentrate
- 1¼ teaspoons almond extract
- 4 eggs, lightly beaten
- 2 packages (10 ounces each) frozen sweetened raspberries, thawed
- 2 tablespoons cornstarch

1. In a small bowl, combine the shortbread cookie crumbs, almonds and 2 tablespoons sugar; stir in the butter. Press into a greased 13-in. x 9-in. baking dish. Cover and refrigerate for at least 15 minutes.

2. In a large bowl, beat the cream cheese and remaining sugar until smooth. Add the orange juice concentrate and extract; beat until smooth. Add eggs; beat on low speed just until combined. Pour over crust.

3. Bake at 350° for 35-40 minutes or until center is almost set. Cool on a wire rack for 1 hour. Cover and refrigerate for 8 hours or overnight.

4. Drain raspberries, reserving juice; set berries aside. In a small saucepan, combine cornstarch and reserved juice until smooth. Bring to a boil; cook and stir for 1-2 minutes or until thickened. Remove from the heat; gently stir in the raspberries. Cool. Serve with cheesecake dessert.

PEANUT BUTTER MERINGUE PIE

My mom discovered her recipe for peanut butter pie in a farmwife magazine in the 1960s. My sons can't get enough of this dessert.
—**JUDY HERNKE** MUNDELEIN, ILLINOIS

PREP: 45 MIN. + CHILLING **BAKE:** 15 MIN. + COOLING
MAKES: 8 SERVINGS

- Pastry for single-crust pie (9 inches)
- ¾ cup confectioners' sugar
- ½ cup creamy peanut butter
- ⅔ cup sugar

- 3 tablespoons cornstarch
- 2 tablespoons all-purpose flour
- Dash salt
- 3 cups 2% milk
- 3 egg yolks
- 2 tablespoons butter
- 1 teaspoon vanilla extract

MERINGUE
- 3 egg whites
- Dash cream of tartar
- ¼ cup sugar

1. Roll out pastry to fit a 9-in. pie plate. Transfer pastry to pie plate. Trim pastry to ½ in. beyond edge of plate; flute edges. Line unpricked pastry with a double thickness of heavy-duty foil. Fill with dried beans, uncooked rice or pie weights.

2. Bake at 450° for 8 minutes. Remove the foil and weights; bake 5-7 minutes longer or until lightly browned. Cool on a wire rack.

3. Meanwhile, in a small bowl, beat the confectioners' sugar and peanut butter until crumbly, about 2 minutes. Set aside.

4. In a large heavy saucepan, combine the sugar, cornstarch, flour and salt. Stir in the milk until smooth. Cook and stir over medium-high heat until thickened and bubbly. Reduce the heat; cook and stir 2 minutes longer.

5. Remove from the heat. Stir a small amount of hot mixture into egg yolks; return all to the pan, stirring constantly. Bring to a gentle boil; cook and stir 2 minutes longer. Remove from the heat. Stir in butter and vanilla.

6. Sprinkle 1 cup peanut butter mixture over the crust. Pour the hot filling over the top.

7. In a large bowl, beat the egg whites and cream of tartar on medium speed until soft peaks form. Gradually beat in the sugar, 1 tablespoon at a time, on high until stiff glossy peaks form and sugar is dissolved. Spread evenly over hot filling, sealing edges to crust. Sprinkle with remaining peanut butter mixture.

8. Bake at 350° for 12-15 minutes or until meringue is golden brown. Cool on a wire rack for 1 hour. Refrigerate for at least 4 hours before serving. Store leftovers in the refrigerator.

Editor's Note: *Let pie weights cool before storing. Beans and rice may be reused as pie weights, but not for cooking.*

SPICED PEACH COBBLER

Each spoonful of this comforting, classic peach cobbler makes you want more! It's best served warm from the oven.

—**MARY RELYEA** CANASTOTA, NEW YORK

PREP: 20 MIN. **BAKE:** 30 MIN. **MAKES:** 8 SERVINGS

- 12 **medium peaches, peeled and sliced**
- ¾ **cup sugar, divided**
- 3 **tablespoons cornstarch**
- 1 **tablespoon lemon juice**
- ½ **teaspoon ground cinnamon**
- ¼ **teaspoon ground cardamom**
- 1 **cup all-purpose flour**
- 2 **teaspoons grated orange peel**
- ¾ **teaspoon baking powder**
- ¼ **teaspoon salt**
- ¼ **teaspoon baking soda**
- 3 **tablespoons cold butter**
- ¾ **cup buttermilk**

1. In a large bowl, combine peaches, ½ cup sugar, cornstarch, lemon juice, cinnamon and cardamom. Transfer to a 2-qt. baking dish coated with cooking spray.

2. In a small bowl, combine flour, orange peel, baking powder, salt, baking soda and remaining sugar; cut in the butter until the mixture resembles coarse crumbs. Stir in buttermilk just until moistened. Drop by tablespoonfuls onto peach mixture.

3. Bake, uncovered, at 375° for 30-35 minutes or until golden brown. Serve warm.

FRESH PUMPKIN PIE

When I have the time, I prepare pumpkin pie using freshly cooked pumpkin rather than the canned variety. The taste of a homemade filling with traditional spices just can't be beat.

—**CHRISTY HARP** MASSILLON, OHIO

PREP: 30 MIN. **BAKE:** 55 MIN. + COOLING **MAKES:** 8 SERVINGS

- 1 **medium pie pumpkin**
  Pastry for single-crust pie (9 inches)
- 2 **eggs**
- ¾ **cup packed brown sugar**
- 1 **teaspoon ground cinnamon**
- ½ **teaspoon salt**
- ½ **teaspoon ground ginger**
- ¼ **teaspoon ground cloves**
- 1 **cup 2% milk**

1. Cut the pumpkin in half lengthwise; discard seeds. Place cut side down in a microwave-safe dish; add 1 in. of water. Cover and microwave on high for 15-18 minutes or until very tender.

2. Meanwhile, roll out the pastry to fit a 9-in. pie plate. Transfer pastry to pie plate. Trim pastry to ½ in. beyond the edge of plate; flute edges. Set aside.

3. Drain pumpkin. When cool enough to handle, scoop out the pulp and mash. Set aside 1¾ cups (save remaining pumpkin for another use).

4. In large bowl, combine mashed pumpkin, eggs, brown sugar, cinnamon, salt, ginger and cloves; beat until smooth. Gradually beat in milk. Pour into crust.

5. Bake at 425° for 15 minutes. Reduce heat to 350°; bake 40-45 minutes longer or until a knife inserted near the center comes out clean. Cover the edges with foil during the last 30 minutes to prevent overbrowning if necessary. Cool pie on a wire rack. Refrigerate leftovers.

LEMON RICOTTA CAKE

Here is a treasured family recipe that was passed down from my grandmother and mother to me. The lemon curd, cake batter and frosting are all made from scratch—and those extra steps are well worth the effort! Garnished with sugared lemon peel, it's the ideal dessert when you want to impress guests.

—NAN SLAUGHTER SAMMAMISH, WASHINGTON

PREP: 1 HOUR + CHILLING **BAKE:** 30 MIN. + COOLING
MAKES: 12-16 SERVINGS

- 3 eggs
- 2 egg yolks
- ⅔ cup sugar
- ⅓ cup lemon juice
- ⅓ cup butter, cubed

CAKE BATTER

- 1 cup butter, softened
- 2 cups sugar
- 3 eggs
- 1 cup ricotta cheese
- 1 cup buttermilk
- 1 tablespoon grated lemon peel
- 1½ teaspoons vanilla extract
- 1 teaspoon lemon juice
- 3 cups all-purpose flour
- ½ teaspoon baking powder
- ½ teaspoon baking soda
- ½ teaspoon salt

SUGARED LEMON PEEL

- 6 medium lemons
- ¼ cup sugar

FROSTING

- ⅔ cup butter, softened
- 5½ cups confectioners' sugar
- ⅓ cup milk
- 1½ teaspoons grated lemon peel
- 1½ teaspoons vanilla extract
- ⅛ teaspoon salt

1. For lemon curd, in a small bowl, combine eggs and egg yolks. In a heavy saucepan, cook and stir sugar, lemon juice and butter over medium heat until smooth. Stir a small amount of the hot mixture into eggs; return all to the pan, stirring constantly. Bring to a gentle boil, cook and stir for 2 minutes. Cool slightly. Cover and chill for 1½ hours or until thickened.

2. In a large bowl, cream the butter and sugar until light and fluffy. Add eggs, one at a time, beating well after each addition. Combine the ricotta cheese, buttermilk, lemon peel, vanilla and lemon juice. Combine the flour, baking powder, baking soda and salt; add to the creamed mixture alternately with the buttermilk mixture, beating well after each addition.

3. Pour into two greased and floured 9-in. round baking pans. Bake at 350° for 30-35 minutes or until a toothpick inserted near the center comes out clean. Cool for 10 minutes before removing from pans to wire racks to cool completely.

4. Using a citrus zester, remove the peel from lemons in long narrow strips; toss with sugar. Let stand for 30 minutes. (Save fruit for another use.) Meanwhile, in a large bowl, cream butter until light and fluffy. Add the confectioners' sugar, milk, lemon peel, vanilla and salt; beat until smooth.

5. Cut each cake in half horizontally. Place one cake layer on a serving plate. Pipe a circle of frosting around the edge of the cake. Spread a third of the lemon curd inside the frosting. Repeat the layers twice. Top with the remaining cake layer. Frost the top and sides of the cake. Garnish with sugared lemon peel. Store in the refrigerator.

MICROWAVE CHOCOLATE BREAD PUDDING

For a fuss-free microwave treat that pleases everyone, try this chocolate bread pudding. I like to top it with whipped cream and a sprinkling of crushed peppermint candies, but you could also add a chocolate kiss or sliced strawberries.

—JULIE JOHNSON WESTMINSTER, COLORADO

PREP: 10 MIN. + STANDING **COOK:** 20 MIN.
MAKES: 9 SERVINGS (2 CUPS WHIPPED CREAM)

- 6 eggs, beaten
- 1 can (12 ounces) evaporated milk
- 1 cup chocolate syrup
- 9 slices white bread, cubed
- 1 cup heavy whipping cream
- 2 tablespoons sugar
- ½ teaspoon vanilla extract
- ⅛ teaspoon peppermint extract
  Crushed peppermint candies, optional

1. In a large bowl, combine the eggs, milk, and syrup. Gently stir in bread; let stand for 15 minutes or until bread is softened.

2. Transfer to a greased 8-in. square baking dish. Microwave at 50% power for 18-22 minutes or until a knife inserted near the center comes out clean.

3. Meanwhile, in a small bowl, beat the heavy whipping cream until it begins to thicken. Add the sugar and extracts; beat until soft peaks form. Serve with the bread pudding. Sprinkle with peppermint candies if desired.

Editor's Note: *This recipe was tested in a 1,100-watt microwave.*

CHERRIES IN THE SNOW

We experimented to create a recipe for guests who have dietary restrictions but still want something sweet after dinner. The result was a sugar-free, fat-free rice pudding dotted with dried cherries. It's a cool, creamy and pretty treat.

—**BARBARA SIDWAY** BAKER CITY, OREGON

PREP: 10 MIN. **COOK:** 40 MIN. + CHILLING **MAKES:** 6 SERVINGS

- 6 **cups fat-free milk**
- ¾ **cup uncooked arborio rice**
  Sugar substitute equivalent to ¾ cup sugar
- ½ **vanilla bean**
- ½ **cup dried cherries**
- 2 **tablespoons dark rum**
- ¼ **teaspoon salt**
- 1 **cup fat-free whipped topping**

1. In a large saucepan, combine milk, rice and sugar substitute. Scrape the seeds from vanilla bean; add bean and seeds to milk mixture. Bring to a boil. Reduce heat; simmer, uncovered, for 40-45 minutes or until rice is tender and pudding is thickened, stirring occasionally.

2. Transfer to a small bowl; discard the vanilla bean. Stir in the cherries, rum and salt. Cover and refrigerate until chilled. Fold in whipped topping before serving.

CHOCOLATE RASPBERRY CAKE

Coffee flavor and a lovely raspberry filling make this moist layer cake even more special. Garnished with chocolate curls and fresh berries, it looks like it came from a bakery.

—**TAMMY BOLLMAN** MINATARE, NEBRASKA

PREP: 45 MIN. **BAKE:** 30 MIN. + COOLING **MAKES:** 16 SERVINGS

- 2 **cups sugar**
- 1 **cup 2% milk**
- 1 **cup strong brewed coffee**
- 1 **cup canola oil**
- 2 **eggs**
- 1 **teaspoon vanilla extract**

- 2 **cups all-purpose flour**
- ¾ **cup baking cocoa**
- 1 **tablespoon instant coffee granules**
- 2 **teaspoons baking soda**
- 1 **teaspoon baking powder**
- 1 **teaspoon salt**

FILLING

- 1 **cup butter, softened**
- 1½ **cups confectioners' sugar**
- ½ **cup seedless raspberry jam**

FROSTING

- 9 **ounces bittersweet chocolate, chopped**
- 1½ **cups butter, softened**
- 3 **cups marshmallow creme**
- ½ **cup confectioners' sugar**
- 1 **teaspoon vanilla extract**
  Fresh raspberries and chocolate curls

1. In a large bowl, beat the sugar, milk, coffee, oil, eggs and vanilla until well blended. In a small bowl, combine the flour, cocoa, coffee granules, baking soda, baking powder and salt; gradually beat into sugar mixture until blended.

2. Pour into two greased and floured 9-in. baking pans. Bake at 325° for 30-35 minutes or until a toothpick inserted near the center comes out clean. Cool for 10 minutes before removing from pans to wire racks to cool completely.

3. For the filling, in a large bowl, beat butter and confectioners' sugar. Add jam; beat until blended.

4. For the frosting, melt the chocolate in a microwave; stir until smooth. In a large bowl, beat butter and chocolate until fluffy. Add marshmallow creme, confectioners' sugar and extract; beat until smooth.

5. Place one cake layer on a serving plate; spread with filling. Top with remaining cake layer. Spread frosting over top and sides of cake. Garnish with berries and chocolate curls. Store in the refrigerator.

LEMON PUDDING DESSERT

We always indulge in my fluffy lemon dessert during the holidays. I really appreciate the fact that I can prepare it in advance and let it chill in the refrigerator until serving time.

—JANICE HURD CHURCH HILL, TENNESSEE

PREP: 35 MIN. + CHILLING **MAKES:** 20 SERVINGS

- 1 cup all-purpose flour
- ½ cup chopped pecans
- ½ cup butter, melted
- 1 tablespoon sugar

FILLING

- 1 package (8 ounces) cream cheese, softened
- 1 cup confectioners' sugar
- 1 carton (12 ounces) frozen whipped topping, thawed, divided
- 4 cups cold 2% milk
- 3 packages (3.4 ounces each) instant lemon pudding mix

1. In a small bowl, combine the flour, pecans, butter and sugar. Press onto the bottom of a greased 13-in. x 9-in. baking dish. Bake at 350° for 12-15 minutes or until the edges are lightly browned. Cool completely on a wire rack.

2. In a large bowl, beat the cream cheese and confectioners' sugar until smooth. Fold in half of the whipped topping. Spread over the crust.

3. In a large bowl, whisk the milk and pudding mix for 2 minutes (mixture will be thick). Spread over cream cheese layer; top with remaining whipped topping. Refrigerate until chilled.

PEAR GINGERBREAD CAKE ROLL

Love the aroma and taste of gingerbread at Christmastime? Why stop at baking cutout cookies? This elegant, impressive roll dresses up a spiced molasses cake with a luscious pear swirl.

—GWEN BEAUCHAMP LANCASTER, TEXAS

PREP: 50 MIN. + CHILLING **BAKE:** 10 MIN. + COOLING
MAKES: 10 SERVINGS

- 3 eggs
- 3 egg yolks
- ⅔ cup sugar
- 2 tablespoons butter, melted
- 2 tablespoons molasses
- ¾ cup cake flour
- 1 teaspoon baking powder
- 1 teaspoon each ground ginger, cinnamon and allspice
- 2 to 3 teaspoons confectioners' sugar

FILLING

- 2 medium pears, peeled and finely chopped
- 1 tablespoon butter
- 2 tablespoons pear brandy or brandy
- 1 cup heavy whipping cream
- 2 tablespoons confectioners' sugar
- ½ teaspoon ground cinnamon
- ¼ teaspoon ground ginger
  Additional confectioners' sugar and ground cinnamon, optional

1. Line a 15-in. x 10-in. x 1-in. baking pan with waxed paper; grease and flour the pan and paper. Set aside. In a large bowl, beat the eggs and egg yolks for 3 minutes. Gradually add the sugar; beat for 2 minutes or until mixture becomes thick and lemon-colored. Beat in butter and molasses. Combine the flour, baking powder and spices; fold into egg mixture. Spread batter into prepared pan.

2. Bake at 375° for 9-11 minutes or until the cake springs back when lightly touched. Cool in pan for 5 minutes. Turn cake onto a kitchen towel dusted with confectioners' sugar. Gently peel off waxed paper. Roll up cake in towel jelly-roll style, starting with a short side. Cool completely on a wire rack.

3. For filling, in a small skillet, saute pears in butter until tender. Remove from the heat; stir in brandy. Cool completely. In a large bowl, beat the cream, confectioners' sugar, cinnamon and ginger until stiff peaks form. Gently fold in pear mixture.

4. Unroll the cake and spread the filling over the cake to within ½ in. of the edges. Roll up again. Cover and refrigerate for 1 hour before serving. Dust with additional confectioners' sugar and cinnamon if desired.

DATE PUDDING CAKE LOAF

For old-fashioned appeal at Christmas, or any time at all, consider this moist cake baked in a loaf pan and dotted with chopped dates and walnuts. It's served with a delectable vanilla sauce.
—**NANCY FOUST** STONEBORO, PENNSYLVANIA

PREP: 20 MIN. **BAKE:** 45 MIN. + COOLING
MAKES: 12 SERVINGS (1⅓ CUPS SAUCE)

- 1   **cup finely chopped dates**
- 1   **cup boiling water**
- 4½ **teaspoons shortening**
- 1   **cup sugar**
- 1   **egg**
- 1   **teaspoon vanilla extract**
- 1   **cup all-purpose flour**
- 1   **teaspoon baking soda**
- ½   **teaspoon baking powder**
- 1   **cup chopped walnuts**

VANILLA SAUCE
- ½   **cup sugar**
- ½   **cup packed brown sugar**
- 1   **tablespoon cornstarch**
- 1   **cup milk**
- 1   **teaspoon butter**
- 1   **teaspoon vanilla extract**

1. Place the dates in a small bowl; add boiling water. Let stand for 5 minutes. Meanwhile, in a small bowl, beat the shortening and sugar until crumbly, about 2 minutes. Add egg and vanilla; mix well. Combine the flour, baking soda and baking powder; add to shortening mixture alternately with dates and water. Fold in walnuts.

2. Transfer to a greased 9-in. x 5-in. loaf pan. Bake at 350° for 45-55 minutes or until a toothpick inserted near the center comes out clean. Cool on a wire rack for 20 minutes.

3. In a small saucepan, combine the sugars and cornstarch. Gradually whisk in the milk until smooth. Bring to a boil over medium heat; cook and stir for 2 minutes or until thickened. Stir in butter and vanilla. Serve warm with cake.

GREAT AMERICAN BROWNIE PIE

A brownie is about as American as you can get. I transform it into a pie as a special treat for our Independence Day celebration.
—**EDIE DESPAIN** LOGAN, UTAH

PREP: 30 MIN. **BAKE:** 30 MIN. + COOLING **MAKES:** 8 SERVINGS

- ½   **cup butter, softened**
- ¾   **cup sugar**
- 2   **eggs**
- 2   **tablespoons corn syrup**
- 1½ **teaspoons almond extract**
- ⅔   **cup all-purpose flour**
- ⅓   **cup baking cocoa**
- ¼   **teaspoon baking powder**
- ⅓   **cup chopped maraschino cherries**
- ⅓   **cup coarsely chopped almonds**
- 1   **cup white baking chips**
     Whipped topping and maraschino cherries with stems, optional

1. In a small bowl, cream butter and sugar. Add the eggs, corn syrup and extract; mix well. Combine the flour, cocoa and baking powder. Add to creamed mixture and mix well. Drain chopped cherries on paper towels. Fold the cherries, almonds and chips into batter.

2. Transfer to a greased and floured 9-in. pie plate. Bake at 325° for 30-35 minutes or until a toothpick inserted near the center comes out clean. Cool on a wire rack. Garnish with whipped topping and cherries if desired.

SHORTCUT STRAWBERRY-VANILLA DESSERT

Here's a yummy way to dress up a frozen pound cake. I cut it into slices and layer it with fresh strawberries and a creamy pudding mixture. Extra berries and whipped topping finish it off perfectly.
—**CHRISTINE JOHNSON** RICETOWN, KENTUCKY

PREP: 15 MIN. + STANDING **MAKES:** 7 SERVINGS

- 2 cups fresh strawberries, sliced
- 1 teaspoon sugar
- 1½ cups cold 2% milk
- 1 package (3.4 ounces) instant vanilla pudding mix
- 2 cups whipped topping, divided
- 1 loaf (10¾ ounces) frozen pound cake, thawed

1. In a small bowl, combine strawberries and sugar; let stand for 30 minutes. Meanwhile, in a large bowl, whisk the milk and vanilla pudding mix for 2 minutes. Let stand for 2 minutes or until soft-set. Fold in 1 cup whipped topping; set aside.
2. Cut the pound cake into 14 slices. Layer seven cake slices with 2 tablespoons strawberries, ⅓ cup vanilla pudding mixture and another cake slice. Top with the remaining strawberries and whipped topping.

DEVIL'S FOOD CAKE WITH CHOCOLATE FUDGE FROSTING

This winning recipe received several blue ribbons at our state fair. Spread with a fudgy made-from-scratch frosting, this homemade chocolate cake is one you won't want to miss.
—**DONNA CARMAN** TULSA, OKLAHOMA

PREP: 45 MIN. **BAKE:** 25 MIN. + COOLING **MAKES:** 12 SERVINGS

- 3 ounces unsweetened chocolate, chopped
- ½ cup butter, softened
- 2¼ cups packed brown sugar
- 3 eggs
- 1½ teaspoons vanilla extract
- 2¼ cups cake flour
- 1 teaspoon baking soda
- ½ teaspoon salt
- ½ teaspoon baking powder
- 1 cup water
- 1 cup (8 ounces) sour cream
FROSTING
- ½ cup butter, cubed
- 4 ounces unsweetened chocolate, chopped
- 3¾ cups confectioners' sugar
- ½ cup milk
- 2 teaspoons vanilla extract

1. In a microwave, melt chocolate; stir until smooth. Set aside. In a large bowl, cream butter and brown sugar until light and fluffy. Add eggs, one at a time, beating well after each addition. Beat in vanilla and melted chocolate.
2. Combine the flour, baking soda, salt and baking powder; add to the creamed mixture alternately with water and sour cream. Transfer to two greased and floured 9-in. round baking pans.
3. Bake at 350° for 25-30 minutes or until a toothpick inserted

near the center comes out clean. Cool for 10 minutes before removing from pans to wire racks to cool completely.
4. For the frosting, in a small heavy saucepan, melt butter and chocolate over low heat. Remove from heat; cool for 5 minutes. In a large bowl, beat the confectioners' sugar, milk and vanilla until smooth. Gradually beat in chocolate mixture until frosting is light and fluffy. Spread between layers and over top and sides of cake. Refrigerate leftovers.

RASPBERRY-SWIRL CHEESECAKE PIE

When I need something special to take to a family gathering, I rely on my raspberry cheesecake pie. But I have to make more than one because some of my relatives worry they won't get a piece!
—**GUSTY CRUM** DOVER, OHIO

PREP: 20 MIN. **BAKE:** 1 HOUR + CHILLING **MAKES:** 6-8 SERVINGS

- 1 package (8 ounces) cream cheese, softened
- 1 tablespoon all-purpose flour
- 1 can (14 ounces) sweetened condensed milk
- 3 tablespoons plus 1 teaspoon lemon juice, divided
- 1 egg, lightly beaten
- 1 graham cracker crust (9 inches)
- ½ cup seedless raspberry preserves
   Fresh raspberries and mint, optional

1. In a small bowl, beat cream cheese and flour until smooth. Beat in milk and 3 tablespoons lemon juice. Add egg; beat on low speed just until combined. Pour half of the filling into crust.
2. In a small bowl, combine raspberry preserves and remaining lemon juice. Drop two-thirds of the mixture by teaspoonfuls over filling; cut through with a knife to swirl. Top with remaining filling and preserves; cut through with a knife to swirl.
3. Bake at 300° for 60-65 minutes or until center is almost set. Cool on a wire rack for 1 hour. Refrigerate until chilled. Garnish with raspberries and mint if desired.

COOKING FOR TWO

Planning on a table for two? You don't have to make more food than you want. Downsize your meal with these smaller-yield recipes, from meaty entrees and standout side dishes to refreshing salads and luscious desserts.

going back to

civilian life

FAVORITE CHICKEN SALAD SANDWICHES

Whether I'm serving just one friend or more, I often get requests for my chicken salad sandwiches on toasted sourdough bread. The dill pickles, ripe olives, green onion and celery combine for a nice blend of flavors and a pleasant crunch.
—**VALERIE ARREDONDO** HACIENDA HEIGHTS, CALIFORNIA

PREP/TOTAL TIME: 20 MIN. **MAKES:** 2 SERVINGS

    1   cup shredded cooked chicken
    ½   cup chopped celery
    1   tablespoon chopped green onion
    2   tablespoons chopped ripe olives
    2   tablespoons chopped dill pickle
    ¼   cup mayonnaise
    ¼   teaspoon pepper
    ⅛   teaspoon salt
    4   slices sourdough bread, toasted
    2   lettuce leaves

In a small bowl, combine the first eight ingredients. Spread over two toast slices; top with lettuce and remaining toast.

SPICED CHICKEN SALAD
To jazz up chicken salad, I sprinkle it with a little cinnamon. I got the idea from a local restaurant.
—**MYRTLE S.** FRANKLIN, NORTH CAROLINA

HAM & PICKLE WRAPS

I decided to try out a new appetizer on the members of my card club, and these creamy ham slices were a big success. I've since found that I can change them up a bit by swapping ingredients— the versatile wraps always turn out well.
—**DETRA LITTLE** MOULTRIE, GEORGIA

PREP: 10 MIN. + CHILLING **MAKES:** 1 DOZEN

    2   ounces cream cheese, softened
    1½   teaspoons spicy ranch salad dressing mix
    2   slices deli ham
    2   whole dill pickles

In a small bowl, combine the cream cheese and ranch salad dressing mix. Spread over the deli ham slices. Place a dill pickle on each ham slice. Roll up tightly; wrap in plastic wrap. Refrigerate for at least 1 hour or until firm. Cut each wrap into six slices.

SAUTEED CORN WITH CHEDDAR

My brother-in-law gave me this side dish recipe and told me that his family never ate corn any other way. The first time I sampled the cheesy sauteed kernels, I understood why!
—**SARAH COPE** DUNDEE, NEW YORK

PREP/TOTAL TIME: 10 MIN. **MAKES:** 2 SERVINGS

    1½   cups frozen corn, thawed
    ⅛   teaspoon salt
    ⅛   teaspoon pepper
    1   tablespoon butter
    ¾   cup shredded cheddar cheese

In a small skillet, saute the corn, salt and pepper in butter until tender. Stir in cheddar cheese.

STUFFED PORK CHOPS WITH SHERRY SAUCE

Here's an entree for meat lovers! With a mushroom-ham stuffing and delectable sauce, it's a terrific treatment for pork chops.
—**DALE SMITH** GREENSBORO, NORTH CAROLINA

PREP: 20 MIN. **COOK:** 30 MIN. **MAKES:** 2 SERVINGS

- 2 **bone-in pork loin chops (1 inch thick and 8 ounces each)**
- ½ **cup sliced fresh mushrooms**
- ¼ **cup chopped onion**
- 3 **tablespoons butter, divided**
- ¼ **teaspoon dried oregano**
- ⅛ **teaspoon pepper**
- 2 **slices deli ham**
- ½ **cup sherry or chicken broth**
- 2 **teaspoons cornstarch**
- 1 **tablespoon cold water**

1. Cut a pocket in each pork chop by slicing almost to the bone; set aside.

2. In a large skillet, saute mushrooms and onion in 1 tablespoon butter until tender. Remove from the heat. Stir in oregano and pepper. Place a ham slice in the pocket of each pork chop; fill each with mushroom mixture.

3. In same skillet, brown the pork chops in remaining butter. Add the sherry, stirring to loosen the browned bits from the pan. Bring to a boil. Reduce heat; cover and simmer 20-25 minutes

or until a thermometer reads 160°. Remove the pork chops to a serving platter.

4. Combine cornstarch and water until smooth; gradually stir into the pan. Bring to a boil; cook and stir for 2 minutes or until thickened. Serve with pork chops.

MARSHMALLOW-TOPPED SWEET POTATOES

When I discovered baked sweet potatoes, I had fun experimenting with different ways of preparing them. One of my favorites is this marshmallow-topped version, which is perfectly sized for two.
—**MARY DAVIS** MONTROSE, IOWA

PREP: 1¼ HOURS **BAKE:** 25 MIN. **MAKES:** 2 SERVINGS

- 1 **large sweet potato**
- 1 **tablespoon butter**
- 1 **tablespoon honey**
- 2 **tablespoons chopped walnuts**
- 3 **tablespoons miniature marshmallows**

1. Scrub and pierce the sweet potato. Bake at 375° for 1 hour or until tender. When cool enough to handle, cut potato in half lengthwise. Scoop out the pulp, leaving thin shells.

2. In a small bowl, mash the pulp with butter and honey; stir in walnuts. Spoon into potato shells. Bake, uncovered, at 375° for 20 minutes. Top with marshmallows; bake 5-10 minutes longer or until marshmallows are toasted.

CHICKEN CURRY

My husband is a big fan of curry, so I look at other recipes he likes and try to find ones I can accent with that spice. When I added it to creamy slow-cooked chicken, he couldn't get enough!

—SHARON DELANEY-CHRONIS SOUTH MILWAUKEE, WISCONSIN

PREP: 20 MIN. **COOK:** 3 HOURS **MAKES:** 2 SERVINGS

- 1 small onion, sliced
- 1 tablespoon plus ⅓ cup water, divided
- ½ pound boneless skinless chicken breasts, cubed
- 1 small apple, peeled and chopped
- ¼ cup raisins
- 1 garlic clove, minced
- 1 teaspoon curry powder
- ¼ teaspoon ground ginger
- ⅛ teaspoon salt
- 1½ teaspoons all-purpose flour
- 1 teaspoon chicken bouillon granules
- ¾ teaspoon cornstarch
- ½ cup sour cream
- 1 tablespoon thinly sliced green onion
  Hot cooked rice

1. Place the onion and 1 tablespoon water in a microwave-safe bowl. Cover and microwave on high for 1 to 1½ minutes or until crisp-tender.

2. In a 1½-qt. slow cooker, combine chicken, apple, raisins, garlic, curry, ginger, salt and onion. Combine the flour, chicken bouillon and remaining water; pour over the chicken mixture. Cover and cook on low for 3 to 3½ hours or until the chicken juices run clear.

3. Remove the chicken mixture to a bowl; keep warm. Transfer the juices to a small saucepan. Combine the cornstarch and sour cream until smooth; add to the juices. Bring to a boil; cook and stir for 2 minutes or until thickened. Pour over chicken mixture; toss to coat. Sprinkle with green onion and serve with rice.

CHAPATI BREADS

These traditional Indian flatbreads are so easy and fun to prepare. Even when I might not need the full yield of 10 breads, I bake the entire batch knowing I'll probably have leftovers. They're great to use for wrap sandwiches for lunch the next day.

—JOYCE MCCARTHY SUSSEX, WISCONSIN

PREP: 20 MIN. **COOK:** 5 MIN./BATCH **MAKES:** 10 SERVINGS

- 1½ cups all-purpose flour
- ½ cup whole wheat flour
- 1 teaspoon salt
- ¼ teaspoon garlic powder
- ¾ cup hot water
- 2 tablespoons olive oil

1. In a large bowl, combine flours, salt and garlic powder. Stir in water and oil. Turn onto a floured surface; knead 10-12 times. Divide dough into 10 portions. On a lightly floured surface, roll each portion into a 6-in. circle.

2. In a large nonstick skillet, cook breads over medium heat for 1 minute on each side or until lightly browned. Keep warm.

SPICED GREEN BEANS

Want a new idea for the fresh-picked beans from your garden? Steam them until crisp-tender, then heat them in a buttery mix of ginger, celery seed and mustard. It's a simple, quick and tasty side dish I can pair with just about any entree.

—HOWARD PIERCE NAPERVILLE, ILLINOIS

PREP/TOTAL TIME: 20 MIN. **MAKES:** 2 SERVINGS

- ½ pound fresh green beans, trimmed
- 1 tablespoon butter
- ⅛ teaspoon celery seed
- ⅛ teaspoon ground ginger
- ⅛ teaspoon ground mustard
  Dash salt

1. Place the green beans in a steamer basket; place in a small saucepan over 1 in. of water. Bring to a boil; cover and steam for 8-10 minutes or until crisp-tender.

2. In a large skillet, melt butter. Add green beans, celery seed, ginger, mustard and salt; heat through.

MANGO LASSI

For the ideal thirst-quencher to serve with a home-cooked Indian dinner, try this beverage. The lassi, or yogurt drink, takes many different forms in India. The popular mango variation here is one of our favorite flavors and very refreshing—like a chilled liquid ice cream but without the fat and calories!

—NAMRATA TELUGU TERRE HAUTE, INDIANA

PREP/TOTAL TIME: 10 MIN. **MAKES:** 2 SERVINGS

- 1 cup fat-free plain yogurt
- 1 medium mango, peeled and cubed
- 2 cups ice cubes
- 3 tablespoons sugar
- 5 fresh mint leaves
- 2 cardamom pods, crushed, optional

In a blender, combine the plain yogurt, mango, ice cubes, sugar, mint leaves and cardamom pods if desired. Cover and process for 30-60 seconds or until blended. Pour into two chilled glasses; serve immediately.

CURRY CLUES

- A standard in the cuisine of India, curry powder is a yellowish blend that can contain up to 20 ground spices, herbs and seeds, often including chilies and black pepper.
- Curry's heat level varies based on the ingredients used. It can be found in both mild and hot versions.
- Curry powder imparts a distinctive flavor and rich golden color to recipes such as Curry Chicken (top left). Many cooks season dishes lightly with curry powder at first, then add more as desired to reach an acceptable spice level.

GRILLED SAUSAGES WITH PEPPERS

Try these zippy Italian sausages for your next cookout, and they just might become a new family favorite. Sweet-and-sour sautéed peppers make the perfect topping for the smoky links.

—TASTE OF HOME TEST KITCHEN

PREP/TOTAL TIME: 25 MIN. **MAKES:** 2 SERVINGS

- 2 teaspoons olive oil
- 1 small green pepper, julienned
- 1 small onion, thinly sliced
- 1 tablespoon brown sugar
- 1 tablespoon red wine vinegar
- 1 garlic clove, minced
   Dash salt
   Dash pepper
- 2 Italian sausage links (4 ounces each)
- 2 brat buns
   Spicy brown mustard, optional

1. Heat oil in a large skillet over medium-high heat. Add the green pepper and onion; cook and stir until softened. Stir in the brown sugar, vinegar, garlic, salt and pepper. Reduce the heat to medium-low; cook, stirring occasionally, 12-15 minutes or until golden brown.

2. Meanwhile, grill the sausages, covered, over medium heat 12-15 minutes or until no longer pink, turning occasionally. Serve in buns with the pepper mixture and, if desired, mustard.

BROCCOLI-CASHEW SALAD

Here's one of my go-to summer dishes. It's crunchy, refreshing and low in calories, too. Sometimes I turn it into a main course by adding cooked pasta and either chicken or shrimp.

—PEGGY STILSON SIDNEY, NEW YORK

PREP: 20 MIN. + CHILLING **MAKES:** 3 SERVINGS

- ⅔ cup fresh cauliflowerets
- ⅔ cup fresh broccoli florets
- ½ cup chopped zucchini
- ⅓ cup canned garbanzo beans or chickpeas, rinsed and drained
- ¼ cup chopped celery
- 3 tablespoons chopped red onion
- 2 tablespoons plain yogurt
- 2 tablespoons reduced-fat mayonnaise
- ⅛ teaspoon celery seed
- ⅛ teaspoon salt
- ⅛ teaspoon pepper
- 3 tablespoons chopped cashews

1. In a large bowl, combine the first six ingredients. In a small bowl, combine yogurt, mayonnaise, celery seed, salt and pepper. Pour over broccoli mixture and toss to coat.

2. Cover and refrigerate for 2 hours or until chilled. Just before serving, stir in cashews.

MACARONI SALAD

When everyone raved over my co-worker's macaroni salad, she shared the recipe. Now I often rely on it as a fast-to-fix, meatless lunch or dinner. Using leftover macaroni and cheese from the day before, I can whip up a meal in just 15 minutes.

—CHARLENE WORKMAN ATCHISON, KANSAS

PREP/TOTAL TIME: 15 MIN. **MAKES:** 2 SERVINGS

- 2 cups prepared macaroni and cheese
- ½ cup frozen peas, thawed
- ¼ cup chopped celery
- 1 tablespoon chopped onion
- 3 tablespoons mayonnaise
- ¼ teaspoon celery salt
- ¼ teaspoon celery seed

In a small bowl, combine the macaroni and cheese, peas, celery and onion. Combine the mayonnaise, celery salt and seed. Add to macaroni mixture; stir to coat.

TOASTED CORNED BEEF SANDWICHES

After finding inspiration in one of my old cookbooks, I assembled these toasted sandwiches. Anyone who likes corned beef will love them! They're quick, easy and satisfying.
—**SUSAN WESTERFIELD** ALBUQUERQUE, NEW MEXICO

PREP/TOTAL TIME: 30 MIN. **MAKES:** 2 SERVINGS

- ½ cup chopped cooked corned beef
- 2 tablespoons plus 1 teaspoon mayonnaise
- 2 tablespoons finely chopped celery
- 1 green onion, finely chopped
- ½ teaspoon prepared mustard
- 4 slices pumpernickel bread
- 2 slices Swiss cheese
- 1 tablespoon butter, softened

1. In a small bowl, combine the first five ingredients. Spread over two slices of bread. Top with cheese and remaining bread. Spread outside of sandwiches with butter.

2. In a small skillet over medium heat, toast the sandwiches for 2-3 minutes on each side or until cheese is melted.

PEPPERMINT BROWNIES

How do you make a brownie even better? Dress it up with creamy peppermint frosting and a drizzle of chocolate ganache!
—**HEIDI FARNWORTH** RIVERTON, UTAH

PREP: 20 MIN. **BAKE:** 30 MIN. + COOLING **MAKES:** 9 BROWNIES

- 1 package fudge brownie mix (8-inch square pan size)
- ⅓ cup semisweet chocolate chips
- 3 tablespoons plus 5 teaspoons heavy whipping cream, divided
- 2 tablespoons butter, softened
- ¾ cup confectioners' sugar
- ⅛ teaspoon peppermint extract
- 1 to 2 drops green food coloring, optional

1. Prepare and bake brownies according to package directions. Cool on a wire rack.

2. Meanwhile, place chocolate chips in a small bowl. In a small saucepan, bring 3 tablespoons cream just to a boil. Pour over the chocolate; whisk until smooth. Set aside.

3. In a small bowl, beat butter until fluffy. Add the confectioners' sugar, extract, remaining cream and food coloring if desired. Beat until smooth. Frost brownies. Drizzle chocolate over top.

Just Like Mom Made

*Craving the comfort of a home-style meal? Savor the heartwarming recipes here...
from creamy potato soup and classic chocolate cake to crunchy coleslaw and flaky biscuits.*

HOME-STYLE POTATO SOUP

I experimented with an old soup recipe until I hit on a variation
I love. Mashed potato flakes serve as a thickening agent, and bacon
lends savory flavor. Enjoy a bowlful with fresh-baked breadsticks
or your favorite sandwich on a chilly day.

—CAROL HENSON INDEPENDENCE, KANSAS

PREP/TOTAL TIME: 30 MIN. **MAKES:** 2 SERVINGS

- 2 **tablespoons finely chopped onion**
- 2 **tablespoons chopped celery**
- 1 **teaspoon canola oil**
- 2 **medium Yukon Gold potatoes, peeled and diced**
- 1½ **cups water**
- ½ **teaspoon chicken bouillon granules**
- ¼ **teaspoon salt**
- ¼ **teaspoon pepper**
- ½ **cup 2% milk**
- ¼ **cup mashed potato flakes**
- 1 **ounce process cheese (Velveeta), cubed**
- 1 **bacon strip, cooked and crumbled**

1. In a small saucepan, saute the onion and celery in oil until
tender. Add potatoes, water, chicken bouillon, salt and pepper.
Bring to a boil. Reduce heat; cover and simmer for 10-12 minutes
or until potatoes are tender.

2. Stir in milk and potato flakes; cook and stir 8 minutes longer.
Stir in cheese until melted. Sprinkle servings with bacon.

MOM'S COLESLAW

Mom came up with her signature coleslaw when I was a child, and
I made a few changes to suit my taste. It's the only coleslaw I'll eat!
Reduced-fat mayo and sour cream make it a little lighter.

—RONNI RUSSELL BEACON FALLS, CONNECTICUT

PREP/TOTAL TIME: 20 MIN. **MAKES:** 2 SERVINGS

- 1½ **cups shredded cabbage**
- 2 **tablespoons shredded carrot**
- 1 **tablespoon chopped sweet red pepper**
- 1 **tablespoon chopped green pepper**
- 2 **tablespoons plus 1 teaspoon reduced-fat sour cream**
- 1½ **teaspoons reduced-fat mayonnaise**
- 1 **teaspoon red wine vinegar**
- ½ **teaspoon sugar**
- ¼ **teaspoon celery seed**
- ¼ **teaspoon salt**

In a large bowl, combine the cabbage, carrot and peppers. In a
small bowl, whisk the sour cream, mayonnaise, vinegar, sugar,
celery seed and salt. Pour over the cabbage mixture; toss to coat.
Chill until serving.

OLD-FASHIONED CHOCOLATE CAKE

Here's a classic cake you'll want to bake again and again. Mashed potatoes give it a hearty texture, and the chocolate flavor isn't too rich. For a pretty finish, add a dusting of confectioners' sugar.
—**CHARLIE ADKINS** PRESTONSBURG, KENTUCKY

PREP: 20 MIN. **BAKE:** 25 MIN. **MAKES:** 9 SERVINGS

- ½ cup shortening
- 1 cup sugar
- 2 eggs
- ⅓ cup mashed potatoes (without added milk and butter)
- 1 teaspoon vanilla extract
- 1 cup all-purpose flour
- 3 tablespoons baking cocoa
- ½ teaspoon baking soda
- ½ teaspoon salt
- ⅓ cup buttermilk
- ½ cup chopped walnuts
  Confectioners' sugar

1. In a large bowl, cream the shortening and sugar until light and fluffy. Add the eggs, one at a time, beating well after each addition. Stir in the mashed potatoes and vanilla. Combine the flour, cocoa, baking soda and salt; add to the creamed mixture alternately with buttermilk, beating well after each addition.
2. Pour into a greased and floured 9-in. square baking pan; sprinkle with walnuts. Bake at 350° for 30-35 minutes or until a toothpick inserted near the center comes out clean. Cool completely. Dust with confectioners' sugar.

OLD-FASHIONED BUTTERMILK BISCUITS

My family keeps grabbing more of these goodies until the basket is empty. The tender, golden-brown biscuits go with many different meals and are best served warm from the oven.
—**WENDY MASTERS** GRAND VALLEY, ONTARIO

PREP/TOTAL TIME: 20 MIN. **MAKES:** 8 BISCUITS

- 1¾ cups all-purpose flour
- 2 teaspoons baking powder
- ½ teaspoon baking soda
- ½ teaspoon sugar
- ¼ teaspoon salt
- ⅔ cup buttermilk
- 2 tablespoons canola oil
- 1 tablespoon reduced-fat sour cream

1. In a large bowl, combine the flour, baking powder, baking soda, sugar and salt. Combine buttermilk, oil and sour cream; stir into flour mixture just until moistened. Turn onto a lightly floured surface; knead 8-10 times.
2. Pat or roll out dough to ½-in. thickness; cut with a floured 2½-in. biscuit cutter. Place 2 in. apart on an ungreased baking sheet. Bake at 400° for 8-12 minutes or until lightly golden brown. Serve warm.

BISCUIT BOOST
When I don't have time to fix biscuits from scratch, I use refrigerated dough and brush the tops of the biscuits with Italian salad dressing before baking. They're great, especially with spaghetti.
—**LAURA HELFRITZ** NEW ORLEANS, LOUISIANA

SWITCHMAN SANDWICHES

I reproduced one of the specialties served at a unique Ramona, California restaurant. The eatery was housed in the original town telephone office, complete with memorabilia, and all menu items were named after old telephone lingo. The open-face sandwiches I duplicated are loaded with flavor and visual appeal.

—JOYCE HRIN SURPRISE, ARIZONA

PREP/TOTAL TIME: 25 MIN. **MAKES:** 2 SANDWICHES

- 4 slices dark rye bread
- 4 teaspoons reduced-fat mayonnaise
- ¼ pound sliced deli turkey
- ¼ pound sliced deli ham
- 4 medium fresh mushrooms, sliced
- 1 small tomato, thinly sliced
- ½ cup alfalfa sprouts
- ½ cup shredded reduced-fat cheddar cheese

1. Spread bread slices with mayonnaise. Layer two slices with turkey, ham, mushrooms, tomato, sprouts and cheese. Top with remaining bread.

2. Transfer to an ungreased baking sheet. Bake at 350° for 10-12 minutes or until cheese is melted.

DOUBLE CHOCOLATE MALTS

In the heat of summertime, what could be more of a treat than a chocolate malt? I top off each cool glass with crushed malted milk balls, whipped cream and a maraschino cherry.

—TARYN KUEBELBECK PLYMOUTH, MINNESOTA

PREP/TOTAL TIME: 10 MIN. **MAKES:** 2 SERVINGS

- ¾ cup 2% milk
- 2 tablespoons malted milk powder
- 2 tablespoons chocolate syrup
- 2 cups low-fat chocolate frozen yogurt
  Whipped cream, maraschino cherries and crushed malted milk balls

1. In a blender, combine the milk, malted milk powder and chocolate syrup; cover and process until blended. Add yogurt; cover and process for 30 seconds or until smooth.

2. Pour into chilled glasses. Garnish malts with whipped cream, cherries and crushed candies; serve immediately.

ZESTY SPINACH DIP

When I wanted a low-fat appetizer for a get-together, I whipped up a simple but zippy spinach dip in 15 minutes. Pair it with your favorite veggies or bread cubes as dippers.

—NOELLE MYERS GRAND FORKS, NORTH DAKOTA

PREP: 15 MIN. + CHILLING **MAKES:** 1 CUP

- ½ cup fat-free plain yogurt
- 1 ounce fat-free cream cheese
- 2 teaspoons thinly sliced green onion
- 2 teaspoons finely chopped sweet yellow pepper
- 2 teaspoons finely chopped sweet red pepper
- 2 teaspoons Italian salad dressing mix
- ⅛ teaspoon ground nutmeg
- 1 cup frozen leaf spinach, thawed and squeezed dry
  Carrot sticks

In a small bowl, combine the first eight ingredients. Cover and refrigerate for at least 1 hour before serving. Serve dip with carrot sticks.

PEACH-BERRY PIE

The sweeter and fresher your fruit, the yummier this pie will be. Colorful blueberries, strawberries and bits of peach make each slice pretty as a picture—and absolutely irresistible!

—GENISE KRAUSE STURGEON BAY, WISCONSIN

PREP: 35 MIN. + CHILLING **MAKES:** 2 SERVINGS

- ½ cup all-purpose flour
- ⅛ teaspoon salt
- 2 tablespoons shortening
- 2 tablespoons cold water

FILLING

- ⅓ cup sugar
- 1 tablespoon cornstarch
- ⅛ teaspoon salt
- ¼ cup water
- ½ cup chopped peeled fresh peach
- ½ cup fresh blueberries
- ½ cup sliced fresh strawberries
  Whipped cream, optional

1. In a small bowl, combine the flour and salt; cut in shortening until crumbly. Gradually add the water, tossing with a fork until dough forms a ball. Cover and refrigerate for 15 minutes or until easy to handle.

2. Roll out the pastry to fit a 5-in. pie plate. Transfer the pastry to pie plate. Trim the pastry to ½ in. beyond the edge of plate; flute the edges. Line the unpricked pastry shell with a double thickness of heavy-duty foil. Fill with dried beans, uncooked rice or pie weights.

3. Bake at 450° for 5 minutes. Remove the foil and weights; bake 5-7 minutes longer or until golden brown. Cool on a wire rack.

4. In a small saucepan, combine the sugar, cornstarch and salt. Stir in the water until smooth; add the peach. Bring to a boil, stirring constantly. Cook and stir for 2 minutes or until thickened. Remove from the heat; stir in the berries. Let stand for 15 minutes. Pour into crust.

5. Refrigerate for 3 hours before serving. Garnish with whipped cream if desired.

Editor's Note: *Let pie weights cool before storing. Beans and rice may be reused for pie weights, but not for cooking.*

JUST PEACHY

Buy peaches that give slightly to palm pressure and have an intense fragrance. Avoid peaches that are hard or have soft spots. Store ripe fruit in a plastic bag in the refrigerator for up to 5 days.

In a small bowl, combine orange yogurt and whipped topping; fold in the mandarin oranges and miniature marshmallows. Refrigerate for 30 minutes before serving. Garnish servings with banana slices.

THE BEST SALSA

The name of this zippy, not-too-spicy salsa says it all. At parties, I always get requests for the recipe. My husband once spotted a woman eating it out of the bowl with a spoon!

—KIMMEL KONKA DAVIDSONVILLE, MARYLAND

PREP/TOTAL TIME: 15 MIN. **MAKES:** 1½ CUPS

- ½ cup canned drained diced tomatoes
- ¼ cup tomato sauce
- 4 teaspoons canned chopped green chilies
- 4 teaspoons chopped pitted ripe olives
- 2 teaspoons thinly sliced green onion
- 2 teaspoons red wine vinegar
- 2 teaspoons olive oil
- 1 small garlic clove, minced
   Dash salt
   Dash cayenne pepper
   Tortilla chips

In a large bowl, combine all ingredients; chill until serving. Serve with tortilla chips.

WATERMELON-BLUEBERRY SALAD

For a great summertime salad, try tossing chunks of watermelon and blueberries with a dressing of honey, lemon juice and mint. The flavor combination is cool and refreshing.

—TASTE OF HOME TEST KITCHEN

PREP/TOTAL TIME: 5 MIN. **MAKES:** 2 SERVINGS

- 1 tablespoon honey
- ¾ teaspoon lemon juice
- ½ teaspoon minced fresh mint
- 1 cup seeded chopped watermelon
- ½ cup fresh blueberries

In a small bowl, combine the honey, lemon juice and mint. Add the watermelon and blueberries; toss gently to coat. Chill until serving.

ORANGE CREAM DELIGHT

This creamy, fluffy dessert is guaranteed to satisfy anyone's sweet tooth. It comes together in only 5 minutes and chills in the fridge until mealtime. For a garnish, I add sliced bananas.

—CHRISTINA SMITH DUNMORE, PENNSYLVANIA

PREP: 5 MIN. + CHILLING **MAKES:** 2 SERVINGS

- 1 carton (4 ounces) whipped orange yogurt
- ¾ cup fat-free whipped topping
- ½ cup canned mandarin oranges
- ¼ cup miniature marshmallows
- 1 small banana, sliced

COCONUT KISSES

Made with just three ingredients, my coconut goodies are a nice option when you want something a little bit lighter for your holiday cookie tray. They're crisp on the outside and chewy on the inside.

—**DOROTHY BEAUDRY** ALBERTVILLE, MINNESOTA

PREP: 15 MIN. **BAKE:** 20 MIN. **MAKES:** 1 DOZEN

- 1 **egg white**
- ½ **cup confectioners' sugar**
- 1 **cup flaked coconut**

1. Place the egg white in a small bowl; let stand at room temperature for 30 minutes.

2. Beat the egg white on medium speed until soft peaks form. Gradually beat in the confectioners' sugar, 1 tablespoon at a time, on high until stiff peaks form. Fold in the coconut. Drop by rounded tablespoonfuls 2 in. apart onto a parchment paper-lined baking sheet.

3. Bake at 325° for 18-20 minutes or until firm to the touch. Cool for 1 minute before removing to a wire rack. Store in an airtight container.

ITALIAN FRITTATA

Here's an old family favorite. The veggie-packed, meatless frittata is a satisfying choice for breakfast—or even dinner.

—MARLENE KROLL CHICAGO, ILLINOIS

PREP/TOTAL TIME: 25 MIN. **MAKES:** 2 SERVINGS

- 1 **package (6 ounces) fresh baby spinach**
- 4 **eggs, lightly beaten**
- 1 **tablespoon diced pimientos, drained**
- 2 **teaspoons Italian seasoning**
- 2 **teaspoons minced fresh parsley or ¾ teaspoon dried parsley flakes**
- 1⅓ **cups sliced fresh mushrooms**
- 4 **green onions, finely chopped**
- 2 **tablespoons butter**
- 2 **teaspoons olive oil**
- 4 **teaspoons grated Parmesan cheese**
  Dash salt

1. In a large saucepan, bring ½ in. of water to a boil. Add the spinach; cover and boil for 3-5 minutes or until wilted. Meanwhile, in a large bowl, whisk the eggs, pimientos, Italian seasoning and parsley; set aside.

2. Drain the spinach and pat dry. In a 7-in. ovenproof skillet, saute the mushrooms and green onions in butter and oil until tender. Reduce heat; sprinkle with spinach, Parmesan cheese and salt. Top with egg mixture. Cover and cook for 4-6 minutes or until nearly set.

3. Uncover skillet. Broil 3-4 in. from the heat for 2-3 minutes or until the eggs are completely set. Let stand for 5 minutes before cutting.

BLUEBERRY LEMON BREAD

With the texture of pound cake, this special blueberry quick bread featuring a twist of citrus might remind you of a dessert. I like to serve thick slices with honey butter or lemon curd.

—NANCY KUSCH MADISON, WISCONSIN

PREP: 15 MIN. **BAKE:** 50 MIN. + COOLING **MAKES:** 1 MINI LOAF

- 2 **tablespoons butter, softened**
- ½ **cup sugar**
- 1 **egg**
- 1 **teaspoon grated lemon peel**
- 1 **cup all-purpose flour**
- ½ **teaspoon baking powder**
- ¼ **teaspoon salt**
- ¼ **cup 2% milk**
- ½ **cup fresh or frozen blueberries**

TOPPING

- 1 **tablespoon sugar**
- 1 **teaspoon lemon juice**

1. In a small bowl, cream butter and sugar. Add egg and lemon peel; beat well. Combine the flour, baking powder and salt; add to creamed mixture alternately with milk. Fold in blueberries. Pour into a greased 5¾-in. x 3-in. x 2-in. loaf pan.

2. Bake at 350° for 45-50 minutes or until a toothpick inserted near the center comes out clean. Cool for 10 minutes before removing from pan to a wire rack. Combine topping ingredients; spread over warm bread.

Editor's Note: *If using frozen blueberries, use without thawing to avoid discoloring the batter.*

GLAZED BACON

Sprinkled with a nutty brown-sugar mixture, these glazed strips boast a wonderful sweet-and-salty flavor combination. Once you taste them, you may never want to go back to plain bacon!

—HEATHER CARDEIRO KING OF PRUSSIA, PENNSYLVANIA

PREP: 10 MIN. **BAKE:** 25 MIN. **MAKES:** 2 SERVINGS

- ¼ **cup finely chopped walnuts**
- 2 **tablespoons dark brown sugar**
- ½ **teaspoon all-purpose flour**
- 6 **thick-sliced bacon strips**

In a small bowl, combine the walnuts, brown sugar and flour. Place bacon on a greased broiler pan; sprinkle with the walnut mixture. Bake at 350° for 25-30 minutes or until golden brown.

BUTTERMILK-OAT PANCAKES

My buttermilk flapjacks have the hearty, healthy addition of oats. Just choose your favorite pancake syrup, and you'll have a filling treat to get everyone going in the morning.

—BARBARA BRUNNER STEELTON, PENNSYLVANIA

PREP/TOTAL TIME: 30 MIN. **MAKES:** 8 PANCAKES

- ¾ **cup buttermilk**
- ½ **cup old-fashioned oats**
- 1 **egg**
- ¼ **cup 2% milk**
- 2 **tablespoons canola oil**
- ½ **cup all-purpose flour**
- 1 **tablespoon sugar**
- 1 **teaspoon baking powder**
- ½ **teaspoon baking soda**
  Strawberry pancake syrup

1. In a large bowl, combine the buttermilk and oats; let stand for 5 minutes. Stir in the egg, milk and oil. Combine the flour, sugar, baking powder and baking soda; stir into the oat mixture just until moistened.

2. Pour the batter by ¼ cupfuls onto a greased hot griddle; turn when bubbles form on top of pancakes. Cook until second side is lightly browned. Serve with syrup.

POURING PANCAKES

To make pancakes in a fuss-free way, I mix prepared pancake batter in a pitcher. There are no messy drips when I'm pouring, and any extra batter can be refrigerated in the covered pitcher.

—LINDA J. TOIVOLA, MICHIGAN

1. In a large bowl, combine flour, cornmeal and sugar. In a small bowl, combine the egg, milk, oil, vanilla and butter flavoring. Stir into dry ingredients just until moistened.

2. Fill greased muffin cups three-fourths full. Bake at 400° for 15-18 minutes or until a toothpick inserted near the center comes out clean. Cool for 10 minutes before removing from pan to a wire rack to cool completely.

Editor's Note: *As a substitute for self-rising flour, place 1 teaspoon baking powder and ¼ teaspoon salt in a measuring cup. Add all-purpose flour to measure ⅔ cup.*

APPLE RAISIN PIE

Want something comforting for dessert? Try a good old-fashioned apple pie featuring raisins and a crunchy walnut topping.
—**ARNOLD BEATLEY** PORTOLA, CALIFORNIA

PREP: 15 MIN. **BAKE:** 50 MIN. **MAKES:** 4 SERVINGS

- 1 sheet refrigerated pie pastry
- 2 medium tart apples, peeled and thinly sliced
- 1 tablespoon plus ½ cup sugar, divided
- 1½ teaspoons ground cinnamon
- ½ cup all-purpose flour
- ¼ cup chopped walnuts
- ¼ cup raisins
- ¼ cup butter, melted
- 2 tablespoons beaten egg

1. Cut the pastry sheet in half. Repackage and refrigerate one half of sheet for another use. On a lightly floured surface, roll out the remaining half into an 8-in. circle. Transfer to a 7-in. pie plate; flute the edges.

2. In a large bowl, combine the apples, 1 tablespoon sugar and cinnamon; place in the crust. In a small bowl, combine the flour, walnuts, raisins, butter, egg and remaining sugar; spoon over the top. Bake at 350° for 50-55 minutes or until the topping is golden brown and the fruit is tender, covering edges with foil to prevent overbrowning if necessary. Cool on a wire rack.

TACO SALAD

In spring, we replace the heavier fare of winter with menus that are light and refreshing. Featuring popular taco fixings such as olives and tomatoes, my Southwestern salad really fills the bill.
—**MURIEL BERTRAND** SHOREVIEW, MINNESOTA

PREP/TOTAL TIME: 25 MIN. **MAKES:** 2 SERVINGS

- ½ pound ground beef
- ⅓ cup bean dip
- 1 teaspoon chili powder
- ¼ teaspoon salt
- 1 cup canned diced tomatoes plus 2 tablespoons liquid
- 2 cups chopped lettuce
- ½ cup shredded cheddar cheese
- 2 green onions, sliced
- 2 tablespoons sliced ripe olives
- ½ cup corn chips

1. In a large skillet, cook beef over medium heat until no longer pink; drain. Stir in bean dip, chili powder, salt and tomato liquid. Remove from the heat.

2. In a large bowl, combine tomatoes, lettuce, cheddar cheese, onions and olives. Add beef mixture; toss to coat. Top with chips. Serve immediately.

BUTTERY CORN MUFFINS

I love the sweet taste of these corn muffins warm from the oven. They're especially good with butter and honey for breakfast, but I've also baked them in miniature muffin pans and served them for afternoon tea. It's easy to make a larger batch if needed.
—**CATHERINE LAMPMAN** HENDERSONVILLE, TENNESSEE

PREP/TOTAL TIME: 25 MIN. **MAKES:** 6 SERVINGS

- ⅔ cup self-rising flour
- ⅓ cup yellow cornmeal
- 2 tablespoons sugar
- 1 egg
- ½ cup 2% milk
- 2 tablespoons canola oil
- ¼ teaspoon vanilla extract
- ½ teaspoon butter flavoring

PINEAPPLE-BACON BAKED BEANS

Here's great way to dress up a can of baked beans. Tangy bits of pineapple and crumbled bacon add fantastic flavor.
—**WILLIAM & JEAN BLACK** LIVINGSTON, TEXAS

PREP/TOTAL TIME: 30 MIN. **MAKES:** 3 SERVINGS

- 1 **can (16 ounces) baked beans**
- ¼ **cup unsweetened crushed pineapple**
- ¼ **cup ketchup**
- 3 **bacon strips, cooked and crumbled**
- 1 **teaspoon prepared mustard**
- ½ **teaspoon ground mustard**
- ¼ **cup packed brown sugar**
- 1 **tablespoon butter, cubed**

1. In a small bowl, combine the first six ingredients. Transfer to a greased 1-qt. baking dish. Sprinkle with brown sugar and dot with butter.
2. Cover and bake at 400° for 20-25 minutes or until heated through.

POOR MAN'S HASH

More than 75 years old, my mother's recipe for hash still goes over well with everyone who tries it. I like the fact that this simple but tasty dish comes together on the stovetop in less than half an hour, so a hot lunch or dinner is on the table fast.
—**DOROTHY BROYLES** PETERSTOWN, WEST VIRGINIA

PREP/TOTAL TIME: 25 MIN. **MAKES:** 2 SERVINGS

- 1 **tablespoon butter**
- 2 **cups cubed peeled potatoes**
- 5 **ounces SPAM luncheon meat, finely chopped**
- ¾ **cup 2% milk**
- 1 **small onion, chopped**
- 1 **tablespoon minced fresh parsley**
- ¼ **teaspoon pepper**
- ⅛ **teaspoon salt**

In a large skillet, melt butter over medium-high heat. Stir in the remaining ingredients. Cook and stir for 10-12 minutes or until browned and potatoes are tender.

PINEAPPLE-GLAZED FRUIT MEDLEY

This recipe adds a tangy glaze to pineapple chunks, banana slices and grapes. It can be served as either a dessert or a side dish.

—TASTE OF HOME TEST KITCHEN

PREP/TOTAL TIME: 15 MIN. **MAKES:** 2 SERVINGS

- 1 can (8 ounces) pineapple chunks
- 1 small banana, sliced
- 6 green grapes, halved
- 1 tablespoon sugar
- 1 teaspoon cornstarch
- 1 teaspoon apricot preserves
- ½ teaspoon lemon juice

1. Drain pineapple, reserving juice. In a small bowl, combine the pineapple, banana and grapes; set aside.
2. In a small saucepan, combine sugar, cornstarch and reserved pineapple juice. Bring to a boil. Reduce heat; cook and stir for 2-3 minutes or until thickened. Remove from the heat; stir in preserves and lemon juice. Cool completely. Pour over fruit and toss gently to coat.

HERBED FRENCH FRIES

Love French fries but not all the fat? They're just as delicious—and healthier, too—when you toss the potato strips with a combination of fresh herbs and other seasonings, then bake.

—LORA GLENN ELKADER, IOWA

PREP: 15 MIN. **BAKE:** 40 MIN. **MAKES:** 2 SERVINGS

- 1 tablespoon olive oil
- ¾ teaspoon minced fresh basil
- ¾ teaspoon minced fresh oregano
- ¾ teaspoon minced fresh rosemary
- 1 small garlic clove, minced
- ¼ teaspoon Italian seasoning
- ⅛ teaspoon salt
- ⅛ teaspoon pepper
  Dash chili powder
- 2 medium potatoes, peeled and cut into thin strips

1. In a small bowl, combine the first nine ingredients. Add the potatoes; toss to coat.
2. Transfer to a 15-in. x 10-in. x 1-in. baking pan coated with cooking spray. Bake at 400° for 40-45 minutes or until tender, turning once.

PUMPKIN PUDDING DESSERTS

Pumpkin is a treat usually reserved for fall and winter, but I enjoy this pudding so much, I indulge year-round! If you like, garnish it with a dash of cinnamon after the dollop of whipped topping.

—STEPHANIE CARLEY DODGEVILLE, WISCONSIN

PREP/TOTAL TIME: 10 MIN. **MAKES:** 2 SERVINGS

- ¾ cup canned pumpkin
- ½ teaspoon ground cinnamon
- ¼ teaspoon ground ginger
- ¾ cup cold 2% milk
- 1 package (3.3 ounces) instant white chocolate pudding mix
- ¼ cup whipped topping

1. In a small bowl, whisk the pumpkin, cinnamon and ginger. Add the milk and chocolate pudding mix; whisk for 2 minutes (mixture will be thick).
2. Transfer to individual serving dishes. Refrigerate until serving. Garnish servings with whipped topping.

BEST-EVER GRILLED CHEESE SANDWICHES

When it comes to classic grilled cheese sandwiches, these are the best! Feel free to experiment with different ingredients, such as a sprinkling of Parmesan cheese or a spoonful of salsa.

—**EDIE DESPAIN** LOGAN, UTAH

PREP/TOTAL TIME: 20 MIN. **MAKES:** 2 SERVINGS

- 2 **tablespoons mayonnaise**
- 1 **teaspoon Dijon mustard**
- 4 **slices sourdough bread**
- 2 **slices Swiss cheese**
- 2 **slices cheddar cheese**
- 2 **slices sweet onion**
- 1 **medium tomato, sliced**
- 6 **cooked bacon strips**
- 2 **tablespoons butter, softened**

1. Combine the mayonnaise and Dijon mustard; spread over two bread slices. Layer with the cheeses, sweet onion, tomato and bacon; top with the remaining bread. Spread the outsides of sandwiches with butter.

2. In a small skillet over medium heat, toast the sandwiches for 2-3 minutes on each side or until the cheese is melted.

CUT-OUT BISCUITS

These biscuits come out so light and fluffy, I think of them as cloud puffs! They can be enjoyed hot or cold any time of day, whether for breakfast, tea, lunch, snacking or dinner.

—**SANDRA KREUTER** BURNEY, CALIFORNIA

PREP/TOTAL TIME: 25 MIN.   **MAKES:** 3 BISCUITS

  1 **cup self-rising flour**
 4½ **teaspoons cold butter**
  ¼ **cup ginger ale**
  1 **tablespoon sour cream**
  1 **tablespoon mayonnaise**
TOPPING
  2 **teaspoons butter, melted**
  ½ **teaspoon sugar**

1. Place the flour in a small bowl. Cut in the butter until the mixture resembles coarse crumbs. In another bowl, combine the ginger ale, sour cream and mayonnaise; stir into the flour mixture just until moistened. Turn onto a lightly floured surface; knead 8-10 times.

2. Pat out to ¾-in. thickness; cut with a floured 2½-in. biscuit cutter. Place 2 in. apart on an ungreased baking sheet. Brush with butter; sprinkle with sugar. Bake at 400° for 9-11 minutes or until lightly browned. Serve warm.

Editor's Notes: *As a substitute for 1 cup of self-rising flour, place 1½ teaspoons baking powder and ½ teaspoon salt in a measuring cup. Add all-purpose flour to measure 1 cup. Reduced-fat or fat-free mayonnaise is not recommended for this recipe.*

COFFEE ALMOND FLOATS

I experimented until I created a homemade version of my favorite coffeehouse drink. It's fun to serve these floats in fancy glasses. For an extra treat, add a maraschino cherry on top.

—**JILL GARN** CHARLOTTE, MICHIGAN

PREP/TOTAL TIME: 10 MIN.   **MAKES:** 2 SERVINGS

  2 **tablespoons instant coffee granules**
  1 **tablespoon hot water**
  2 **cups 2% milk**
  2 **tablespoons brown sugar**
  ⅛ **teaspoon almond extract**
  2 **scoops vanilla ice cream**

In a small pitcher, dissolve coffee granules in hot water. Add the milk, brown sugar and extract. Place a scoop of ice cream in each of two chilled glasses; pour coffee mixture over top.

ICE CREAM EASE

If your ice cream is too hard to scoop, put the whole container in the microwave on high for 15-20 seconds. The ice cream will soften just enough.

—**SUE B.** APOLLO, PENNSYLVANIA

CABBAGE & MEATBALLS

A dill pickle is the secret ingredient in this simple yet satisfying meatball dish. When our children were young, they weren't very fond of cabbage—but they loved this!

—**CHARLOTTE COLE** POINT ORCHARD, WASHINGTON

PREP: 20 MIN. **COOK:** 15 MIN. **MAKES:** 2 SERVINGS

- 3 cups chopped cabbage
- 1 cup tomato juice
- 1 egg, beaten
- 1 small onion, chopped
- 1 tablespoon chili powder
- 1 tablespoon cider vinegar
- 1 tablespoon chopped dill pickle
- ½ teaspoon salt
- ¼ teaspoon pepper
- ¾ pound lean ground beef (90% lean)

1. Place the cabbage in a large saucepan; add the tomato juice. Cover and simmer over low heat. Meanwhile, combine the egg, onion, chili powder, vinegar, pickle, salt and pepper. Crumble beef over the mixture and mix well. Shape into 2-in. balls. Add to the cabbage mixture.

2. Cover and cook over low heat for 15-20 minutes or until meat is no longer pink, stirring occasionally.

SAVORY GREEN BEANS WITH BACON

As a busy working mom, I'm always looking for ways to reduce my time in the kitchen. Through the years, I've tried different ways of livening up canned and frozen vegetables. My family was thrilled when I mixed beans and mushrooms with bacon.

—**DANETTE FOX** MONTGOMERY, ALABAMA

PREP/TOTAL TIME: 25 MIN. **MAKES:** 2 SERVINGS

- 2 cups frozen cut green beans
- 2 tablespoons canned mushroom stems and pieces

- 1½ teaspoons dried minced onion
- 1 bacon strip, diced
- ¼ teaspoon salt
- ¼ teaspoon butter
- ⅛ teaspoon garlic powder
- ⅛ teaspoon pepper

In a small saucepan, combine all ingredients; add enough water to cover. Bring to a boil. Reduce the heat; cover and simmer for 13-15 minutes or until bacon is cooked. Drain.

EFFORTLESS BROCCOLI SOUP

Want a soup recipe that serves just a few people? This broccoli blend is easy to fix and makes a wonderful meal for two.

—**BETTY VAUGHN** ELKHART, INDIANA

PREP/TOTAL TIME: 30 MIN. **MAKES:** 2 SERVINGS

- ¼ cup chopped onion
- 2 tablespoons butter
- 2 cups chopped fresh broccoli
- 1 can (14½ ounces) reduced-sodium chicken broth
- ½ teaspoon garlic powder
- ¼ teaspoon pepper
- ⅛ teaspoon salt
  Sour cream, optional

1. In a large saucepan, saute the onion in butter until tender. Add the broccoli, chicken broth, garlic powder, pepper and salt. Bring to a boil. Reduce heat; cover and simmer for 10-12 minutes or until broccoli is tender. Cool slightly.

2. In a blender, cover and process the soup until smooth. Return to the pan and heat through. Garnish servings with sour cream if desired.

MEALS IN MINUTES

A super-fast main dish helps get breakfast, lunch or dinner on the table in a flash. Your family will be sitting down to eat in no time when you choose from the tasty entrees here— all ready to serve in just 30 minutes or less!

TURKEY PENNE WITH LEMON CREAM SAUCE

You'll please even the pickiest palates at the table when you serve a colorful mixture of penne pasta, turkey, broccoli, carrots and more. It's a great way to get fresh veggies on your menu.
—TASTE OF HOME TEST KITCHEN

PREP/TOTAL TIME: 30 MIN. **MAKES:** 4 SERVINGS

- 2 **cups uncooked penne pasta**
- ½ **pound turkey breast cutlets, cut into ¾-inch pieces**
- 3 **tablespoons butter, divided**
- 2 **cups fresh broccoli florets**
- 3 **small carrots, thinly sliced**
- 2 **garlic cloves, minced**
- 2 **tablespoons all-purpose flour**
- 1½ **teaspoons chicken bouillon granules**
- ½ **teaspoon dried thyme**
- ¼ **teaspoon pepper**
- ⅛ **teaspoon salt**
- 2½ **cups half-and-half cream**
- ¼ **cup lemon juice**
- 2 **plum tomatoes, seeded and chopped**

1. Cook pasta according to package directions. Meanwhile, in a large skillet, saute turkey in 1 tablespoon butter until no longer pink. Remove and keep warm.

2. In the same skillet, saute broccoli and carrots in remaining butter until crisp-tender. Add the garlic; cook 1 minute longer. Stir in the flour, chicken bouillon granules, thyme, pepper and salt until blended. Combine cream and lemon juice; gradually stir into the broccoli mixture. Bring to a boil; cook and stir for 2-3 minutes or until thickened.

3. Drain the pasta; add to the skillet. Stir in turkey and tomatoes and heat through.

SPICED PORK MEDALLIONS WITH BOURBON SAUCE

I don't remember where I discovered this recipe, but it has since become one of my favorite entrees for company. I usually pair the saucy medallions with a side of roasted vegetables.
—KATHY KANTRUD FENTON, MICHIGAN

PREP/TOTAL TIME: 25 MIN. **MAKES:** 4 SERVINGS

- ½ **cup bourbon or reduced-sodium chicken broth**
- ¼ **cup packed dark brown sugar**
- 3 **tablespoons white vinegar**
- 3 **tablespoons reduced-sodium soy sauce**
- 2 **garlic cloves, minced**
- ½ **teaspoon pepper**
- ½ **teaspoon chili powder**
- ¼ **teaspoon ground cinnamon**
- ⅛ **teaspoon salt**
- ⅛ **teaspoon ground allspice**
- 1 **pork tenderloin (1 pound), cut into 12 slices**

1. In a small saucepan, combine bourbon, brown sugar, vinegar, soy sauce, garlic and pepper. Bring to a boil; cook until liquid is reduced to about ½ cup, stirring occasionally.

2. Meanwhile, combine the chili powder, cinnamon, salt and allspice; rub over pork slices.

3. In a large skillet coated with cooking spray, cook the pork over medium heat for 2-4 minutes on each side or until tender. Serve with sauce.

HAMBURGER STEAKS WITH MUSHROOM GRAVY

Here's a real meat-and-potatoes dinner no one will want to miss. The simple mushroom gravy adds wonderful flavor.

—DENISE WHEELER NEWAYGO, MICHIGAN

PREP/TOTAL TIME: 25 MIN. **MAKES:** 4 SERVINGS

- 1 egg
- ½ cup dry bread crumbs
- 1 envelope onion soup mix, divided
  Dash pepper
- 1 pound ground beef
- 3 tablespoons all-purpose flour
- 1¾ cups cold water
- 1 teaspoon Worcestershire sauce
- 1 jar (4½ ounces) whole mushrooms, drained
  Hot cooked mashed potatoes

1. In a large bowl, combine the egg, bread crumbs, 2 tablespoons soup mix and pepper. Crumble beef over mixture and mix well. Shape into four patties.

2. In a large skillet, cook the patties over medium heat for 4-5 minutes on each side or until a thermometer reads 160° and juices run clear. Set aside and keep warm.

3. Combine flour, water, Worcestershire sauce and remaining soup mix until blended; stir into skillet. Add mushrooms. Bring to a boil; cook and stir for 5 minutes or until thickened. Serve with patties and mashed potatoes.

TILAPIA TOSTADAS

Even my non-fish-loving family likes these tilapia-topped tostadas. Reduced-fat ingredients make them a little lighter.

—JENNIFER KOLB OVERLAND PARK, KANSAS

PREP/TOTAL TIME: 30 MIN. **MAKES:** 4 SERVINGS

- ¼ cup all-purpose flour
- 1 teaspoon chili powder
- ½ teaspoon salt
- ½ teaspoon pepper
- ¼ teaspoon garlic powder
- 4 tilapia fillets (6 ounces each)
- 1 tablespoon butter
- 8 corn tortillas (6 inches)
- 2 cups angel hair coleslaw mix
- 2 tablespoons reduced-fat mayonnaise
- 2 tablespoons reduced-fat sour cream
- 1 tablespoon lime juice
- 1 teaspoon grated lime peel
- 1 cup canned black beans, rinsed and drained
- ½ cup sliced avocado

1. In a large resealable plastic bag, combine flour, chili powder, salt, pepper and garlic powder. Add tilapia fillets, one at a time, and shake to coat.

2. In a large nonstick skillet over medium heat, cook fillets in butter for 5-6 minutes on each side or until fish flakes easily with a fork. Meanwhile, place the tortillas on a baking sheet and spritz with cooking spray. Broil 3-4 in. from the heat for 2-3 minutes on each side or until crisp.

3. In a small bowl, toss coleslaw mix, mayonnaise, sour cream, lime juice and peel. Cut fish into large pieces. On each tortilla, layer coleslaw, black beans, fish and avocado.

PECAN-CRUSTED TURKEY CUTLETS

As this quick main course proves, turkey isn't just for Thanksgiving dinner. These stovetop cutlets are a great option for busy nights because they're ready to eat in just 25 minutes. Ground pecans give them an extra-crisp and flavorful crust.
—**LISA VARNER** EL PASO, TEXAS

PREP/TOTAL TIME: 25 MIN. **MAKES:** 4 SERVINGS

- ⅓ cup all-purpose flour
- 2 egg whites
- 1 egg
- 3 tablespoons honey Dijon mustard
- ½ teaspoon cayenne pepper
- ¼ teaspoon salt
- ⅔ cup dry bread crumbs
- ⅔ cup ground pecans
- 1 package (17.6 ounces) turkey breast cutlets
- ¼ cup canola oil

1. Place the flour in a shallow bowl. In another shallow bowl, whisk the egg whites, egg, mustard, cayenne pepper and salt. In another shallow bowl, combine bread crumbs and pecans. Coat cutlets with flour, then dip in egg mixture and coat with bread crumb mixture.

2. In a large skillet, cook turkey in oil in batches over medium heat for 2-3 minutes on each side or until juices run clear.

PEPPER JACK MAC

What a way to dress up ordinary macaroni and cheese! If I have a bit of extra time, I top off the prepared mac with some Parmesan bread crumbs and bake it, uncovered, in a casserole dish at 375° for about 30 minutes or until golden brown.
—**SARAH GILBERT HARTWELL** BEAVERTON, OREGON

PREP/TOTAL TIME: 25 MIN. **MAKES:** 2 SERVINGS

- 1 cup uncooked elbow macaroni
- 2 bacon strips, chopped
- ¼ cup chopped onion
- ¼ cup sliced fresh mushrooms
- 1½ teaspoons butter
- 1 tablespoon all-purpose flour
- ¼ cup plus 2 tablespoons chicken broth
- ¼ cup plus 2 tablespoons 2% milk
- ¾ cup shredded pepper Jack cheese
- ¼ teaspoon Italian seasoning
    Dash salt and pepper

1. Cook macaroni according to package directions. Meanwhile, in a small skillet, cook the bacon over medium heat until crisp. Remove to paper towels with a slotted spoon; drain, reserving ¾ teaspoon drippings.

2. In the same skillet, saute onion and mushrooms in drippings and butter until tender. Stir in flour until blended; gradually stir in broth and milk. Bring to a boil; cook and stir for 1-2 minutes or until thickened. Stir in the cheese, Italian seasoning, salt and pepper. Cook and stir over medium heat until cheese is melted.

3. Drain macaroni; stir macaroni and bacon into sauce mixture.

SHRIMP & TOMATO LINGUINE TOSS

Want something light, refreshing and stress-free? Try my seafood pasta and round out the meal with a salad and garlic bread.
—**LOUISE GILBERT** QUESNEL, BRITISH COLUMBIA

PREP/TOTAL TIME: 15 MIN. **MAKES:** 3 SERVINGS

- 6 ounces uncooked linguine
- ⅓ pound uncooked medium shrimp, peeled and deveined
- 3 garlic cloves, minced
- 1 tablespoon olive oil
- 1 can (14½ ounces) fire-roasted diced tomatoes, undrained
- 2 teaspoons minced fresh basil or ½ teaspoon dried basil
  Dash pepper
- ½ cup crumbled feta cheese
  Additional minced fresh basil, optional

1. Cook the linguine according to the package directions.
2. Meanwhile, in a large skillet, cook the shrimp and garlic in oil over medium heat until shrimp turn pink. Add the tomatoes, basil and pepper. Bring to a boil; cook and stir for 1-2 minutes or until heated through.
3. Drain linguine; toss with tomato mixture. Sprinkle with feta and additional basil if desired.

HOW TO PEEL AND DEVEIN SHRIMP
Starting on the underside by the head area, pull the legs and first section of shell to one side. Continue pulling the shell up around the top and to the other side. Pull off the shell by the tail if desired. Cut a shallow slit along the back from the head area to the tail; rinse with cold water to remove the vein.

STOVETOP ITALIAN MACARONI

Adults and kids alike will enjoy this Italian beef-and-noodle supper featuring two kinds of cheese. If your family prefers food that's on the milder side, simply skip the red pepper flakes.
—**LAILA ZVEJNIEKS** STONEY CREEK, ONTARIO

PREP/TOTAL TIME: 25 MIN. **MAKES:** 5 SERVINGS

- 1 pound ground beef
- 1 can (28 ounces) diced tomatoes, undrained
- 2 cups water
- 1 envelope onion soup mix
- 1 teaspoon Italian seasoning
- ¼ teaspoon crushed red pepper flakes, optional
- 2 cups uncooked elbow macaroni
- ½ cup grated Parmesan cheese
- 1 cup (4 ounces) shredded part-skim mozzarella cheese

1. In a Dutch oven, cook the beef over medium heat until no longer pink; drain. Add the tomatoes, water, soup mix, Italian seasoning and red pepper flakes if desired. Bring to a boil. Stir in macaroni. Reduce heat; cover and simmer for 8-9 minutes or until macaroni is tender.
2. Remove from the heat; stir in the Parmesan cheese. Sprinkle with the mozzarella cheese. Cover and let stand for 2 minutes or until cheese is melted.

GREEK CHICKEN PENNE

Here's a special but simple entree. You may be surprised that a dish this fast to fix can deliver so much Mediterranean flavor.

—**DAWN FRIHAUF** FORT MORGAN, COLORADO

PREP/TOTAL TIME: 25 MIN. **MAKES:** 5 SERVINGS

2½ cups uncooked penne pasta
  1 pound boneless skinless chicken breasts, cubed
  ½ cup chopped red onion
  2 garlic cloves, minced
  1 tablespoon olive oil
  2 jars (7½ ounces each) marinated quartered artichoke hearts, drained and chopped
  1 large tomato, chopped
  ½ cup crumbled feta cheese
  3 tablespoons minced fresh parsley
  2 tablespoons lemon juice
  2 teaspoons dried oregano
  ¼ teaspoon salt
  ¼ teaspoon pepper
    Fresh oregano, optional

1. Cook the penne pasta according to the package directions.
2. Meanwhile, in a large skillet, cook chicken, onion and garlic in oil over medium heat for 4-5 minutes or until the chicken is no longer pink. Stir in artichokes, tomato, cheese, parsley, lemon juice, oregano, salt and pepper; heat through.
3. Drain pasta; toss with chicken mixture. Garnish with oregano if desired.

ASIAN CHICKEN SKILLET

I combine a Rice-A-Roni mix with chicken, frozen veggies, teriyaki sauce and ginger to create an all-in-one meal. It requires only one pan, so cleanup time is as short as the prep time.

—**TERRI CHRISTENSEN** MONTAGUE, MICHIGAN

PREP/TOTAL TIME: 30 MIN. **MAKES:** 4 SERVINGS

  1 package (5.9 ounces) chicken and garlic-flavored rice and vermicelli mix
  2 tablespoons butter
  1 pound boneless skinless chicken breasts, cut into strips
2¼ cups water
  ¼ cup reduced-sodium teriyaki sauce
  ½ teaspoon ground ginger
  1 package (16 ounces) frozen stir-fry vegetable blend, thawed

1. In a large skillet, saute rice mix in butter until golden brown. Stir in the chicken, water, teriyaki sauce, ginger and contents of the rice seasoning packet. Bring to a boil. Reduce heat; cover and simmer for 10 minutes.
2. Stir in vegetable blend. Cover and cook 5-8 minutes longer or until rice is tender and chicken is no longer pink.

CHICKEN BREAST BASICS
Buying skinned and boned chicken breasts can cut up to 15 minutes off of your cooking time. Save money by buying larger-size packages, then rewrap the chicken in smaller portions and freeze.

PORK CHOPS WITH MUSTARD SAUCE

Dress up ordinary pork chops with a delectable golden reduction sauce made of bold ingredients, including Dijon mustard, white wine and lots of garlic. You won't be disappointed!
—**SHARLA REEL** ST. CHARLES, MISSOURI

PREP/TOTAL TIME: 30 MIN. **MAKES:** 4 SERVINGS

- 4 **boneless pork loin chops (6 ounces each)**
- ¼ **teaspoon salt**
- ¼ **teaspoon pepper**
- 2 **tablespoons olive oil**
- ¼ **cup white wine or chicken broth**
- 3 **garlic cloves, minced**
- ½ **cup chicken broth**
- 1 **tablespoon butter**
- 1 **tablespoon lemon juice**
- 1 **tablespoon Dijon mustard**
- ¼ **teaspoon Worcestershire sauce**

1. Sprinkle pork chops with salt and pepper. In a large skillet, brown pork chops in oil. Add wine and garlic, stirring to loosen browned bits from pan. Bring to a boil; cook for 2 minutes.

2. Add the chicken broth; cover and cook for 8-10 minutes or until a thermometer reads 160°. Remove pork and keep warm. Bring pan juices to a boil; cook until liquid is reduced to ⅓ cup. Stir in butter, lemon juice, mustard and Worcestershire sauce; heat through. Serve with pork.

MEDITERRANEAN ROASTED SALMON

These colorful roasted fillets are topped with chopped vegetables and a wonderful homemade vinaigrette. Try serving the salmon over quick-cooking angel hair pasta and sprinkle on some feta.
—**WOLFGANG HANAU** WEST PALM BEACH, FLORIDA

PREP/TOTAL TIME: 30 MIN. **MAKES:** 4 SERVINGS

- 4 **salmon fillets (6 ounces each)**
- ½ **teaspoon salt, divided**
- ½ **cup olive oil**
- 2 **tablespoons balsamic vinegar**
- 2 **teaspoons honey**
- 1 **teaspoon Dijon mustard**
- 3 **plum tomatoes, chopped**
- ¼ **cup chopped red onion**
- ¼ **cup chopped green pepper**
- 2 **tablespoons chopped pitted green olives**
- 2 **tablespoons chopped ripe olives**

1. Place the salmon in a greased 15-in. x 10-in. x 1-in. baking pan; sprinkle with ¼ teaspoon salt. In a small bowl, whisk oil, vinegar, honey, mustard and remaining salt. Spoon 1 tablespoon over each fillet.

2. In a large bowl, combine the tomatoes, onion, green pepper, olives and remaining oil mixture. Spoon over fillets.

3. Bake at 425° for 12-15 minutes or until the fish flakes easily with a fork.

FAMILY-FAVORITE ITALIAN CHICKEN

Whether you're serving guests or just need a fast meal, consider saucy chicken, pasta and cheese. It all combines for an Italian feast.

—**CAROL HEEREN** PARKER, SOUTH DAKOTA

PREP/TOTAL TIME: 30 MIN. **MAKES:** 4 SERVINGS

- 2 cans (8 ounces each) tomato sauce
- 2 teaspoons dried basil
- ½ teaspoon garlic powder
- 4 boneless skinless chicken breast halves (4 ounces each)
- ¾ cup dry bread crumbs
- 2 teaspoons dried oregano
- ¼ teaspoon salt
- 2 eggs
- 2 tablespoons water
- ½ cup all-purpose flour
- ¼ cup olive oil
- 1 cup (4 ounces) shredded part-skim mozzarella cheese
- ¼ cup shredded Parmesan cheese
  Hot cooked angel hair pasta

1. In a small saucepan, combine tomato sauce, basil and garlic powder; heat through.

2. Meanwhile, flatten chicken breasts to ¼-in. thickness. In a shallow bowl, combine the bread crumbs, oregano and salt. In a separate shallow bowl, whisk the eggs and water. Place flour in another shallow bowl. Coat chicken with flour, then dip in egg mixture and coat with bread crumb mixture.

3. In a large skillet, cook the chicken in oil in batches for 4-6 minutes on each side or until juices run clear. Spoon sauce over chicken; sprinkle with cheeses. Serve with pasta.

PEPPERED FILETS WITH HORSERADISH CREAM SAUCE

For a satisfying meat-and-potatoes supper, add a side of chunky mashed spuds to this peppered beef tenderloin. The creamy sauce has the perfect balance of horseradish and mustard.

—**MARIE RIZZIO** INTERLOCHEN, MICHIGAN

PREP/TOTAL TIME: 25 MIN. **MAKES:** 4 SERVINGS

- 4 beef tenderloin steaks (6 ounces each)
- 1 tablespoon plus ⅛ teaspoon coarsely ground pepper, divided
- ¾ teaspoon salt, divided
- 5 tablespoons butter, divided
- 2 teaspoons all-purpose flour
- ⅔ cup heavy whipping cream
- 2 tablespoons horseradish
- 1 teaspoon Dijon mustard

1. Sprinkle steaks with 1 tablespoon pepper and ½ teaspoon salt. In a large skillet over medium heat, cook the steaks in 1 tablespoon butter for 4-5 minutes on each side or until the meat reaches the desired doneness (for medium-rare, a thermometer should read 145°; medium, 160°; well-done, 170°).

2. Meanwhile, in a small saucepan, melt the remaining butter. Stir in the flour and remaining salt and pepper until smooth; gradually add whipping cream. Bring to a boil; cook and stir for 1-2 minutes or until thickened. Stir in horseradish and mustard. Serve with steaks.

CREAMY SAUSAGE & BOW TIES

It's so easy to dress up a package of noodles with smoked sausage, frozen peas and mozzarella cheese. I stumbled across the recipe when I was running late for dinner, and my kids devoured it!
—**LINDA NILSON** MELROSE PARK, ILLINOIS

PREP/TOTAL TIME: 25 MIN. **MAKES:** 4 SERVINGS

- 1 **package (4.1 ounces) four cheese bow tie pasta mix**
- ½ **pound fully cooked smoked sausage, cut into ¼-inch pieces**
- 1 **cup frozen peas**
- 1 **cup (4 ounces) shredded part-skim mozzarella cheese**

Prepare pasta mix according to package directions. Meanwhile, in a large skillet, brown sausage; drain. Add the peas and pasta. Simmer, uncovered, for 1-2 minutes or until heated through. Sprinkle with mozzarella cheese. Cover and cook for 1-2 minutes or until the cheese is melted.

MORE CHEESE, PLEASE

Cheese can be frozen for longer storage time, but keep in mind that the freezing process will change the cheese's texture slightly. Because of this, it's best to use frozen cheese for cooking or baking.

SMOKY CHICKEN ENCHILADA SKILLET

Here in Texas, we love Mexican food, and this stovetop version of enchiladas is a popular choice in our house. It's quick and fuss-free because you don't have to roll up tortillas or wait for them to bake.
—**CAROLYN COLLINS** FREEPORT, TEXAS

PREP/TOTAL TIME: 25 MIN. **MAKES:** 5 SERVINGS

- 1 **pound boneless skinless chicken breasts, cubed**
- 1 **small onion, chopped**
- 1 **tablespoon canola oil**
- 1 **can (10¾ ounces) condensed cream of chicken soup, undiluted**
- 1 **can (10 ounces) enchilada sauce**
- 1 **can (4 ounces) chopped green chilies**
- 1 **tablespoon minced chipotle pepper in adobo sauce**
- 12 **corn tortillas (6 inches), cut into 1-inch strips**
- 1¼ **cups shredded Mexican cheese blend, divided**
- ¼ **cup minced fresh cilantro**
  Sour cream

1. In a large skillet, cook chicken and onion in oil over medium heat for 6-8 minutes or until chicken is no longer pink. Stir in the soup, enchilada sauce, chilies and chipotle pepper. Add tortillas and 1 cup cheese.
2. Bring to a boil. Reduce heat; cover and simmer for 5-7 minutes or until heated through, stirring occasionally. Sprinkle with cilantro and remaining cheese. Serve with sour cream.

Busy-Day Breakfast

Thanks to these quick and easy favorites, you and your family will have time to enjoy a delicious homemade breakfast on even the busiest mornings. What a way to start the day!

SMOKED SALMON AND EGG WRAPS

Here's a convenient choice when you need to feed a crowd in the morning. The tortilla roll-ups feature plenty of smoked salmon, which is nicely accented by a hint of dill in the eggs.
—**MARY LOU WAYMAN** SALT LAKE CITY, UTAH

PREP/TOTAL TIME: 25 MIN. **MAKES:** 10 SERVINGS

- 12 **eggs, lightly beaten**
- ¼ **cup snipped fresh dill or 4 teaspoons dill weed**
- 2 **tablespoons 2% milk**
- ½ **teaspoon seasoned salt**
- 10 **flour tortillas (8 inches)**
- 1 **package (4 ounces) smoked salmon or lox**
- ½ **cup finely chopped red onion**
- 6 **ounces Havarti cheese, thinly sliced**

1. In a large bowl, whisk the eggs, dill, milk and seasoned salt. Coat a large nonstick skillet with cooking spray and place over medium heat. Add egg mixture. Cook and stir over medium heat until eggs are completely set.

2. Spoon a scant ⅓ cup egg mixture down the center of each tortilla. Top with the salmon, onion and cheese. Fold opposite sides of tortilla over filling (sides will not meet in center). Roll up tortilla, beginning at one of the open ends. Place the wraps, seam side down, in a 15-in. x 10-in. x 1-in. baking pan coated with cooking spray.

3. Cover wraps and bake at 350° for 10 minutes or until the cheese is melted.

CHORIZO SALSA OMELET

Want a new idea for an omelet? Fill it with plenty of zippy chorizo sausage and any chunky salsa you prefer.
—**TASTE OF HOME TEST KITCHEN**

PREP/TOTAL TIME: 20 MIN. **MAKES:** 1 SERVING

- 1 **tablespoon butter**
- 3 **eggs**
- 3 **tablespoons water**
- ⅛ **teaspoon salt**
- ⅛ **teaspoon pepper**
- ¼ **cup cooked chorizo or sausage**
- 2 **tablespoons chunky salsa**

1. In a small nonstick skillet, melt butter over medium-high heat. Whisk the eggs, water, salt and pepper. Add egg mixture to skillet (mixture should set immediately at edges).

2. As the eggs set, push the cooked edges toward center, letting uncooked portion flow underneath. When eggs are set, spoon chorizo and salsa on one side; fold other side over filling. Slide omelet onto a plate.

CREAMY SCRAMBLED EGGS WITH HAM

These just might be the creamiest, richest scrambled eggs you'll ever taste! Complete a special yet down-home breakfast by adding a side of hash browns and a bowl of fresh fruit.

—SUZY HORVATH GLADSTONE, OREGON

PREP/TOTAL TIME: 20 MIN. **MAKES:** 4 SERVINGS

- 8 eggs
- ⅓ cup heavy whipping cream
- ⅔ cup cubed fully cooked ham
- 1 green onion, chopped
  Dash salt
  Dash pepper
- 4 teaspoons butter
- 4 ounces cream cheese, cubed

In a large bowl, whisk eggs and cream; stir in the ham, onion, salt and pepper. In a large skillet, heat butter over medium heat. Add egg mixture; cook and stir until almost set. Stir in cream cheese. Cook and stir until completely set.

GREEN ONION EASE

When a recipe calls for green onions, cut them with kitchen scissors instead of a knife. If the recipe calls for quite a few, grab a bunch at once and snip away. You'll be done before you know it!

—LOUISE B. COLUMBIA, SOUTH CAROLINA

RICOTTA PANCAKES WITH CINNAMON APPLES

At my Harbour House Inn Bed & Breakfast, I love surprising guests with a stack of fluffy ricotta pancakes topped with spiced apples. They're yummy with or without maple syrup.

—EVA AMUSO CHESHIRE, MASSACHUSETTS

PREP/TOTAL TIME: 25 MIN. **MAKES:** 8 SERVINGS

- 2 medium apples, sliced
- 1 tablespoon butter
- ½ cup plus 2 tablespoons sugar, divided
- 2 teaspoons ground cinnamon
- 1¼ cups cake flour
- 3 teaspoons baking powder
- ¼ teaspoon salt
- 1 cup ricotta cheese
- 1 cup 2% milk
- 3 eggs, separated
- 1 teaspoon grated lemon peel
- 1 teaspoon lemon juice
  Maple syrup

1. In a large saucepan, cook apples in butter over medium heat for 6-8 minutes or until tender. Sprinkle with ½ cup sugar and cinnamon; set aside.

2. In a large bowl, combine the flour, baking powder and salt. In another bowl, combine the cheese, milk, egg yolks, lemon peel, juice and remaining sugar. Stir into the dry ingredients just until combined. In a small bowl, beat egg whites until stiff peaks form; fold into batter.

3. Pour the batter by ¼ cupfuls onto a greased hot griddle; turn when bubbles form on top. Cook until the second side is golden brown. Serve with apples and maple syrup.

QUICKER CHICKEN AND DUMPLINGS

Here's a speedy version of a down-home classic. I use convenience items such as frozen mixed vegetables and canned cream soup. The biscuits go together quickly with a purchased baking mix.
—**WILLIE DEWAARD** CORALVILLE, IOWA

PREP/TOTAL TIME: 30 MIN. **MAKES:** 6 SERVINGS

1½ cups 2% milk
1½ cups frozen mixed vegetables, thawed
2½ cups cubed cooked chicken
 1 can (10¾ ounces) condensed cream of chicken soup, undiluted
 ½ teaspoon garlic powder
 ¼ teaspoon poultry seasoning

DUMPLINGS
 1 cup biscuit/baking mix
 ⅓ cup French-fried onions, coarsely chopped
 7 tablespoons 2% milk
 ½ teaspoon dried parsley flakes

1. In a Dutch oven, combine the first six ingredients; bring to a boil, stirring occasionally.
2. Meanwhile, in a small bowl, combine the biscuit mix, French-fried onions, milk and parsley just until moistened. Drop by heaping teaspoonfuls onto simmering stew. Cook, uncovered, for 10 minutes.
3. Cover and simmer 10-12 minutes longer or until a toothpick inserted in a dumpling comes out clean (do not lift the cover while simmering).

ONE SKILLET LASAGNA

After sampling this dish, a panel of taste testers called this the best skillet lasagna they'd ever tried. The traditional Italian flavors and cheesy layers appeal to children and adults alike.
—**TASTE OF HOME TEST KITCHEN**

PREP/TOTAL TIME: 30 MIN. **MAKES:** 6 SERVINGS

 ¾ pound ground beef
 2 garlic cloves, minced
 1 can (14½ ounces) diced tomatoes with basil, oregano and garlic, undrained
 2 jars (14 ounces each) spaghetti sauce
 ⅔ cup condensed cream of onion soup, undiluted
 2 eggs, lightly beaten
1¼ cups 1% cottage cheese
 ¾ teaspoon Italian seasoning
 9 no-cook lasagna noodles
 ½ cup shredded Colby-Monterey Jack cheese
 ½ cup shredded part-skim mozzarella cheese

1. In a large skillet, cook beef and garlic over medium heat until the meat is no longer pink; drain. Stir in tomatoes and spaghetti sauce; heat through. Transfer to a large bowl.
2. In a small bowl, combine the soup, eggs, cottage cheese and Italian seasoning.
3. Return 1 cup meat sauce to the skillet; spread evenly. Layer with 1 cup cottage cheese mixture, 1½ cups meat sauce and half of the lasagna noodles, breaking to fit. Repeat layers of cottage cheese mixture, meat sauce and noodles. Top with the remaining meat sauce. Bring to a boil. Reduce heat; cover and simmer for 15-17 minutes or until noodles are tender.
4. Remove from the heat. Sprinkle with shredded cheeses; cover and let stand for 2 minutes or until melted.

CHICKEN MARSALA

In the mood for an elegant, restaurant-quality dinner? You won't have to leave the comforts of home—or pay high prices—when you choose this special entree. The lightly breaded chicken boasts a delicate marsala wine sauce with sauteed mushrooms. Best of all, you'll need only 30 minutes in the kitchen.
—**CHER SCHWARTZ** ELLISVILLE, MISSOURI

PREP/TOTAL TIME: 30 MIN. **MAKES:** 4 SERVINGS

- 4 boneless skinless chicken breast halves (4 ounces each)
- 2 tablespoons all-purpose flour
- 2 tablespoons olive oil
- 2 cups sliced fresh mushrooms
- 2 tablespoons butter
- ¾ cup marsala wine or chicken broth
- 2 tablespoons minced fresh parsley
- ¼ teaspoon dried rosemary, crushed
- 2 tablespoons grated Parmesan cheese, optional

1. Flatten the chicken to ¼-in. thickness. Place the flour in a large resealable plastic bag. Add chicken, two pieces at a time, and shake to coat.

2. In a large skillet over medium heat, cook the chicken in oil for 3-5 minutes on each side or until a thermometer reads 170°. Remove and keep warm.

3. In the same skillet, saute mushrooms in butter until tender. Add the wine, parsley and rosemary. Bring to a boil; cook until the liquid is reduced by half. Serve with chicken; sprinkle with cheese if desired.

GAME-NIGHT NACHO PIZZA

Bring a little excitement to game night or any day of the week with a nacho-style pie. Some like it hot with sliced jalapeno peppers; others prefer it cool with a dollop of sour cream.
—**JAMIE JONES** MADISON, GEORGIA

PREP/TOTAL TIME: 20 MIN. **MAKES:** 6 SLICES

- 1 prebaked 12-inch pizza crust
- 1 tablespoon olive oil
- 1 cup refried beans
- 1 cup refrigerated fully cooked barbecued shredded beef
- ½ cup chopped seeded tomatoes
- ½ cup pickled jalapeno slices
- 1 cup (4 ounces) shredded Colby-Monterey Jack cheese
  Shredded lettuce, sour cream and salsa, optional

1. Place crust on an ungreased pizza pan. Brush with oil. Spread beans over crust. Top with beef, tomatoes, jalapenos and cheese.
2. Bake at 450° for 10-15 minutes or until the cheese is melted. Serve with lettuce, sour cream and salsa if desired.

SOUTH-OF-THE-BORDER PIE
When I have leftover taco meat, I top a pizza crust with a blend of refried beans and sour cream, then add the meat and bake until heated through. When serving, I sprinkle on tomato, lettuce and cheese.
—**MICHELLE KOORN** OAK HARBOR, WASHINGTON

BASIL-BUTTER STEAKS WITH ROASTED POTATOES

Treat youself and your family to a memorable steak feast in only half an hour. Topped with a delectable basil butter, the tenderloins are accompanied by roasted potatoes and tomatoes.

—TASTE OF HOME TEST KITCHEN

PREP/TOTAL TIME: 30 MIN. **MAKES:** 4 SERVINGS

- 1 package (15 ounces) frozen Parmesan and roasted garlic red potato wedges
- 4 beef tenderloin steaks (1¼ inches thick and 6 ounces each)
- ½ teaspoon salt
- ½ teaspoon pepper
- 5 tablespoons butter, divided
- 2 cups grape tomatoes
- 1 tablespoon minced fresh basil

1. Bake the potato wedges according to the package directions.
2. Meanwhile, sprinkle the steaks with salt and pepper. In a 10-inch cast-iron skillet, brown steaks in 2 tablespoons butter. Add the tomatoes to the skillet. Bake, uncovered, at 425° for 15-20 minutes or until the meat reaches desired the doneness (for medium-rare, a thermometer should read 145°; medium, 160°; well-done, 170°).
3. In a small bowl, combine basil and remaining butter. Spoon over steaks and serve with potatoes.

ORANGE-GLAZED HAM STEAKS

This citrusy ham combines orange marmalade and maple syrup for a taste that goes beyond dinnertime. I like to serve any leftovers at brunch with scrambled eggs and fruit.

—BONNIE HAWKINS ELKHORN, WISCONSIN

PREP/TOTAL TIME: 20 MIN. **MAKES:** 4 SERVINGS

- ½ cup orange marmalade
- 2 tablespoons maple syrup
- 4½ teaspoons orange juice
- 1½ teaspoons chili powder
- 4 boneless fully cooked ham steaks (5 ounces each)

1. In a small bowl, combine the marmalade, syrup, orange juice and chili powder.
2. Grill ham steaks, covered, over medium heat or broil 4 in. from the heat for 3-4 minutes on each side or until heated through, brushing occasionally with marmalade mixture.

CRUMB-COATED COD FILLETS

Salad dressing mix and other pantry items transform cod into a special entree. It's a delicious way to get more fish in your diet.

—CANDY SUMMERHILL ALEXANDER, ARKANSAS

PREP/TOTAL TIME: 30 MIN. **MAKES:** 4 SERVINGS

- ¼ cup all-purpose flour
- ¼ teaspoon pepper
- ⅛ teaspoon salt
- 2 eggs
- 1 teaspoon water
- 1 cup panko (Japanese) bread crumbs
- ¼ cup shredded Parmesan cheese
- 4½ teaspoons ranch salad dressing mix
- 1 tablespoon salt-free Italian herb seasoning
- 4 cod fillets (4 ounces each)

1. In a shallow bowl, combine flour, pepper and salt. In another shallow bowl, whisk the eggs and water. In a third shallow bowl, combine the bread crumbs, cheese, dressing mix and seasoning. Coat the fillets with flour mixture, then dip in egg mixture and coat with crumb mixture.
2. Place the fillets on a greased baking sheet. Bake at 425° for 15-20 minutes or until fish flakes easily with a fork, turning once.

PORK & TOMATO PASTA SAUCE

Loaded with sausage, this five-ingredient sauce is popular with my husband and two children. Serve it over fettuccine or your favorite type of noodles, and you'll have a sure winner.

—JACKIE HUGHES BALTIMORE, MARYLAND

PREP/TOTAL TIME: 30 MIN. **MAKES:** 5 SERVINGS

- 1 **pound bulk pork sausage**
- 2 **cups heavy whipping cream**
- 1 **can (14½ ounces) diced tomatoes with basil, oregano and garlic, undrained**
- ½ **cup julienned oil-packed sun-dried tomatoes**
  Hot cooked fettuccine

1. In a large skillet, cook the sausage over medium heat until no longer pink; drain.
2. Stir in the cream and tomatoes. Bring to a boil. Reduce heat; simmer, uncovered, for 15-20 minutes or until liquid is reduced by half. Serve with fettuccine.

SOUTHWESTERN VEGETABLES & RICE

Short on time? Here's a spicy, satisfying dish that comes together in just 20 minutes. With vegetarian meat crumbles, it's also a great choice when you want a meatless meal.

—TASTE OF HOME TEST KITCHEN

PREP/TOTAL TIME: 20 MIN. **MAKES:** 4 SERVINGS

- 1 **can (14½ ounces) fire-roasted diced tomatoes, undrained**
- 1 **package (12 ounces) frozen vegetarian meat crumbles, thawed**
- 1 **package (12 ounces) frozen Southwestern corn, thawed**

- 1 **can (10¾ ounces) condensed tomato soup, undiluted**
- 1 **cup water**
- 1 **teaspoon ground cumin**
- ¼ **teaspoon salt**
- 1 **cup uncooked instant rice**
- 1 **cup (4 ounces) shredded Monterey Jack cheese**

In a Dutch oven, combine the first seven ingredients. Bring to a boil. Stir in rice. Remove from the heat; cover and let stand for 5-7 minutes or until rice is tender. Sprinkle with cheese.

SCALLOPED SHRIMP AND POTATOES

Shrimp and spinach take the flavor level up a notch in this cheesy, comforting supper. Packaged scalloped potatoes speed along the recipe so you'll be out of the kitchen in a hurry.

—TASTE OF HOME TEST KITCHEN

PREP/TOTAL TIME: 20 MIN. **MAKES:** 4 SERVINGS

- 1 **package (4.9 ounces) scalloped potatoes**
- 2¼ **cups water**
- ⅓ **cup 2% milk**
- 1 **pound peeled and deveined cooked medium shrimp**
- 3 **cups fresh baby spinach, coarsely chopped**
- 1 **cup (4 ounces) shredded Colby-Monterey Jack cheese**

1. In a large skillet, combine the potatoes, contents of the sauce mix packet, water and milk. Bring to a boil. Reduce heat; cover and simmer for 8-10 minutes or until the potatoes are tender, stirring occasionally.
2. Add the shrimp and spinach. Cook and stir until spinach is wilted. Stir in cheese until melted.

MEMORABLE MEALS

Whether you're serving breakfast, lunch or dinner, turn to this chapter for complete menus—six delicious options in all. You'll soon be serving a meal that's unforgettable, from the savory entree to the luscious dessert!

SCRAMBLED EGG SPINACH CASSEROLE

Nutmeg is a wonderful complement to the Italian sausage, spinach and feta in this company-perfect casserole. It's a great make-ahead option when you don't have a lot of time in the morning.

—LISA SPEER PALM BEACH, FLORIDA

PREP: 40 MIN. + CHILLING **BAKE:** 45 MIN. + STANDING
MAKES: 8 SERVINGS

- 2 tablespoons butter
- 2 tablespoons all-purpose flour
- ½ teaspoon ground nutmeg
- ⅛ teaspoon plus ½ teaspoon salt, divided
- ⅛ teaspoon plus ¼ teaspoon pepper, divided
- 2 cups 2% milk
- ½ pound bulk Italian sausage
- ½ cup chopped sweet onion
- 12 eggs
- 3 tablespoons half-and-half cream
- 1 package (10 ounces) frozen chopped spinach, thawed and squeezed dry
- 1½ cups (6 ounces) crumbled feta cheese

TOPPING
- ¾ cup soft bread crumbs
- 1 tablespoon butter, melted
- 2 tablespoons grated Parmesan cheese
- ¼ teaspoon paprika

1. In a small saucepan, melt the butter. Stir in the flour, nutmeg and ⅛ teaspoon each salt and pepper until smooth; gradually add the milk. Bring to a boil; cook and stir for 2 minutes or until thickened. Remove from the heat; cool completely.

2. Meanwhile, in a large skillet, cook the sausage, onion and remaining salt and pepper over medium heat until the meat is no longer pink; drain. Transfer to a greased 13-in. x 9-in. baking dish; set aside.

3. In a large bowl, whisk the eggs and cream. Stir in the spinach, feta and cooled white sauce. Pour over sausage mixture. Cover and refrigerate overnight.

4. Remove from the refrigerator 30 minutes before baking. For the topping, toss bread crumbs and melted butter; sprinkle over casserole. Top with Parmesan cheese and paprika.

5. Bake, uncovered, at 350° for 45-50 minutes or until a knife inserted near the center comes out clean. Let casserole stand for 10 minutes before serving.

STRAWBERRY BRUNCH BRUSCHETTA

Here's an indulgent treat for a holiday brunch or special weekend breakfast. The goat cheese, fresh herbs, sweet strawberries and arugula make every bite seem like a luxury.

—JOHANNA HAUER KENNEBUNK, MAINE

PREP/TOTAL TIME: 30 MIN. **MAKES:** 1½ DOZEN

- 3 tablespoons olive oil
- 1 teaspoon minced fresh thyme or ¼ teaspoon dried thyme
- 1 teaspoon minced fresh rosemary or ¼ teaspoon dried rosemary, crushed
- ¼ teaspoon salt
- ¼ teaspoon pepper
- 24 slices French bread baguette (½ inch thick)
- ½ pound fresh goat cheese
- 2 cups chopped fresh strawberries
- 2 cups fresh arugula or fresh baby spinach, chopped

1. In a small bowl, combine the first five ingredients. Place the bread on ungreased baking sheets; brush with oil mixture.

2. Broil 3-4 in. from the heat for 1-2 minutes or until lightly browned. Spread with goat cheese. Broil 2-3 minutes longer or until cheese begins to melt.

3. In a small bowl, combine the strawberries and arugula; layer over cheese.

RICOTTA SCONES WITH RHUBARB-ORANGE COMPOTE

Enjoyed warm from the oven with a hot cup of coffee or tea, these golden scones are a little piece of heaven. If you'll be serving them to guests, be prepared to share copies of the recipe! Don't forget a dollop of the accompanying fruit compote.

—MARILYN RODRIGUEZ FAIRBANKS, ALASKA

PREP: 30 MIN. **BAKE:** 15 MIN.
MAKES: 1 DOZEN (¾ CUP COMPOTE)

- ¾ cup sugar
- 2 tablespoons cornstarch
- ½ cup orange juice
- 1 cup finely chopped fresh or frozen rhubarb, thawed
- ½ small navel orange, peeled and pureed

SCONES
- 3 cups all-purpose flour
- ⅓ cup sugar
- 2 teaspoons baking powder
- ¾ teaspoon salt
- ½ teaspoon baking soda
- ½ cup cold butter
- 1 egg, beaten
- 1 cup heavy whipping cream
- 1 cup ricotta cheese
- 2 teaspoons grated orange peel

TOPPING
- 2 tablespoons heavy whipping cream
- 2 tablespoons sugar
- ¼ teaspoon ground cinnamon

1. In a small saucepan, combine sugar, cornstarch and orange juice until smooth. Stir in rhubarb and orange. Bring to a boil;

cook and stir until thickened and the rhubarb is tender. Remove from the heat; cool.

2. In a large bowl, combine the flour, sugar, baking powder, salt and baking soda. Cut in the butter until the mixture resembles coarse crumbs. Combine the egg, cream, cheese and orange peel; stir into the crumb mixture just until moistened. Turn onto a floured surface; knead 10 times.

3. Divide dough in half; pat each into a 7-in. circle. Cut each into six wedges. Separate wedges and place on a greased baking sheet. Brush with cream; sprinkle with sugar and cinnamon. Bake at 375° for 15-20 minutes or until golden brown. Remove to a wire rack. Serve warm with compote.

Editor's Note: *If using frozen rhubarb, measure rhubarb while still frozen, then thaw completely. Drain in a colander, but do not press liquid out.*

MOCK CHAMPAGNE

Everyone can join in the toast when I fix my simple nonalcoholic drink. It tastes just like champagne, complete with bubbles! Using white grape juice instead of water for the ice cubes prevents the beverage from getting watered down as the cubes melt.

—PAM ION GAITHERSBURG, MARYLAND

PREP: 10 MIN. + FREEZING **MAKES:** 8 SERVINGS

- 3 cups white grape juice, divided
- 2 cans (12 ounces each) ginger ale, chilled
- ½ cup chilled club soda
  Orange slices and sliced fresh strawberries

1. Pour 2 cups grape juice into ice cube trays; freeze until set.

2. Transfer the ice cubes to a pitcher; add the remaining juice. Slowly stir in ginger ale and club soda. Garnish with oranges and strawberries. Serve immediately.

TASTY SHRIMP SPREAD

A festive occasion at my mother's house just wouldn't be complete without her popular shrimp spread. She's been making it for more than 25 years, and it never fails to get raves from guests.

—**SARA MCDONALD** RICHMOND, ONTARIO

PREP: 20 MIN. + CHILLING **MAKES:** 2½ CUPS

- 1 package (8 ounces) cream cheese, softened
- ¼ cup butter, softened
- ¼ cup mayonnaise
- ½ pound peeled and deveined cooked medium shrimp, finely chopped
- 1 medium onion, chopped
  Assorted crackers and/or fresh vegetables

In a small bowl, combine cream cheese, butter and mayonnaise. Stir in the shrimp and onion. Cover and refrigerate until serving. Serve with crackers and/or vegetables.

CHEESE ASPARAGUS ROLL-UPS

These warm roll-ups look special but are surprisingly easy to fix. They bake up crispy and have a colorful touch of paprika on top.

—**LINDA FINN** LOUISVILLE, MISSISSIPPI

PREP/TOTAL TIME: 25 MIN. **MAKES:** 14 SERVINGS

- 1 pound fresh asparagus, trimmed
- 1 jar (8 ounces) process cheese sauce
- ½ cup mayonnaise
- 1 loaf (1 pound) sliced sandwich bread, crusts removed
- ⅓ cup butter, melted
  Paprika

1. Place the asparagus in a steamer basket; place in a large saucepan over 1 in. of water. Bring to a boil; cover and steam for 3-5 minutes or until crisp-tender. Place the asparagus on paper towels; pat dry.

2. In a small bowl, combine the process cheese sauce and mayonnaise. Flatten the bread slices with a rolling pin. Spread the cheese mixture over each to within ½ in. of the edges. Top each with 2 pieces of asparagus; roll up. Brush with butter; sprinkle with paprika.

3. Place in an ungreased 15-in. x 10-in. x 1-in. baking pan. Bake at 350° for 5-8 minutes or until lightly browned. Serve warm.

APPLE, ALMOND & CASHEW WRAPS

After sampling a small bistro's delicious wrap, I decided to try creating my own. The result was smooth, crunchy, sweet and salty.

—**TRISHA KRUSE** EAGLE, IDAHO

PREP: 30 MIN. + CHILLING **MAKES:** 3 DOZEN

- ¾ cup almonds, toasted
- ½ cup unsalted cashews, toasted
- 1 package (8 ounces) reduced-fat cream cheese
- ¼ cup 2% milk
- 2 tablespoons honey
- ½ teaspoon salt
- 6 flavored flour tortillas of your choice (8 inches)
- 2 medium carrots, peeled and shredded
- 1 medium apple, finely chopped
- ½ cup chopped dates
- ¼ cup canned pineapple tidbits

1. Place the first six ingredients in a food processor. Cover and process until blended. Spread over tortillas.

2. Combine the remaining ingredients; sprinkle over the nut mixture. Roll up tightly and wrap in plastic wrap. Refrigerate for 1 hour or until firm.

3. Unwrap and cut each into six slices.

BRIE-BERRY BRUSCHETTA

I love fresh strawberries and enjoy them as much as I can during the growing season. Because so many recipes that include them are quite sweet, I experimented in the kitchen and came up with something savory—this bruschetta featuring berries and Brie.

—**MARY MARLOWE LEVERETTE** COLUMBIA, SOUTH CAROLINA

PREP/TOTAL TIME: 15 MIN. **MAKES:** 1 DOZEN

- 12 slices French bread baguette (¼ inch thick)
- 1 tablespoon olive oil
- 1 round (8 ounces) Brie cheese, rind removed
- 1 cup sliced fresh strawberries
- 1 tablespoon balsamic vinegar
- 1½ teaspoons minced fresh thyme or ½ teaspoon dried thyme

1. Place bread on an ungreased baking sheet; brush with oil. Broil 3-4 in. from the heat for 1-2 minutes or until golden brown.

2. Spread Brie over toast; top with strawberries. Drizzle with vinegar and sprinkle with thyme.

Baseball Bonanza

CARAMELIZED ONION-BACON BURGERS

Want a sure hit for a cookout? These bacon cheeseburgers get even more flavor from barbecue sauce and caramelized onions.

—**JORDAN MASON** BROOKVILLE, PENNSYLVANIA

PREP: 30 MIN. **GRILL:** 15 MIN. **MAKES:** 4 SERVINGS

- ⅓ cup plus ½ cup barbecue sauce, divided
- 1 pound ground beef
- 4 bacon strips, halved
- 1 large sweet onion, sliced
- 4 tablespoons butter, divided
- 4 hamburger buns, split
- 4 slices cheddar cheese

1. Place ⅓ cup barbecue sauce in a small bowl. Crumble beef over barbecue sauce and mix well. Shape into four patties.
2. In a small skillet, cook the bacon over medium heat until crisp. Remove to paper towels; drain. In another skillet, saute the onion in 2 tablespoons butter until softened. Reduce heat to medium-low; cook, stirring occasionally, for 20-25 minutes or until golden brown.
3. Spread buns with remaining butter; set aside. Grill burgers, covered, over medium heat or broil 4 in. from the heat for 5-7 minutes on each side or until a thermometer reads 160° and juices run clear. Top with cheese. Grill 1 minute longer or until cheese is melted.
4. Place the buns, cut side down, on grill for 1-2 minutes or until toasted. Spread buns with barbecue sauce; serve burgers on buns with onion and bacon.

GREEN ONION POTATO SALAD

Ever since I can remember, my Aunt Beverly has fixed her potato salad for special occasions. She gave me the recipe a few years ago.

—**LORI BIASE** SACRAMENTO, CALIFORNIA

PREP: 30 MIN. + CHILLING **MAKES:** 4 SERVINGS

- 5 medium red potatoes, cubed
- 2 hard-cooked eggs, chopped
- ¼ cup chopped dill pickle
- 1 green onion, chopped
- ¾ cup mayonnaise
- 2 tablespoons plus ¾ teaspoon green onion dip mix
- 2¼ teaspoons cider vinegar
- ¾ teaspoon sugar
- ¾ teaspoon minced fresh parsley
- ¾ teaspoon prepared mustard
- ¼ teaspoon salt
- ⅛ teaspoon pepper

1. Place potatoes in a large saucepan; cover with water. Bring to a boil. Reduce heat; cover and cook for 10-15 minutes or until tender. Drain and cool to room temperature.
2. In a small bowl, combine the potatoes, eggs, pickle and green onion. In another bowl, combine the remaining ingredients. Pour over potato mixture and toss gently to coat. Refrigerate for 1 hour or until chilled.

BUTTERMILK VEGETABLE DIP

Creamy and tangy, this dip is wonderfully versatile. Enjoy it not only as a dip for fresh vegetables, but also as a dressing for salad.

—**JULISSA COBLENTZ** WESTMINSTER, SOUTH CAROLINA

PREP/TOTAL TIME: 5 MIN. **MAKES:** 1 CUP

- ¾ cup mayonnaise
- ¼ cup buttermilk
- 2½ teaspoons Italian salad dressing mix
  Assorted fresh vegetables

In a small bowl, combine the mayonnaise, buttermilk and Italian salad dressing mix. Cover and refrigerate until serving. Serve with vegetables.

BASEBALL CUPCAKES

Transforming cupcakes into cute little baseballs is as easy as can be. I simply top the cooled cakes with a basic homemade frosting and add pieces of red shoestring licorice for the lacing. To save time, use your favorite cake mix instead.

—**JANE PEARSON** DAYTON, OHIO

PREP: 15 MIN. **BAKE:** 20 MIN. + COOLING **MAKES:** 4 CUPCAKES

- 2 tablespoons shortening
- ¼ cup sugar
- ¼ cup 2% milk
- 1 egg white
- ¼ teaspoon vanilla extract
- ⅔ cup cake flour
- ¾ teaspoon baking powder
- ¼ teaspoon salt

FROSTING

- 2 tablespoons butter
- ½ cup confectioners' sugar
- 2 teaspoons 2% milk
  Red shoestring licorice

1. In a small bowl, cream shortening and sugar until crumbly, about 2 minutes. Beat in milk, egg white and vanilla. Combine flour, baking powder and salt; gradually add to creamed mixture and mix well.
2. Fill paper-lined muffin cups two-thirds full. Bake at 350° for 16-20 minutes or until a toothpick inserted near the center comes out clean. Cool for 10 minutes before removing from the pan to a wire rack to cool completely.
3. In a small bowl, beat the butter, confectioners' sugar and milk until smooth. Frost the cupcakes. Decorate with licorice pieces to form lacing.

COWBOY STEW

Yee-haw! This stick-to-your-ribs combination of ground beef, hot dogs, beans, barbecue sauce and cheese is a hit with everyone.
—**VAL RANANAWSKI** MILLVILLE, NEW JERSEY

PREP/TOTAL TIME: 30 MIN. **MAKES:** 11 SERVINGS

- 2 pounds ground beef
- 4 cans (16 ounces each) baked beans
- 8 hot dogs, sliced
- ½ cup barbecue sauce
- ½ cup grated Parmesan cheese

In a Dutch oven, cook beef over medium heat until no longer pink; drain. Stir in remaining ingredients. Bring to a boil. Reduce heat; cover and simmer for 4-6 minutes or until flavors are blended.

STRAW BALE STICKS

I keep my simple breadsticks in mind whenever I need a quick and easy side. They're best served warm from the oven.
—**BETTY SLIVON** SUN CITY, ARIZONA

PREP/TOTAL TIME: 25 MIN. **MAKES:** 2 DOZEN

- 2 cups biscuit/baking mix
- ½ cup shredded Mexican cheese blend
- ½ cup 2% milk
- ¼ cup butter, melted
- 1 tablespoon sesame seeds
- ⅛ teaspoon garlic powder

1. In a large bowl, combine the mix, cheese and milk just until moistened. Turn onto a lightly floured surface; knead 8-10 times.
2. Roll into a 9-in. x 6-in. rectangle; cut in half lengthwise. Cut into ¾-in. strips. Brush with the melted butter; sprinkle with the sesame seeds and garlic powder.
3. Transfer to a greased 15-in. x 10-in. x 1-in. baking pan. Bake at 425° for 12-15 minutes or until golden brown. Serve warm.

COWPOKE CORRAL CAKE

Saddle up for a cake decorated with cereal hay bales, a pretzel fence and more. It's fun for both the young and young at heart.
—**MERRI RICKERT** MESA, ARIZONA

PREP: 25 MIN. **BAKE:** 25 MIN. + COOLING **MAKES:** 12 SERVINGS

- 3 eggs, separated
- 1 cup 2% milk
- 1 tablespoon white vinegar
- ½ cup shortening
- 1½ cups sugar
- 2 ounces unsweetened chocolate, melted
- 1 teaspoon vanilla extract
- 2 cups cake flour
- 1 teaspoon baking soda
- ½ teaspoon salt

FROSTING
- ½ cup shortening
- 4½ cups confectioners' sugar
- 1 teaspoon vanilla extract
- 5 to 6 tablespoons 2% milk
  Brown paste food coloring

DECORATING
- 1 teaspoon water
- 4 drops green food coloring
- 1½ cups flaked coconut
- ¼ cup graham cracker crumbs
- 16 pretzels
- 2 cups bite-sized shredded wheat
  Toy horses

1. Place the egg whites in a large bowl; let stand at room temperature for 30 minutes. In a small bowl, combine milk and vinegar. Let stand for 10-15 minutes or until it begins to curdle.
2. In a large bowl, cream shortening and sugar until light and fluffy. Add yolks, one at a time, beating well after each addition. Beat in chocolate and vanilla. Combine the cake flour, baking soda and salt; add to the creamed mixture alternately with milk mixture, beating well after each addition. Beat egg whites with clean beaters until stiff peaks form. Fold into batter.
3. Transfer to two greased and floured 9-in. round baking pans. Bake at 350° for 25-30 minutes or until a toothpick inserted near the center comes out clean. Cool for 10 minutes before removing from pans to wire racks to cool completely.
4. In a large bowl, cream shortening until light and fluffy. Beat in confectioners' sugar, vanilla and enough milk to achieve desired consistency. Spread 1¼ cups frosting between layers and over top of cake. Tint 1¼ cups frosting brown. Cut a small hole in the corner of a pastry or plastic bag; insert #48 basket weave tip. Fill the bag with brown frosting. Pipe vertical lines on sides of cake.
5. In a large resealable plastic bag, combine water and food coloring; add coconut. Seal the bag and shake to tint. Sprinkle coconut and crumbs over the top of cake. For fence, lightly press pretzels around top of cake. Stack cereal as desired for hay bales, attaching each with frosting. Arrange horses as desired.

CACTUS PUNCH

The flavors of lime and pineapple give this punch a pleasant tang. Crowned by a foamy topping, it's pretty and refreshing.
—**TASTE OF HOME TEST KITCHEN**

PREP/TOTAL TIME: 10 MIN. **MAKES:** 21 SERVINGS (¾ CUP EACH)

- 1 can (46 ounces) unsweetened pineapple juice
- ¾ cup frozen limeade concentrate, thawed
- 1 bottle (1 liter) ginger ale, chilled
- 1 quart lime sherbet, softened

In a punch bowl, combine juice and limeade concentrate. Add soda and sherbet; stir until blended. Serve immediately.

Treats for Halloween

PUMPKIN TURKEY CHILI

I love pumpkin, and my husband loves chili. So I combined the two into a warm-you-up dish we both enjoy on cool fall days.

—**CATHERINE WALMSLEY** PHOENIX, ARIZONA

PREP: 20 MIN. **COOK:** 1¾ HOURS
MAKES: 6 SERVINGS (2¼ QUARTS)

- 1 pound ground turkey
- 1 medium sweet yellow pepper, chopped
- 1 medium onion, chopped
- 3 garlic cloves, minced
- 2 teaspoons olive oil
- 2 cups chicken broth
- 1 can (15 ounces) kidney beans, rinsed and drained
- 1 can (15 ounces) black beans, rinsed and drained
- 1 can (15 ounces) solid-pack pumpkin
- 1 can (15 ounces) tomato sauce
- 4 medium tomatoes, chopped
- ⅔ cup chili sauce
- 3 tablespoons brown sugar
- 1 tablespoon dried oregano
- 1 tablespoon dried parsley flakes
- 1 teaspoon dried tarragon
- ¾ teaspoon salt
- ¾ teaspoon pepper
  Dash crushed red pepper flakes
  Dash cayenne pepper

In a Dutch oven, cook the turkey, yellow pepper, onion and garlic in oil over medium heat until the meat is no longer pink; drain. Stir in the remaining ingredients. Bring to a boil. Reduce heat; simmer, uncovered, for 1½ hours or until the chili reaches the desired thickness.

HOT DOG MUMMIES WITH HONEY MUSTARD DIP

These flaky sandwiches go over well with everyone who samples them. The accompanying mustard dip adds just the right kick.

—**JESSIE SARRAZIN** LIVINGSTON, MONTANA

PREP: 25 MIN. **BAKE:** 10 MIN.
MAKES: 20 APPETIZERS (ABOUT 1 CUP DIP)

- 1 tube (8 ounces) refrigerated crescent rolls
- 20 miniature hot dogs
- 1 egg
- 2 teaspoons water
  Dijon mustard

DIP
- ½ cup mayonnaise
- 3 tablespoons Dijon mustard
- 3 tablespoons honey
- 1 tablespoon cider vinegar
  Dash hot pepper sauce

1. Separate crescent roll dough into two rectangles; seal seams and perforations. Cut each rectangle horizontally into 10 strips. Wrap one strip around each hot dog.

2. Place 1 in. apart on an ungreased baking sheet. In a small bowl, whisk the egg and water; brush over the tops. Bake at 375° for 10- 15 minutes or until golden brown. Add the eyes with the mustard. In a small bowl, combine dip ingredients; serve with the mummies.

CARAMEL-TOFFEE APPLE DIP

My friend Jami shared her husband's special apple dip with me. It requires just a handful of ordinary ingredients and always gets lots of compliments at autumn parties. Serve both red and green apple wedges for a colorful presentation.

—**ANGIE HILLMAN** COTTONWOOD, ARIZONA

PREP/TOTAL TIME: 15 MIN. **MAKES:** 4¼ CUPS

- 1 carton (12 ounces) whipped cream cheese
- 1¼ cups caramel apple dip
- 1 package (8 ounces) milk chocolate English toffee bits
  Apple wedges

Spread cream cheese into a serving dish. Layer with apple dip and sprinkle with toffee bits. Serve with apple wedges.

WICKED DEVILED EGGS

Here's my variation on a recipe from my stepdaughter, who came up with it while trying to remember her mother's recipe. I think the eggs taste even better when made a day in advance.

—**JANICE PARKER** HUMBOLDT, IOWA

PREP/TOTAL TIME: 30 MIN. **MAKES:** 2 DOZEN

- 12 hard-cooked eggs
- ½ cup Miracle Whip
- 2 tablespoons cider vinegar
- 2 tablespoons prepared mustard
- 1 tablespoon minced fresh parsley or 1 teaspoon dried parsley flakes
- 1 tablespoon butter, melted
- 1 tablespoon sweet pickle relish
- 2 teaspoons Worcestershire sauce
- 1 teaspoon sweet pickle juice
- ½ teaspoon salt
- ½ teaspoon cayenne pepper
- ½ teaspoon pepper
  Paprika

1. Cut the eggs in half lengthwise. Remove the yolks; set the whites aside. In a small bowl, mash the yolks. Add the Miracle Whip, vinegar, mustard, parsley, butter, relish, Worcestershire sauce, pickle juice, salt, cayenne and pepper; mix well. Stuff or pipe into the egg whites.

2. Refrigerate until serving. Sprinkle with paprika.

1. In a large skillet, cook steak in canola oil over medium-high heat for 3-4 minutes on each side or until meat reaches desired doneness (for medium-rare, a thermometer should read 145°; medium, 160°; well-done, 170°). Add 1 tablespoon soy sauce, salt and pepper; cook 1 minute longer. Remove from the pan and keep warm.

2. In the same skillet, saute the mushrooms, onion and pepper in olive oil until tender. Stir in the remaining soy sauce. Remove from the heat; add the tomato. Spread mustard over rolls. Slice steak; place on rolls. Add mushroom mixture; replace tops.

BURGER JOINT ONION RINGS

I never tire of these fried onion rings. Crisp and golden brown, they make a great side for burgers, hot dogs and more.
—**BETSY KING** DULUTH, MINNESOTA

PREP: 20 MIN. **COOK:** 5 MIN./BATCH **MAKES:** 4 SERVINGS

- 1 large onion
- ½ cup all-purpose flour
- ½ teaspoon baking powder
- ½ teaspoon salt
- 1 egg
- ½ cup 2% milk
- ¼ cup plus 2 tablespoons dry bread crumbs
  - Oil for deep-fat frying
- ½ teaspoon seasoned salt

1. Cut onion into ¼-in. slices; separate into rings. In a shallow bowl, combine flour, baking powder and salt. In another shallow bowl, whisk egg and milk. Place bread crumbs in a third shallow bowl. Coat onion with flour mixture, then dip in egg mixture and coat with bread crumbs.

2. In an electric skillet or deep fryer, heat oil to 375°. Fry onion rings, a few at a time, for 30 seconds on each side or until golden brown. Drain on paper towels. Sprinkle with seasoned salt.

SCRUMPTIOUS BANANA SPLITS

Here's an old-time dessert no one will be able to resist. Bananas are smothered with scoops of chocolate ice cream, lots of yummy toppings and—of course—a maraschino cherry!
—**MARGIE WILLIAMS** MT. JULIET, TENNESSEE

PREP/TOTAL TIME: 10 MIN. **MAKES:** 4 SERVINGS

- 4 medium bananas
- 8 scoops chocolate ice cream
- 2 tablespoons pineapple ice cream topping
- 2 tablespoons strawberry ice cream topping
- 2 tablespoons black cherry ice cream topping
  - Whipped cream, chopped pecans and maraschino cherries

Slice each banana in half lengthwise. Place two banana halves in each of four dessert dishes; top with ice cream. Spoon toppings over ice cream. Top each with whipped cream, nuts and a cherry.

STRAWBERRY YOGURT SHAKES

These rich, creamy treats give you the taste of fresh strawberries in every sip. Plus, the shakes are ready to enjoy in just 10 minutes.
—**LEE LUST** ANTWERP, OHIO

PREP/TOTAL TIME: 10 MIN. **MAKES:** 4 SERVINGS

- 1 cup 2% milk
- 2 cups fresh strawberries, sliced
- 2 cups (16 ounces) strawberry yogurt
- 2 cups vanilla ice cream
- ¼ teaspoon vanilla extract

In a blender, combine all ingredients; cover and process until smooth. Pour into chilled glasses; serve immediately.

MUSHROOM STEAK SANDWICHES

With one 12-ounce steak, you can serve four people satisfying, flavorful sandwiches. Portobello mushrooms, sweet pepper and other veggies make them even more appealing.
—**MARTHA BENOIT** PROCTORSVILLE, VERMONT

PREP: 15 MIN. **COOK:** 20 MIN. **MAKES:** 4 SERVINGS

- 1 beef top sirloin steak (12 ounces)
- 2 teaspoons canola oil
- 2 tablespoons soy sauce, divided
- ¼ teaspoon salt
- ¼ teaspoon pepper
- 3 large portobello mushrooms, thinly sliced
- 1 large onion, thinly sliced
- 1 medium sweet yellow pepper, thinly sliced
- 1 tablespoon olive oil
- 1 large tomato, seeded and chopped
- ¼ cup Dijon mustard
- 4 kaiser rolls, split

Substitutions & Equivalents

EQUIVALENT MEASURES

3 teaspoons	= 1 tablespoon		16 tablespoons	= 1 cup
4 tablespoons	= 1/4 cup		2 cups	= 1 pint
5-1/3 tablespoons	= 1/3 cup		4 cups	= 1 quart
8 tablespoons	= 1/2 cup		4 quarts	= 1 gallon

FOOD EQUIVALENTS

GRAINS

Macaroni	1 cup (3-1/2 ounces) uncooked	= 2-1/2 cups cooked
Noodles, Medium	3 cups (4 ounces) uncooked	= 4 cups cooked
Popcorn	1/3 to 1/2 cup unpopped	= 8 cups popped
Rice, Long Grain	1 cup uncooked	= 3 cups cooked
Rice, Quick-Cooking	1 cup uncooked	= 2 cups cooked
Spaghetti	8 ounces uncooked	= 4 cups cooked

CRUMBS

Bread	1 slice	= 3/4 cup soft crumbs, 1/4 cup fine dry crumbs
Graham Crackers	7 squares	= 1/2 cup finely crushed
Buttery Round Crackers	12 crackers	= 1/2 cup finely crushed
Saltine Crackers	14 crackers	= 1/2 cup finely crushed

FRUITS

Bananas	1 medium	= 1/3 cup mashed
Lemons	1 medium	= 3 tablespoons juice, 2 teaspoons grated peel
Limes	1 medium	= 2 tablespoons juice, 1-1/2 teaspoons grated peel
Oranges	1 medium	= 1/4 to 1/3 cup juice, 4 teaspoons grated peel

VEGETABLES

Cabbage	1 head	= 5 cups shredded	Green Pepper	1 large	= 1 cup chopped
Carrots	1 pound	= 3 cups shredded	Mushrooms	1/2 pound	= 3 cups sliced
Celery	1 rib	= 1/2 cup chopped	Onions	1 medium	= 1/2 cup chopped
Corn	1 ear fresh	= 2/3 cup kernels	Potatoes	3 medium	= 2 cups cubed

NUTS

Almonds	1 pound	= 3 cups chopped	Pecan Halves	1 pound	= 4-1/2 cups chopped
Ground Nuts	3-3/4 ounces	= 1 cup	Walnuts	1 pound	= 3-3/4 cups chopped

EASY SUBSTITUTIONS

When you need...		Use...
Baking Powder	1 teaspoon	1/2 teaspoon cream of tartar + 1/4 teaspoon baking soda
Buttermilk	1 cup	1 tablespoon lemon juice or vinegar + enough milk to measure 1 cup (let stand 5 minutes before using)
Cornstarch	1 tablespoon	2 tablespoons all-purpose flour
Honey	1 cup	1-1/4 cups sugar + 1/4 cup water
Half-and-Half Cream	1 cup	1 tablespoon melted butter + enough whole milk to measure 1 cup
Onion	1 small, chopped (1/3 cup)	1 teaspoon onion powder or 1 tablespoon dried minced onion
Tomato Juice	1 cup	1/2 cup tomato sauce + 1/2 cup water
Tomato Sauce	2 cups	3/4 cup tomato paste + 1 cup water
Unsweetened Chocolate	1 square (1 ounce)	3 tablespoons baking cocoa + 1 tablespoon shortening or oil
Whole Milk	1 cup	1/2 cup evaporated milk + 1/2 cup water

COOKING TERMS

Here's a quick reference for some of the cooking terms used in *The Best of Country Cooking* recipes:

BASTE To moisten food with melted butter, pan drippings, marinades or other liquid to add more flavor and juiciness.

BEAT A rapid movement to combine ingredients using a fork, spoon, wire whisk or electric mixer.

BLEND To combine ingredients until *just* mixed.

BOIL To heat liquids until bubbles form that cannot be "stirred down." In the case of water, the temperature will reach 212°.

BONE To remove all meat from the bone before cooking.

CREAM To beat ingredients together to a smooth consistency, usually in the case of butter and sugar for baking.

DASH A small amount of seasoning, less than 1/8 teaspoon. If using a shaker, a dash would comprise a quick flip of the container.

DREDGE To coat foods with flour or other dry ingredients. Most often done with pot roasts and stew meat before browning.

FOLD To incorporate several ingredients by careful and gentle turning with a spatula. Used generally with beaten egg whites or whipped cream when mixing into the rest of the ingredients to keep the batter light.

JULIENNE To cut foods into long thin strips much like matchsticks. Used most often for salads and stir-fry dishes.

MINCE To cut into very fine pieces. Used often for garlic or fresh herbs.

PARBOIL To cook partially, usually used in the case of chicken, sausages and vegetables.

PARTIALLY SET Describes the consistency of gelatin after it has been chilled for a short amount of time. Mixture should resemble the consistency of egg whites.

PUREE To process foods to a smooth mixture. Can be prepared in an electric blender, food processor, food mill or sieve.

SAUTE To fry quickly in a small amount of fat, stirring almost constantly. Most often done with onions, mushrooms and other chopped vegetables.

SCORE To cut slits partway through the outer surface of foods. Often used with ham or flank steak.

STIR-FRY To cook meats and/or vegetables with a constant stirring motion in a small amount of oil in a wok or skillet over high heat.

GENERAL RECIPE INDEX

Spicy Cowboy Chili, 25
Sweet and Savory Pulled Beef
   Dinner, 74
Teriyaki Steak, 59
Toasted Corned Beef
   Sandwiches, 135

BEVERAGES
Cactus Punch, 174
Chocolate Chai Frappes, 19
Coffee Almond Floats, 148
Cranberry Fizz, 13
Cranberry Glogg, 16
Double Chocolate Malts, 138
Mango Lassi, 132
Mango Melba Shakes, 17
Mock Champagne, 169
Sangria Wine, 15
Strawberry Yogurt Shakes, 178

BISCUITS & SCONES
Cut-Out Biscuits, 148
Mocha Chip Hazelnut Scones, 89
Old-Fashioned Buttermilk
   Biscuits, 137
Ricotta Scones with Rhubarb-
   Orange Compote, 169
Rosemary-Lemon Scones, 88
Sugar Plum Scones, 88
Whole Wheat Cranberry
   Scones, 89

BLUEBERRIES
Blueberry French Toast, 75
Blueberry Jam, 54
Blueberry Lemon Bread, 142
Peach-Berry Pie, 138
Turkey Burgers with Blueberry
   BBQ Sauce, 27
Watermelon-Blueberry Salad, 140

BREADS
*(see Biscuits & Scones; Corn Bread &
Cornmeal; Muffins; Pancakes & French
Toast; Quick Breads; Rolls, Breadsticks
& Pastries; Yeast Breads)*

BROCCOLI
Broccoli-Cashew Salad, 134
Broccoli with Orange Sauce, 40
Effortless Broccoli Soup, 149
Layered Broccoli Salad, 27

BRUSSELS SPROUTS
Garlic-Roasted Brussels Sprouts
   with Mustard Sauce, 41

Maple & Bacon Glazed Brussels
   Sprouts, 55

CABBAGE
Cabbage & Meatballs, 149
Mom's Coleslaw, 136
Orange-Poppy Seed Coleslaw, 35
Sunflower Noodle Coleslaw, 32

CAKES & COFFEE CAKE
(also see Cheesecakes; Cupcakes)
Caramel Apple Cake Pops, 117
Cherry Pound Cake, 110
Chocolate Raspberry Cake, 124
Citrus-Raspberry Coffee Cake, 82
Cowpoke Corral Cake, 174
Date Pudding Cake Loaf, 126
Devil's Food Cake with Chocolate
   Fudge Frosting, 127
Lemon Ricotta Cake, 123
Old-Fashioned Chocolate
   Cake, 137
Pear Gingerbread Cake Roll, 125
Pumpkin-Citrus Bundt Cake, 113
Zucchini Chocolate Cake, 120

CANDIES
Acorn Treats, 104
Caramel-Nut Candy Bars, 100
Cashew Clusters, 99
Crispy Peanut Butter Balls, 100
Molasses Fudge, 99
Rich Peanut Clusters, 106
So-Easy Truffles, 98
Toffee Candy, 96
Tumbleweeds, 95
White Chocolate Raspberry
   Truffles, 99

CARAMEL
Caramel Apple Cake Pops, 117
Caramel Apple Muffins, 80
Caramel-Nut Candy Bars, 100
Caramel-Toffee Apple Dip, 176

CARROTS
Carrot Fritters, 45
Gingered Orange Carrots, 48

CASSEROLES
Cranberry Corn Bread
   Casserole, 46
Durango Potato Casserole, 50
Potato Bacon Casserole, 48
Scallop Mac & Cheese, 71

Scrambled Egg Spinach
   Casserole, 168
Two-Cheese Spaghetti Bake, 60

CHEESE & CREAM CHEESE
(also see Cheesecakes)
APPETIZERS
Almond-Bacon Cheese
   Crostini, 18
Apricot Brie, 16
Brie-Berry Bruschetta, 170
Brie with Almonds, 12
Cheese Asparagus Roll-Ups, 170
Fried Cheese Ravioli, 7
Herbed Garlic Cheese Dip, 9
Parmesan Pretzel Rods, 16
BREADS
Golden Danish Twists, 83
Jumbo Jalapeno Cheddar
   Rolls, 84
Pumpkin Cheesecake Muffins, 86
Ricotta Scones with Rhubarb-
   Orange Compote, 169
DESSERTS
Almond Cheesecake Bars, 94
Lemon Ricotta Cake, 123
MAIN DISHES
Garden Cheddar Frittata, 59
Ricotta Pancakes with Cinnamon
   Apples, 161
Scallop Mac & Cheese, 71
Two-Cheese Spaghetti Bake, 60
SANDWICHES & SOUP
Best-Ever Grilled Cheese
   Sandwiches, 146
Golden Gouda Mushroom
   Soup, 34
Ham 'n' Swiss Envelopes, 22
Italian Grilled Cheese
   Sandwiches, 23
SIDE DISHES
Beer Macaroni & Cheese, 51
Polenta Fries with Blue Cheese
   Dip, 52
Sauteed Corn with Cheddar, 130

CHEESECAKES
Butter Pecan Cheesecake, 115
Orange Cheesecake Dessert, 121
Raspberry-Swirl Cheesecake
   Pie, 127

CHERRIES
Cherries in the Snow, 124
Cherry Pound Cake, 110

ALPHABETICAL RECIPE INDEX